The Design of Coffee

An Engineering Approach

Third Edition

William Ristenpart & Tonya Kuhl

Department of Chemical Engineering, University of California Davis

Ristenpart / Kuhl Publishing

2021

Ristenpart / Kuhl Publishing
1 Shields Ave
Davis, CA 95616 USA

ISBN: 9798474576558

Contents

Acknowledgments

We thank the many individuals and organizations who have enthusiastically supported the development of *The Design of Coffee*, including the Specialty Coffee Association, Baratza LLC, Rogers Family Coffee, Tony's Coffee, Mishka's Coffee, Chocolate Fish Coffee, Kalita USA, Bunn-o-Matic Corporation, Peet's Coffee and Tea, Cropster, and Folger's Coffee. We are especially grateful for the generous financial support of Chevron Corporation; alumnus John Wasson and his wife Gina; and the College of Engineering at University of California Davis for supporting the renovation of the Coffee Lab in 2015. There are many individuals from the coffee industry who have been extremely helpful, but we especially acknowledge the assistance of Doug Welsh, Phil Maloney, and Roman Bondarenko at Peet's Coffee; Nicholas Cho of Wrecking Ball Coffee; and Peter Giuliano from the Specialty Coffee Association.

At UC Davis, we are indebted to Dr. Bill Doering, both for his excellent management of the Coffee Lab early on and for his thoughtful advice, suggestions, and critical review of the original editions. We are blessed to have worked with excellent head teaching assistants including Kaitlin Johnson, Grace McClintock, Shiva Murali, Ryan Edmonds, and Ana Acosta. The excellent support from the U.C. Davis Center for Educational Effectiveness was instrumental in helping us form a hybridized form of *The Design of Coffee*, and we are particularly grateful to Cecilia Gomez and Mark Wilson for their excellent advice and suggestions. Most recently, we are grateful to Juliet Han, the Probat Roasting Fellow, for her expertise and dedicated, meticulous work as lab manager and her careful review of this edition. Likewise, we thank Jessie Liang for her hard work drafting the new glossary for this edition, and for her beautiful cover photography.

We also thank our colleague Prof. Jean-Xavier Guinard for teaching us so much about sensory and consumer science. The new Coffee Brewing Control Chart presented in this edition is an attempt to summarize the complicated sensory trends reported by Frost et al. (2020) and Batali et al. (2020); we are grateful to both Prof. Guinard and Dr. Mackenzie Batali for helpful discussions regarding the composition of this chart. Research funding provided via the Coffee Science Foundation, with underwriting from Breville Corporation and Toddy LLC, has been instrumental in helping the U.C. Davis Coffee center improve our fundamental understanding of coffee.

The development of *The Design of Coffee* has occurred in tandem with the development of the U.C. Davis Coffee Center, which has only been made possible by the generous support of so many forward-thinking individuals and entities in the coffee industry. We gratefully acknowledge the leadership and generous philanthropic support of: Doug Welsh and Peet's Coffee and Tea for the pilot roastery; Kent Bakke and La Marzocco for the brewing and espresso laboratory; Wim Abbing and Probat for their support of the Probat Roasting Fellowship and the roastery equipment; Edwin Rizo of Rizo-Lopez Foods and Bencafe for the green bean storage laboratory; Jim Trout and Folger's Coffee for the analytical laboratory; Julia Leach and Toddy LLC for the innovation lab; Joe Behm and Behmor Co. for the office space; Patrick and Brant Curtis for the outdoor patio; John and Gina Wasson for the coffee classroom; Melind John and Steph Chu of Josuma Coffee for the conference room; Tim Styczynski and Bridge Coffee for the bridge to the Coffee Center; Pam Fair and Glen Sullivan for the alcove; and many other generous donors including Bill Murray, Mike and Jody Coffey, Mery Santos, and Mohamed Moledina.

Most importantly of all, we thank the many students who have taken *The Design of Coffee* and helped us learn how to improve the labs – this project would not have been possible without you.

Preface to the 3rd Edition

This book is intended for use in the laboratory component of *The Design of Coffee*, a general education science and engineering course originally developed at the University of California Davis. Specifically, the course serves as a non-mathematical introduction to chemical engineering as elucidated by the process of roasting and brewing coffee. The primary focus of the course is a weekly 2-hour lab session where students perform experiments designed to illustrate key chemical engineering principles. As described in this book, students learn about material balances, chemical kinetics, mass transfer, conservation of energy, fluid mechanics, colloidal phenomena, and engineering economics – all examined through the prism of roasting and brewing coffee. Toward the end of the course, the students compete in a design competition where they strive to make the **best** tasting coffee using the **least** amount of energy – a classic engineering optimization problem, but one that is both fun and broadly accessible to a general audience.

The Design of Coffee was originally intended for non-science majors who would like to satisfy their general education requirements for science and engineering. Over the past few years, however, we have found that a much larger audience is eager to learn how to think more scientifically about the beverage that they consume on a regular basis. Although this book is primarily intended to serve those students enrolled in "The Design of Coffee," the material and experiments presented here will be of use to anybody interested in learning more about coffee – or how to think about coffee like an engineer.

Accordingly, we have made the material here as self-contained as possible. Anybody at the college freshmen level or above can perform the experiments described here: no calculus or chemistry is required. Importantly, most of the requisite equipment and supplies, such as hot-air popcorn roasters, drip brewers, and green coffee beans, are inexpensive and readily purchased. All of the experiments described here can be performed in a kitchen or anywhere else with access to a sink and electricity.

This new and improved third edition is considerably expanded in length, with new labs focused on water chemistry, pressure driven flow, colloid science, espresso viscosity, and engineering economics. The new labs are intended for courses taught at schools on the semester system, or for individuals who crave more coffee science content. Toward that end, we have also included many new bonus materials at the end of each lab that further explore various aspects of coffee science.

Over the past five years there has been an explosion of scientific research on coffee, and accordingly we have updated and expanded the text to reflect new findings. Most importantly, the previous version of the "Coffee Brewing Control Chart" (originally developed in the 1950s) has been replaced in this edition with a new chart based on work published in 2020-21 by the U.C. Davis Coffee Center. The new chart summarizes how different sensory attributes vary with key brewing parameters, and thus serves as a powerful tool to guide students as they apply the scientific principles learned here to design their ideal coffee.

As with the first two editions, an important aspect of this guidebook is that we *don't* provide the answers here to many of the questions we pose. The intent is to have students think about and experimentally explore the underlying physical and chemical processes for themselves using the scientific method, rather than simply reading the answer. Our goal is to help you understand how to think like an engineer – and along the way learn how to make excellent coffee!

William Ristenpart & Tonya Kuhl

Davis, California
Summer 2021

Part I

Introduction

Why Coffee and Chemical Engineering?

A cup of coffee

Every morning, millions of people wake up and perform a familiar ritual. Perhaps a bit bleary-eyed and groggy, they make their way to the kitchen and stand in front of a drip coffee brewer. There, they launch into a series of well-practiced actions: filling a glass pot with cold water; pouring the water into a reservoir; placing some filter paper inside a plastic basket; scooping some brown powder into the filter paper; and flipping a switch to turn on the coffee brewer. Of course, the details of the procedure vary from household to household. Some people use a metal or reusable filter instead of a paper filter. Others buy whole coffee beans and grind the beans themselves. Some buy more expensive "pod" machines that dispense single servings of coffee. Whatever the detailed procedure might have been, soon the coffee brewer begins to gurgle, a little steam escapes, and the wonderful fragrance of coffee fills the whole kitchen. Eventually, they pour some of the black liquid into a cup.

As they sit down to enjoy their first sip of coffee, however, very few of these people realize that they just completed the final steps of a very elegant process in chemical engineering.

Huh? Chemical Engineering?

Wait a second, you might object – what does making a cup of coffee have to do with chemical engineering? Don't chemical engineers make complicated chemicals? Or engineer chemical reactions? How could something as customary as making a cup of coffee count as engineering anything?

Before deciding whether something "counts" as chemical engineering, we should first answer the question: what is chemical engineering? It's worth emphasizing that most people have only a vague idea of what chemical engineers actually do, especially as compared to other engineering professions. Computer engineers design computers. Civil engineers design buildings and bridges. Mechanical engineers design motors and things that move. Biomedical engineers design medical implants and devices. Electrical engineers design electrical circuits. Aerospace engineers design things that go into outer space. All of these engineering professions have well defined subject matters that are readily grasped in the public mind, even if the details are complicated.

In contrast, students of chemical engineering often struggle to convey what a chemical engineer actually does. As the name implies, chemical engineers indeed often work on chemistry and chemical reactions – but that by itself is not the whole story. If the work solely involved chemical reactions, how would a chemical engineer be any different from a chemist? By definition, chemists work on chemistry and chemical reactions, so why is there a whole separate profession known as "chemical engineering"?

Some people might claim, "Oh, chemical engineers work at petroleum refineries to make gasoline." These folks would only be partially correct. Many chemical engineers traditionally have worked in refineries, where crude oil is converted into gasoline and many other products. Further, one can trace the early history of chemical engineering through the development of the petrochemical industry in the late 1800s and early 1900s. In modern times, however, only a fraction of chemical engineers (~20%) actually work in petroleum related fields. On top of that, even within the modern petroleum industry you find many talented chemists; are they doing something different than their chemical engineer colleagues?

The Definition of Chemical Engineering

The answer is most definitely yes: chemical engineers are trained to think in a very different way than chemists or other types of engineers. So, what is chemical engineering? The broadest and simplest definition goes like this:

Chemical engineers design ways to convert matter to a more useful form.

This definition is deceptively simple. Note that no specific product or application is mentioned, nor is there even a specific requirement to include something about chemical reactions. Instead, we have only the incredibly broad criterion that we 'convert' matter to something more 'useful.'

What exactly does this mean? Because there are many kinds of matter, and because there are even more kinds of things that human beings consider 'useful,' there is essentially an infinite number of examples of chemical engineering processes. The classic example, for historical reasons, is that of petroleum. Here we take matter in one form, crude oil which has been extracted from underground, and turn it into a bunch of more useful products: gasoline, fertilizers, plastics, and many others.

However, the starting matter doesn't have to be crude oil, or even a liquid. A second great example involves silicon-based computer chips. Here we take silicon (a solid material), and convert it into the chips that run a variety of products, like computers, cell phones and modern TVs. Again, some readers might object, saying "Hold on, computer chips are made by computer engineers, not chemical engineers!" It's absolutely true that computer engineers design the layout of the circuits within a chip – but it's often a chemical engineer that designs the overall process of converting the raw material of silicon into the finished product. Andy Grove, one of the founders of Intel Corporation (arguably the world's largest and most influential producer of computer chips) was trained as a chemical engineer. Likewise, Jack Welch, the long-time CEO of General Electric (one of the world's largest manufacturers of electrical equipment) was also trained as a chemical engineer. Today the computer and semiconductor industries continue to employ a sizable fraction of all chemical engineers (~5%).

A third example of chemical engineering involves a favorite beverage of many college students: beer! Here, just four raw ingredients (barley, hops, yeast and water) are combined and converted into an extremely popular beverage. Unlike the previous two examples, making beer also involves some biology (specifically, the fermentation of sugars into ethanol performed by the yeast), but chemical engineers often design and oversee that process as well. In fact, chemical engineers are heavily recruited not only by brewers (e.g., Anheuser-Busch or Coors), but also by wineries (think Napa Valley) and distillers (think Jack Daniels whiskey or Absolut vodka). Likewise, there are many other examples of modern chemical engineering, including manufacture of consumer products like toothpaste or detergent, pharmaceutical products like antibiotics or vaccines, or new food products like plant-based meat substitutes. Chemical engineers are also heavily employed in equipment design and construction, environmental health and safety, and scientific and technical consulting.

OK, but what about coffee?

It should be clear by now that the process of making coffee absolutely counts as an example of chemical engineering. Here we start with the berries of a certain type of evergreen tree or shrub, *Coffea arabica*, which grows well in tropical regions, especially at high altitudes. These bright red (or yellow) berries contain green seeds that are processed, roasted, ground into a powder, and then mixed with hot water to produce the drink we know as coffee. (Note that coffee beans are technically seeds and have nothing to do with beans, but everybody calls them beans anyway.) In other words, we take matter in one form – green coffee beans – and we convert it to a much more useful form – coffee that we can drink.

Indeed, based on how popular it is, coffee is clearly considered extremely useful. Coffee in its various forms (e.g., drip-brewed, instant, espresso, etc.) is one of the most heavily consumed beverages in the world. In the United States alone, coffee is a $30 billion per year business; Americans consume about 400 *million* cups per *day*!

A key reason for coffee's popularity is the stimulating effect of caffeine, which the seeds of *Coffea arabica* (and other types of coffee trees) have in great abundance. Most of this caffeine stays in the beans during roasting, and then is extracted from the ground beans into the water during brewing. As a person drinks the coffee, the caffeine enters his or her bloodstream through the lining of the mouth, throat, and stomach and ultimately interacts with the central nervous system to produce a whole range of positive effects: increased wakefulness, clearer flow of thought, better focus, and overall better body coordination. Less well known is that coffee can be prepared so that it tastes *sweet*, without adding any sugar. Coffee aficionados are constantly striving to roast and brew coffee that highlights the sweetness and more delicate flavors of high-quality coffees.

The key point here is that all of those millions of people preparing coffee each morning are, whether they know it or not, performing a chemical engineering operation. The drip coffee maker in a person's kitchen might be much smaller than a petroleum refinery, but the underlying principle – of performing some process to convert matter to a more useful form – is exactly the same.

But what makes someone a chemical engineer?

Of course, even though those millions of people making coffee are performing a chemical engineering operation, few of those people would characterize themselves as "chemical engineers." And with good reason: most people making coffee are simply following a protocol that they learned from somebody else.

Note that according to our definition, chemical engineers are individuals who design ways to convert matter to more useful form. There is a lot of meaning packed into that one little word, "design." By "design", we mean that chemical engineers are the ones who plan, simulate, create, and test different procedures for converting some type of matter to a desired more useful form.

The earliest chemical engineers did this design process by trial and error. There is evidence that beer was first brewed in the Neolithic era, more than 10,000 years ago; presumably somebody noticed that if their barley got sufficiently wet, it fermented into something that was intoxicating. Coffee is a more recent invention, probably first made in Ethiopia or Arabia sometime in the 1500s. The coffee beans had to first be roasted and then boiled in water; since chemistry and engineering as disciplines did not develop until much later, presumably the first coffee was likewise developed by a process of trial and error.

Modern chemical engineers often work for companies that are either producing very expensive products (like cell phones), or are producing large quantities of commodity products (like beer), or are designing entirely new processes to make new products (like biofuels). These engineers cannot afford to do things by random trial and error. Instead, they must understand the underlying scientific principles affecting choices in their design, and make decisions about them in a rational manner.

In thinking about coffee, we start to see what differentiates a chemist from a chemical engineer. Typically, chemists focus on just one specific part of the process of converting matter from one form to another: the chemical reaction. Many of the chemical reactions of interest in coffee take place during the roasting. This is when the proteins, sugars and acids originally present in the green coffee beans are converted into other types of chemicals that humans perceive as tasting good. As we explore in Lab 4, even more chemical reactions take place during and after brewing (as evidenced by a sizable change in the pH of heated coffee with time). A good chemist can measure how fast molecules react and characterize the underlying chemical reactions that govern how the various molecules react and transform.

Anybody who has made coffee, however, knows that you need to do more than just roast the beans. That's exactly where chemical engineers enter the picture. Oftentimes in the process of converting matter a chemical reaction is only the first step, and many other steps are required to get the desired "useful form." Anything beyond the chemical reaction – even the design of the reactor vessel in which the reaction occurs – is where chemical engineers come in. Chemical engineers not only have to understand the chemistry, but then they must understand many additional concepts in order to yield a final desired product. Specifically, in the context of coffee, the chemical engineer will design the process with the following questions in mind: How long should I roast the beans? How big of a roaster can I use? How much heat should I deliver to the beans, and what form of energy source should I use? After they're roasted, how small should I grind the beans? What temperature water should I use to brew the coffee? How should I deliver the water to the grind, and how fast should I pump it through? What type of filtration should I use – and how does the filter affect the taste of the end product? How do I keep the coffee hot until we're ready to drink it? And by the way, how much is it all going to cost?

The answers to these questions might seem self-evident to you, probably because you've seen how coffee is traditionally made in a drip coffee brewer and you know how much a cappuccino costs at Starbucks. But close your eyes for a moment, and imagine that you've never actually seen how coffee is made. Let's focus on one specific question: how small should I grind the beans? Of course, you can do the trial-and-error approach, and just try a bunch of different sizes until you get something acceptable. The chemical engineer approach, however, is to understand how the size of the grind affects the rate at which the desired chemicals (e.g., the caffeine and other molecules that taste good) move from inside the solid coffee particles into the liquid water. This process is generally referred to by chemical engineers as "mass transfer," which is just a fancy expression meaning "chemicals move from over here to over there." As we explore in Lab 6, it turns out that the size of the solid particles tremendously affects the rate at which the chemicals move to the liquid – and chemical engineers need to understand how to use this principle to design the overall process in a rational manner.

The Design of Coffee

The laboratory experiences described in this book are intended to serve as a hands-on, non-mathematical introduction to how chemical engineers think, as elucidated by the process of roasting and brewing coffee. The phrase "non-mathematical" is key: the reader needs no prior knowledge of calculus, chemistry, or physics beyond the high school level. The goal is to provide a qualitative overview of key concepts in chemical engineering, so that students get "the big picture," without getting bogged down in complicated calculus or chemistry.

Why coffee? As mentioned above, making coffee is a quintessential operation in chemical engineering. More importantly, unlike the raw materials involved in many other chemical engineering processes (such as petroleum or silicon), green coffee beans are both inexpensive and easy to order online. This means that the reader can personally perform all of the experiments described in this book, and thereby help develop his or her chemical engineering intuition. Even if you think you already know everything there is to know about making coffee, it is unlikely you have approached making coffee the way a trained chemical engineer would. This book will start you down the path of thinking about coffee – and other processes or products – the way a chemical engineer does.

Toward that end, this laboratory guidebook is organized as follows. First, we take care of some essential preliminaries with an overview of all the necessary supplies and equipment for those readers setting up the labs at home. Most importantly, we review key safety aspects and introduce the main concepts of tasting coffee in Lab 1.

The remainder of the book is divided into two distinct parts: analysis and design. Labs 2 through 10 each focus on a core chemical engineering concept, with an emphasis on understanding how to perform "engineering analysis" on each concept. Labs 2 and 3 examine the concept of a "process flow diagram," and how conservation of mass must be satisfied in each step of the process. Lab 4 explores the effect of chemical reactions on how the taste of brewed coffee changes with time, while Lab 5 examines the meaning of "energy" and how it pertains to roasting and brewing coffee. The concepts of "flux" and "mass transfer" are then illustrated in Lab 6 with experiments on the effect of grind size, extraction time, and water temperature on the strength of the brew. Lab 7 examines water chemistry and its impact on coffee brewing. Lab 8 introduces key concepts of pressure and fluid motion through porous media, and Lab 9 discusses coffee "colloids" and their ramifications for filtration of coffee. Lab 10 introduces espresso and viscosity measurements. At the end of each lab, we also include some "bonus material" that highlights key scientific or engineering aspects of the lab topic as they pertain to the process of making coffee.

In the third part, we then shift gears from "analysis" to "design." Labs 11 through 13 are open-ended design trials, with each design trial focusing on a different aspect of design. Lab 11 discusses optimization of brew parameters to achieve specific targets in terms of total dissolved solids and extraction yields, while Lab 12 guides students in "scaling up" their own unique process for roasting and brewing. In Lab 13, the economics of roasting and brewing coffee are considered from an engineering perspective. Finally, everything culminates in Lab 14, which is where students compete in the engineering design challenge: to make the best tasting coffee (as judged by a blind taste panel) using the least amount of energy. It is difficult to make good tasting coffee – but it is even more difficult to make good tasting coffee while using little energy!

If the material presented here is used in a semester-long course, we recommend that all 14 labs be performed in sequence. At schools on the quarter system (which typically only allow for 10 weeks), or for semester schools that desire a smaller number of lab experiences, we recommend that students complete at least the five "core" labs 1, 2, 3, 5, and 6, then one of labs 4 or 7 through 10 (whichever is of most interest), a couple of the design trials and the design competition. Of course, since all the labs are independent, instructors or students at home should feel free picking and choosing the labs of most interest to perform.

As emphasized in this introduction, the main point of The Design of Coffee is to teach students how to think like an engineer. Nonetheless, even if you decide your interests lie outside of engineering, you definitely will understand on a deeper level how to make a truly excellent cup of coffee – a useful skill no matter what you choose to do in life!

Supplies & Equipment – What Do We Need?

If you are reading this book as part of a course offered at a school or a workshop, then you don't need to worry about this section. The instructor will already have gathered all of the necessary equipment and supplies that you will need to perform the upcoming labs. Unless you are curious, you can skip this section and move on to Lab 1 to review very important safety considerations and begin learning about tasting coffee.

If, however, you are setting up the labs to do on your own, then you need to give some thought and attention to procuring all of the necessary supplies and equipment. The goal of this section is to help interested individuals identify what they need to borrow or purchase.

Before getting into the details, some comments are necessary. First, all of the specific items listed here have been found by us to be useful for the purpose of learning about the science and engineering of coffee. There are many great brewing and roasting vendors, and their inclusion or exclusion on this list should not be construed as a recommendation either for or against them in terms of their quality. The items listed here were chosen with an eye toward elucidating key principles inexpensively – not for making the "best" coffee.

Second, we strongly recommend that individual readers team up with other interested people to do the labs. One reason for this is practical: it's easier to split up some of the work while doing the labs, and it's kind of silly to hold a design contest (Lab 14) if there is only one coffee to taste! But another reason is philosophical: in industry, engineers almost invariably work on teams, and indeed most engineering schools emphasize teamwork and group activities in their curricula. We recommend that you find a few other friends interested in coffee to do the experiments collaboratively, and to do the coffee design contest competitively. We think you'll find that it's also much more fun!

Items marked below with an asterisk are used in every lab, and so won't be listed under the necessary equipment for each lab overview – you will still need them even though they are not specifically listed there. For every category, items needed in Labs 11 to 14 are only potentially needed because of the open-ended nature of those labs. For easy reference, the table at the end of this section lists all needed equipment and supplies by lab number.

Infrastructure

First, you'll need a room that has access to a sink, electricity, and a few feet of table space per group of participants. About six feet of table-top space is adequate for a group of three standing participants. Modern electrical codes require electrical outlets near sinks to have GFCI protection, and it's a good idea that your outlets have that (in case you drop an electrical apparatus in the sink). A dishwasher is convenient but not necessary.

The room should have at least standard ventilation. Never roast coffee in an enclosed or unventilated space. If there is no mechanical ventilation in your space (an unusual situation in most modern buildings), then open a window and use a standard room fan to help exhaust roasting fumes. If you use a kitchen hood to vent, make sure it vents to the outside and doesn't simply recirculate back into the kitchen – if it does, open a window instead.

In terms of time commitment, each lab is designed to take about 2 hours, including set up and clean up. Although you can combine multiple labs in one day, it's better to space them out by at least one or two days. This gives roasted beans time to off-gas and develop their full flavor, and gives you time to absorb the lessons learned in previous labs.

Coffee beans

☐ Roasted coffee beans, about 1 pound   (Labs 1 – 4)

☐ Green coffee beans, about 6 pounds, at least two varieties   (Labs 3 – 13)

Roasted coffee beans are available at basically every grocery store and cafe. Green coffee beans are less expensive but need to be specially ordered from an online vendor such as Sweet Maria's, or their wholesale branch (Coffee Shrub) for larger purchases. How many green beans you use will depend on the time spent in the design trials (Labs 11 to 13). If you prefer less caffeine, you can also order decaffeinated green coffee beans to roast. The quantities listed here are adequate for a group of three participants who share the coffee.

Other ingredients

☐ Caffeine and citric acid   (Lab 1)

☐ Epsom salt, baking soda, and distilled water   (Lab 7)

Understanding the difference between "bitter" and "sour" is crucial for coffee, so in Lab 1 we strongly recommend tasting sensory references of dilute caffeine (which is very bitter) and citric acid (which is very sour). Make sure you purchase each in pure powder form without other additives (which will affect the taste); you will dilute these in water before tasting. The Epsom salt, baking soda, and distilled water are necessary to adjust the alkalinity and hardness of your brewing water in Lab 7.

Grinders

☐ Baratza Encore grinder *   (Labs 1 – 14)

☐ Pestle and mortar   (Lab 6)

Coffee aficionados swear by the more expensive cone-and-burr grinders like those made by Baratza, which yield a more uniform grind size and allows better control over the extraction during brewing. If cost is an issue, we find that a standard $20 electric blade grinder is sufficient for the labs described here. If you do use a standard electric blade grinder, gently shake the grinder up and down while it's grinding to help make sure the beans are evenly ground. The pestle and mortar is optional but fun to use in Lab 6 when examining how grind size affects extraction, but it isn't strictly necessary – you could also put the roasted coffee beans in a plastic bag and hit them with something heavy.

Roasters

☐ Fresh Roast SR540 fluid air roaster   (Labs 3 – 13)

☐ Nostalgia Electric Popcorn Popper   (Labs 5 – 13)

These are both small "table-top" roasters, perfect for the small batches we'll be making here. The Fresh Roast is specifically designed for coffee and is a bit more expensive (about $200). The popcorn roaster is much less expensive ($30) but works great on coffee. If cost is an issue, you can do almost all the roasting described here just with the popcorn roaster. Note that the popcorn popper must have air vents designed to swirl the air (either clockwise or counter-clockwise when looking into it). Don't buy one with a mesh that blows the hot air straight up, the beans won't rotate and they'll eventually catch on fire.

Brewing Equipment

- ☐ Mr. Coffee Drip Brewer, 4-cup (TF4-RB)   (Labs 1–3, 11–14)
- ☐ Clever Coffee Dripper, large   (Labs 3 – 7, 9, 11–14)
- ☐ AeroPress Coffee Maker   (Labs 7 – 14)
- ☐ Bodum 4-cup French Press   (Labs 9, 11 – 14)
- ☐ Bonavita 1.7 L Variable Temp Gooseneck Electric Kettle   (Labs 1, 4 – 14)

The Mr. Coffee is a standard drip brewer that has a built-in water heater. Any simple drip brewer can be used – but you will be taking it apart and reassembling it. The other three brewers (Clever Coffee, AeroPress, and French Press) require an external source of hot water. We find the Bonavita electric kettle to be convenient since it has a built-in thermostat, and the gooseneck simplifies pouring. A smaller kettle is less convenient but will still work.

Glassware and Kitchenware

- ☐ Bormioli Rocco Easy Bar Espresso Cups, Clear, 3.5 oz *   (Labs 2 – 14)
- ☐ Cupping spoons   (Lab 1)
- ☐ Large glass mugs (12 oz)   (Labs 1 – 14)
- ☐ Small paper cups   (Labs 4, 6)
- ☐ Large measuring cup with spout   (Labs 4 – 14)
- ☐ Large & small mixing bowls   (Labs 2 – 14)
- ☐ Vacuum-insulated stainless-steel thermal carafe, 1 liter   (Lab 14)

Transparent glass mugs are preferred because they allow you to see the coffee. You only need big ones for some of the brewing methods; the small espresso mugs are perfect for tasting. Small paper cups are useful for several of the time sensitive measurements (e.g., pH or TDS versus time) because you can write the sample time on the side. The large measuring cup is convenient for filling reservoirs and for pouring coffee samples into the espresso cups. A large bowl is useful for catching chaff from the popcorn roaster, while small bowls are useful for measuring masses. A thermal carafe keeps your coffee warm and is essential for the blind taste test.

Filters and Bags

- ☐ Appropriate size filter papers for various brewers*   (Labs 2 – 14)
- ☐ Metallic round reusable filters for AeroPress   (Labs 9 – 14)
- ☐ Clear plastic coffee bags with one-way degassing valves, ¼ lb size   (Labs 3 – 13)

Make sure you get the right filter paper for each of your brewers. Melitta makes nice paper filters both for a standard 4-cup Mr. Coffee (get the 4-cup flat bottom filters), as well as for the conical Clever Coffee dripper (get the #4 size). AeroPress brewers require a flat circular filter; their paper filters are marketed as "microfilters." Lab 9 requires a metal filter for the AeroPress to compare paper and metal filtration. (It makes a difference!) The coffee bags are super convenient for storing roasted beans, since they're designed to allow carbon dioxide to off-gas (without over-pressurizing a container). Allow beans to cool to room temperature before you put them in the plastic bag!

Analytical Measurements

☐ ACAIA digital scale (Pearl or Luna)*   (Labs 1 – 14)

☐ Analog bathroom scale, 1 lb (or .5 kg) resolution   (Labs 8, 10)

☐ Digital thermometer and thermocouple, 6" and 12"   (Labs 2 – 5)

☐ Handheld pH meter (e.g., Ecotestr pH2)   (Labs 4, 7)

☐ P4400 Kill-A-Watt Electricity Usage Meter   (Labs 5 – 14)

☐ Coffee Digital Refractometer   (Labs 6 – 14)

☐ Optical microscope & glass microscopy slides   (Lab 9)

A digital scale with 0.1-gram resolution is absolutely essential since you will be weighing things many times in every lab; brands like Acaia are good because they have a built-in timer useful for monitoring extraction time. The bathroom scale is for measuring the force applied by hand to an AeroPress brewer, a simple analog scale (non-digital) is best, and 1-pound resolution is fine. The digital thermometer is convenient, but if necessary could you use a regular (spirit-filled) thermometer. The pH meter is primarily used in Lab 3, so if cost is an issue you could skip it or try using paper pH strips. The Kill-a-Watt electricity meter is indispensable since our main engineering goal is to minimize the energy usage, but fortunately it's only about $20. Finally, the most expensive item by far is the coffee refractometer (which tells you the total dissolved solids, or "strength," of your coffee). This is a crucial measurement, though, so if you're serious about coffee (and can afford it) you'll get one. If cost is an issue, however, you could buy a hand-held conductivity meter (about $20) to estimate the TDS. It's much cheaper, but also far less accurate. If you have access to a simple optical or USB microscope, then you can observe the effects of filtration on the coffee colloids in Lab 9. A microscope with 400x total magnification and phase contrast is nice but not necessary.

Miscellaneous

☐ Screwdriver   (Lab 2)

☐ Standard ruler (12 inch)   (Lab 8)

☐ Glass graduated cylinders (500 mL and 100 mL)   (Lab 3 and Lab 10)

☐ Metal mesh colander   (Labs 2 – 12)

☐ Pastry brush   (Labs 3 – 13)

☐ Silicone mitts   (Labs 1 – 12)

☐ Gong and drumstick   (Lab 14)

You'll need a screwdriver to take apart the Mr. Coffee, and you'll need an inexpensive ruler to measure the thickness of the coffee grounds in the AeroPress in Lab 8. The graduated cylinder allows you to visualize how much the beans expand in volume during roasting (Lab 3) and the crema thickness of espresso (Lab 10). The metal mesh colander is great for quickly cooling your beans after the roast, and the pastry brush is helpful for cleaning chaff out of the roasters. The mitts are highly recommended for handling hot items, especially the roasters. Finally, it's totally optional, but it's a lot of fun to ring a gong to begin the design competition and to announce the winners.

The table below illustrates which supplies and equipment are necessary in which labs. Items denoted by an "X" are essential for that lab, while items denoted by an "o" are optional. Note that you need only purchase roasted coffee for the first three labs; in labs 5 through 14 it is assumed that you use coffee that you roasted yourself during the previous lab sessions (denoted by a hyphen).

		1 Safety & Tasting	2 Reverse Engineering	3 Mass Balances	4 pH and Chemistry	5 Energy Usage	6 Mass Transfer	7 Water Chemistry	8 Pressure Driven Flow	9 Colloids & Filtration	10 Espresso & Viscosity	11 1st Trials: Optimization	12 2nd Trials: Scaling Up	13 3rd Trials: Economics	14 Design Competition
Ingredients	Roasted coffee beans	X	X	X	X	–	–	–	–	–	–	–	–	–	–
	Green coffee beans		X	X	X	X	X	X	X	X	X	X	X	X	
	Caffeine & citric acid	o													
	Epsom salt, baking soda, distilled water							X							
Roasting & Grinding	Baratza grinder (or other grinder)	X	X	X	X	X	X	X	X	X	X	X	X	X	X
	Pestle and mortar						o								
	Fresh Roast 540 coffee roaster			X	X	X	o	o	o	o	o	o	o	o	
	Popcorn popper					X	o	o	o	o	o	o	o	o	
Brewing Equipment	Bonavita 1.7L Electric Kettle	X			X	X	X	X	X	X	X	X	X	X	X
	Mr. Coffee drip brewer		X	X	X							o	o	o	o
	Clever Coffee Dripper				X	X	X	X		X		o	o	o	o
	AeroPress Coffee Maker								X	X	X	o	o	o	o
	Bodum 4-cup French Press									X		o	o	o	o
	Espresso machine										X	o	o	o	o
Filters & Bags	Appropriate size filter papers		X	X	X	X	X	X	X	X	X	X	X	X	X
	Metallic round reusable Aeropress filters									X	o	o	o	o	o
	Clear valve coffee bags (1/4 lb)			X	X	X	X	X	X	X	X	X	X	X	
Glassware & Kitchenware	Cupping spoons	X													
	Large glass coffee mugs	X	X	X	X	X	X	X	X	X	X	o	o	o	o
	Small glass espresso mugs		X	X	X	X	X	X	X	X	X	X	X	X	X
	Large & small mixing bowls		X	X	X	X	X	X	X	X	X	X	X	X	X
	Large measuring cup with spout			X	X	X	X	X	X	X	X	o	o	o	o
	Small paper cups			X	X										
	Vacuum insulated thermal carafe (1 L)														X
Analytical Equipment	Acaia digital scale	X	X	X	X	X	X	X	X	X	X	X	X	X	X
	Digital thermometer and thermocouple		X	X	X	X					X				
	Handheld pH meter				X			X							
	Kill-a-watt electricity usage meter					X	X	X	X	X	X	X	X	X	X
	Digital refractometer for coffee						X	X	X	X	X	X	X	X	X
	Analog bathroom scale								X		X				
	Optical microscope and glass slides									X					
	Viscometer (Canon-Fenske, 1-10 cSt)										X				
Miscellaneous	Screwdriver		X												
	Graduated cylinders (500 mL / 100 mL)			X							X				
	Pastry brush			X	X	X	X	X	X	X	X	X	X	X	
	Silicone mitts			X	X	X	X	X	X	X	X	X	X	X	
	Metal mesh colander			X	X	X	X	X	X	X	X	X	X	X	
	Ruler							X							
	Gong and drumstick														o

Lab 1 – Safety Overview and Introduction to Tasting

Objectives: In this preliminary lab we will first review important safety issues associated with hot coffee in the laboratory. We will then perform a traditional "cupping" to get experience with the taste of high-quality brewed coffee, and learn about the difference between "bitter" and "sour" using sensory references. The goal is for you to learn the key sensory attributes that you will use to judge your coffee.

Equipment:

☐ Electric kettle ☐ Glasses or mugs ☐ Spoon ☐ Two different roasted coffees

☐ Caffeine sensory reference ☐ Citric acid sensory reference

Lab Activities:

☐ Part A – safety review

☐ Part B – traditional cupping of at least two different coffees, with sensory references

Report:

☐ Signed safety sheet

Part A – Safety Review

Before you step foot in lab, the first crucial activity is for you to review the safety rules and expectations for the coffee lab. Your pre-lab assignment for Lab 1 is straightforward: simply read the safety rules and laboratory orientation, then sign the written safety sheet at the bottom of the next page. Submit the signed safety sheet, either as an image (e.g., a cell phone photo) or a PDF scan. You don't need to submit this page; the pictorial overview is intended only to reinforce the written material on the safety sheet. If you have any questions about safety or procedure at any time, do not hesitate to ask your teaching assistant and/or instructor, or your colleagues or friends if performing experiments at home. Better safe than sorry!

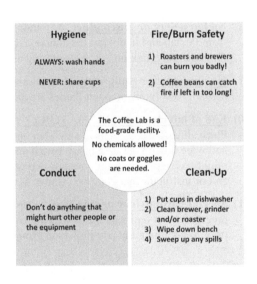

Because this is a preliminary lab, you don't need to write a formal lab report (for either Part A or Part B). If you are part of a class then you simply need to sign and submit the safety sheet; if you are at home, then make sure you understand the safety aspects described here. Make sure you know where a fire blanket and first aid kit are located, in the remote chance that an accident occurs and you do need them. Also make sure you understand what is expected in terms of cleanup after you are done.

If you are performing the experiments in this book on your own at home or elsewhere, it's still a good idea to follow these safety guidelines – please don't set anything on fire!

Safety Orientation for "The Coffee Lab"

1) **Food grade facility.** The "coffee lab" is a food grade facility. Unlike many laboratories, you may eat and drink food. This means, however, that absolutely NO HAZARDOUS CHEMICALS / MATERIALS are allowed inside the coffee lab. Do not bring any chemicals inside the lab.

2) **No lab coats or goggles.** Since there are no chemicals, you do **not** need a lab coat, lab gloves, or eye protection. Regular clothing and shoes are fine.

3) **Store backpacks out of the way.** Upon entering the lab, store your backpack or bag on the designated shelving. Backpacks on the ground become tripping hazards, which is unsafe around hot water.

4) **Hygiene – washing hands.** You must wash your hands with soap and water upon entering the lab. Likewise, wash your hands after you use the restroom; after coughing, sneezing, or blowing your nose; or after doing anything else that soils your hands.

5) **Hygiene – no sharing cups.** Do not share cups with anybody else. Use sticky labels to identify your personal cup at the beginning of each lab session. Avoid the temptation to take "just a small sip" from somebody else's cup. If you think your cup is dirty or was accidentally shared, get a new one.

6) **Burn safety.** The main safety hazard with coffee is the risk of burns. The coffee pots and roasters can get hot enough to cause severe burns if contacted with bare skin. Exercise great caution around them; only handle the brewers and roasters by their designated handles. **Always pour hot coffee into a cup placed on the lab bench, never into a cup in somebody's hand.** If you do receive a burn, immediately begin running cool water over it in the sink and notify your teaching assistant and/or instructor.

7) **Fire safety.** Just like bread can catch fire in a toaster, coffee beans can catch fire in a roaster. Never leave your roaster unattended. If it begins to smoke heavily, turn it off immediately. If the beans stop moving, turn it off immediately. If the beans do catch on fire, turn off the roaster and, if feasible, place a 'fire blanket' over the roaster to smother the flames. Notify the teaching assistant and/or instructor of any observed open flames, no matter how insignificant they might seem. Pay special attention on safe use of all roasters. Note the location of the room exits, the first aid kit, and the fire extinguisher.

8) **No horseplay or misconduct.** Any individual who purposely engages in unsafe behavior will be expelled from the lab and likely fail the course. Examples of misconduct include: throwing things, horseplay, (wrestling, pushing, tickling, etc.), or putting anything other than coffee beans into a roaster or brewer.

9) **No unapproved equipment.** No personal brewing or roasting equipment may be brought from home into the lab. Absolutely no open flames are allowed in the lab (no camp stoves, candles, etc.)

10) **End of lab cleanup (MANDATORY).** At the end of each lab session, your group must clean your station. Place all coffee cups in the dishwasher and wash all brewing glassware you used with soap and water. Spray and wipe down your area of lab bench and use a hand-broom to sweep up any coffee grounds or beans you might have spilled on the ground. IMPORTANT: Before you leave, confirm with your teaching assistant and/or instructor that your lab cleanup is adequate to receive full points.

11) **Special coronavirus precautions.** Depending on the current situation, there might be additional safety precautions in terms of mask-wearing or physical distancing. Find out what the current requirements are prior to taking part in any in-person group activities.

I affirm that I have carefully read and I understand the expectations for conduct and safety in the Coffee Lab.

Signature: _____ Date: _____

Print name: _____

Student ID Number: _____ Section number: _____

Part B Background – Tasting Coffee

Coffee tasting is challenging. Experts spend years developing their palate to identify subtle differences in each cup. Here we provide just the basic definitions of the main sensory attributes that we will use to judge coffees in our blind taste tests.

When tasting, you first smell the coffee, then loudly **slurp** some in your mouth. By slurping, you create smaller droplets (aerosols), which accomplish two goals. First, they help coat all of your taste buds throughout your mouth, so that your entire palate is involved in the evaluation. Second, the smaller droplets have a higher surface area-to-volume ratio, which accelerates volatilization of the aroma molecules that travel up your "retro-nasal" passage way. (A great deal of "taste" is actually "smell"!) Some tasters find it helpful to "chew" the coffee in their mouth to make sure everything is maximally distributed. Finally, after you swallow, continue to assess the aftertaste. The main scoring categories are defined as follows.

Fragrance	The aromatic aspects of the coffee, as detected by an initial smell before tasting in the mouth. A better fragrance receives a higher score. (In the coffee industry, some use "fragrance" to refer to the smell of the dry coffee grounds, and "aroma" to refer to the smell of brewed coffee. In this book we will use these terms interchangeably.)
Flavor	The coffee's taste character, in between the first impressions given by the first aroma and acidity to its final taste (also known as the "mid-range" notes). It is the combined impression of all the taste bud sensations and retro-nasal aromas that go from mouth to nose.
Aftertaste	The length or duration of positive flavor (both taste and aroma) emanating from the back of the palate and remaining after the coffee is swallowed. If the aftertaste is either short or unpleasant, a lower score should be given.
Acidity	Often described as "bright" when favorable, "sour" when unpleasant, or "dull" or "flat" when missing. (In coffee, "bright" means "good acidity"!) Compare to Italian salad dressing: you want an appropriate amount of acidity from the vinegar, but too much vinegar makes it unpleasantly sour. Acidity contributes to the liveliness, sweetness, and fresh-fruit character, especially when the coffee is first slurped. A lack of acidity (a "dullness" or "flatness") receives a low score, but too much acidity ("sourness") also receives a low score. Give a high score to a "bright," lively acidity that enhances the coffee flavor.
Body	The tactile feeling of the coffee liquid in the mouth, highly related to the "viscosity" of the liquid. The presence of colloids and sucrose in the coffee contribute to higher body. A "watery" coffee can have good flavor but lack body, while a "thick" coffee can have strong body but bad flavor. Give high scores for pleasant body.
Balance	The overall impression of the coffee. Ideally a coffee is balanced between all of the above attributes, with none dominating over any other. Think of this category as a subjective "fudge factor"… if smelling and tasting the coffee overall was a

positive experience, give it a high balance score. If, on the other hand, you over-all had a negative experience, then give it a negative score.

Sweetness   How sweet is the coffee? When we talk about sweetness, we don't mean to add sugar to the cup! Perhaps surprisingly, certain coffees can be perceived as having a sweetness due to the presence of sugars and some complex carbohydrates. Black coffee is never as sweet as soda (which has a huge amount of added sugar!), but high quality coffees have a pronounced sweetness that is highly prized.

Defects   Defects are off flavors that detract from the taste. For example, a recent problem with some Rwandan coffees is known as the potato defect. As its name suggests, the potato defect results in the aroma of freshly-peeled potatoes, which is not what you want in a quality coffee.

Many coffee experts advocate a pretty straightforward way to approach tasting coffee, perhaps best summarized by Nick Cho (co-founder of Wrecking Ball Coffee in San Francisco): "The four steps to critical coffee tasting, in order, are sweetness, negatives, acidity, and flavor notes." Nick emphasizes that having a naturally sweet tasting cup of coffee is the most important feature or attribute. Next is avoiding negatives in all attributes, followed by good acidity. Finally, those flavor notes that differentiate the coffee based on its varietal, or postharvest processing, and roast profile. Together, these attributes can culminate in "nirvana in a cup" – distinguishing a truly great cup of coffee from average.

Part B Activity – Cupping Coffee Like a Professional

Time to brew and taste some awesome coffee! For this preliminary laboratory experiment, we will loosely follow the professional cupping guidelines developed by the Specialty Coffee Association (SCA). These guidelines might seem unusual to you, because traditionally the coffee is tasted without any filtration: you simply dump some coffee grounds into a cup, add hot water, and then taste directly out of that cup! **We will not worry about assigning numerical scores here, we will only record your qualitative impressions.**

First, you should ideally have two different, freshly roasted coffees with a light to light-medium roast. According to the SCA the beans should have been roasted within the last 24 hours with a minimum of 8 hours of resting time after roasting. Quality coffees can be brewed with beans roasted up to 2 weeks prior, but part of professionally cupping is to determine what beans you should buy – so the beans are frequently roasted the day before the cupping.

Take the opportunity to compare the aroma of the roasted beans to the aroma of the green (unroasted) beans… the difference is remarkable! Can you detect a difference in aroma of the green beans of two different origins?

The cups themselves have specific requirements (don't just use any old mugs you have lying around). The cups should be made out of either white ceramic or tempered glass, and they should hold about 5 to 6 fluid ounces (about 150 mL), with a top diameter of about 3 to 3.5 inches. All of the cups that you taste out of should be identical, since your perceptions can be affected by the shape, color, or feel of the cup. If you're using a larger cup, scale up the amounts of coffee and water proportionally.

Note that it's better if the beans are *not* ground in advance. In fact, the closer in time the grinding is to brewing the better. The wonderful aromas of freshly ground coffee that you

Cupping Procedure (Tasting Like a Professional)

1. Measure about 9 grams of ground coffee beans into an 8-oz cup for each individual participating. Repeat for each type of coffee.
2. Add enough water to the water kettle for about 155 grams of water per cup and heat to 93°C. (So, for 3 people and 2 cups each, heat about 1 kilogram of water.)
3. Before adding water, evaluate the fragrance of the dry ground coffees and record your impressions into your cupping data sheet.
4. Once the water is 93°C, carefully fill each cup with water to the top (about 150 grams of water), making sure to fully wet the ground coffee. Start your timer.
5. After the timer reaches 4 minutes, "break the crust" at the top of the cup by skimming the spoon from front to back 3 times, while simultaneous smelling. Write down your impressions of the aroma. Repeat with the other. Don't taste yet… it's still too hot!
6. After smelling, use the spoon to carefully scoop out the solids floating on top of each brew. Try not to mix the contents of the cup. Rinse your spoon between brews.
7. After the timer reaches 10 minutes, use the spoon to taste the first coffee and evaluate the flavor, acidity, body, aftertaste, and balance. Do your best to slurp loudly! This helps aerosolize the coffee in your mouth, thereby releasing more aroma into your retronasal passages. Record your impressions.
8. Rinse your mouth with some water, and rinse the spoon. Then taste the other coffee, again slurping loudly. How does it compare?

smell mean that you are losing those volatile components to the air, and we want to capture as much as possible in the brew. The recommended size is just slightly coarser than you would typically use in an automatic drip coffee – a setting of about 20 on a Baratza Encore grinder.

After grinding place 9 grams of ground coffee into your cup. Start heating fresh water to 93°C. While the water is heating, smell the aromas of the freshly ground coffees. Record your impressions of the aromas in the data sheet on the next page. The coffee flavor wheel (see Bonus Box 1) can help you identify aromas, beyond "it smells like coffee." For example, some coffees are known for berry or fruit aromas while others have chocolate or nuts.

Once the water is 93°C, carefully pour water into your cup until it is full (about 150 grams of water). Make sure you fully wet the ground coffee. Set your timer and allow the cup to sit undisturbed for at least 3 but no more than 5 minutes. Break the crust of ground coffee at the top of your cup and again smell the aromas. There's even an official way to break the crust – scrape the crust, trying not to stir the brew too much but moving the solids out of the way. Pull the spoon from the cup – while the foam and liquid is running down the back of the spoon (into your cup, not onto the floor or table). Smell and record your impressions of the aromas of the dry and wet grounds.

While you are waiting for the brewed coffee to cool, you can turn your attention to the bitter and sour sensory references. If you are part of a course, the instructor will likely have prepared the references for you; if you are doing this at home, you will have to prepare the references using the recipe as follows:

Bitter reference: 0.1% caffeine dissolved in water (e.g., 1 gram in 1 kg of water)
Sour reference: 1.25% citric acid dissolved in water (e.g., 12.5 grams in 1 kg of water)

Make sure you procure pure caffeine powder and pure citric acid powder (without any additives that might add flavors), and that the powders are fully dissolved in the water before tasting.

To taste, pour a few milliliters of each reference into a small glass (espresso cup). Smell each one separately; do you smell anything? Then, take a small sip of the bitter reference. Rinse your mouth with some fresh water, and take a small sip of the sour reference. Repeat a few times, until you are confident you have a good sense of what is meant by "bitter" and "sour." Keep those impressions in mind as you taste the coffees. If you happen to be a "supertaster," the bitter taste will be very strong. Dilute the bitter sample by half with plain water, and by half again, to taste each dilution and see how sensitive you are to bitterness.

After the grounds have been allowed to steep for about ten minutes you can start tasting (or slurping!) the brew. While the coffee is hot, your initial impressions should focus on the flavor and aftertaste. As it starts to cool, turn your attention to the acidity and the body. Next, assess the balance, mouth feel, and sweetness. Continue to taste and adjust your evaluations as your perception of the flavors and qualities change with temperature. In particular, how do the coffees differ in their bitterness and sourness? Is one particularly more sour or bitter?

Once you're done with tasting, clean up your area. There is no lab report associated with this lab, simply make sure you have signed and submitted your safety sheet. But make sure you remember the definitions of all the sensory attributes (body, acidity, balance, etc.) as you progress through the upcoming labs. Your ultimate design goal is to make the best tasting coffee using the least amount of energy… and these sensory attributes are what your coffee will be judged on!

Cupping Data Sheet

Coffee type_____

Fragrance evaluation of ground coffee: _____

Fragrance evaluation of brewed coffee: _____

Tasting evaluations of Flavor: _____

Aftertaste: _____ Acidity: _____

Body: _____ Sweetness: _____

Defects:_____ Balance: _____

Comments: _____

Coffee type_____

Fragrance evaluation of ground coffee: _____

Fragrance evaluation of brewed coffee: _____

Tasting evaluations of Flavor: _____

Aftertaste: _____ Acidity: _____

Body: _____ Sweetness: _____

Defects:_____ Balance: _____

Comments: _____

Lab 1 Bonus Box – Why Do Coffees Taste Different?

Now that you've seen and smelled some green and roasted coffee beans, we should discuss a key point: coffee is a highly variable biological material! Much like the grapes used to make fine wines, coffee beans vary tremendously in taste depending on where they are grown and with how much care they are picked and processed. High quality, specialty coffee is mainly produced in tropical, equatorial zones at elevations greater than 3000 feet (equivalent to 1000 meters above sea level). Coffee "beans" are the seeds of the fruit (coffee cherry) of the *Coffea* shrub or tree. A mature plant typically produces about 20-60 pounds of coffee cherries each year, yielding between 3 and 9 pounds of green coffee beans. To maximize the quality of the green beans, the cherries must be harvested at their peak ripeness – typically bright red, yellow, or orange in color depending on the variety. Because the cherries ripen at different rates, harvesting of optimally ripe coffee cherries is very labor-intensive with multiple picks.

Workers on a coffee farm (typically in a developing tropical country) have to care for the coffee trees, pick the ripe cherries, de-pulp the cherries to remove the fruity flesh, wash and dry the beans, sort out the bad beans by hand, bag the good beans, and then transport them to the nearest buyer – oftentimes by mule down the side of a mountain. In a sense, by the time the consumer or the commercial roaster receives a shipment of green coffee beans, most of the hard work has already been done.

There are fascinating scientific aspects to the processing of coffee cherries to usable green beans, which is done primarily through two main processing methods: wet or dry processing. Ultimately, the goal of processing is to separate the beans from the fruit and reduce their moisture content to about 12%. This enables transport and storage of the green beans for up to one year with little degradation, making it easy to ship the beans all over the world.

In dry processing the growers lay the coffee cherries out in the sun to dry. Over the course of 3 to 4 weeks the cherries are raked and rotated every few hours and protected from moisture to ensure even drying without mildew or spoilage. In some cases, mechanical dryers are used after a few days to accelerate the drying process. Once the cherries are dried sufficiently, the outer hull is removed to release the coffee beans. Dry processing is used in production areas with limited access to water and is more variable due to the reliance on climate conditions during the drying process. On the other hand, wet processing uses a hand or mechanical depulper to remove the outer skin and some of the pulp from the cherries immediately after harvest, and then a lot of water to ultimately separate the seeds from the fruit. After depulping there is a lot of mucilage (a slimy fruit residue) on the seeds, so they are stored for a few hours to a couple of days and allowed to "ferment" to breakdown the mucilage and allow it to be removed from the seeds more easily by washing. Fermentation also occurs during dry processing, but it is not controlled by washing steps.

The word "fermentation" refers to a biological process in which yeast or bacteria convert sugars into different chemicals (such as the alcohol in beer). Moreover, it has long been held that a crucial step in the final flavor and aroma profile of roasted coffee is the fermentation step during the processing of the coffee cherries, as the coffee beans produced via the different methods yield notably different taste profiles. Some growers and coffee processors are experimenting with various yeasts (like those used for different kinds of beer or wine) to try to enhance the flavor characteristics by better controlling the fermentation portion of the process. The impact of these experiments is still up in the air, but in the future you might have green coffee beans fermented with an IPA yeast, or an ale yeast, or even a Chardonnay yeast. More recently, variations in the partial germination of the coffee beans (recall the "beans" are really seeds) during wet vs. dry processing steps are being studied more closely as germination may be just as, or even more, important to the final flavors. The word "germination" refers to the process by which a seed yields a plant. Given that coffee bean processing has evolved through a trial and error process - limited or impacted by the local environment (humidity and temperature), availability of water, equipment, time and resources – we hope that an even better understanding of how to produce great coffee will be available in the near future.

The key point is that both a huge amount of manual labor and a great deal of biological activity go into the preparation of green coffee beans. Despite all this hard work and the interesting scientific aspects, for the purpose of this book we focus on what happens to green coffee beans after all this processing. In other words, we treat green coffee beans as our starting material. There is nothing unusual about this; many other chemical engineering processes involve "raw" starting materials that were actually pre-processed in some way. Moreover, from a practical perspective, in the US it is difficult to obtain unprocessed coffee cherries.

An important point, however, must be emphasized: because coffee is a biological material, it is subject to tremendous variability. Green coffee beans vary wildly in their precise composition depending on what region they're grown. Beans grown in Brazil are distinct from those grown in Indonesia, Ethiopia or anywhere else. Even beans from ostensibly identical coffee plants in the same plantation can also differ, depending on soil characteristics, how wet or dry the local microclimate is, or even the precise altitude of the coffee plant. (Recall many coffee plants are grown in mountainous terrain.) Moreover, the coffee cherry processing method will alter otherwise similar green coffee beans into dramatically different beans.

All of these factors will influence the taste of the final brewed coffee! Perhaps surprisingly, black coffee can have amazing flavors, including berry, floral, citrus, chocolate, and vanilla. Black coffee can even have a pronounced sweet taste – without adding sugar. The image below shows a part of the "Coffee Taster's Flavor Wheel," developed by a collaboration between the Specialty Coffee Association, World Coffee Research, and UC Davis. The full wheel lists 104 different flavors that have been detected in coffee!

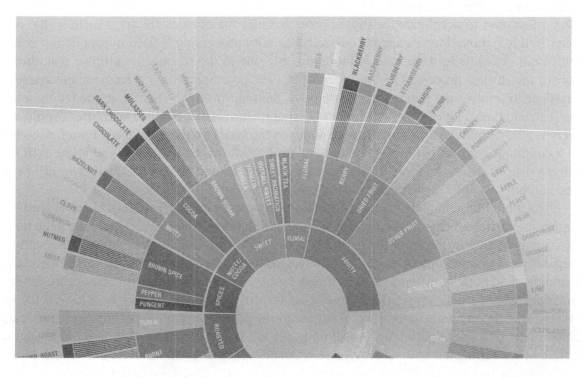

To give an idea of the tremendous flavor profiles possible, here is an example review of a particular 2021 coffee from the Kangunu Farmers Cooperative Society in Kenya (on the east side of central Africa):

The fragrance from the dry grounds is boldly potent, with a strong cane sugar syrupy sweetness, and caramelized sugar notes like flambe dessert. Adding hot water, the wet aroma has mild fruited character, like tamarind chews, enveloped in caramel-vanilla sweetness, and raw sugar smells. The cup is perhaps tamer than some other Kenyas on our list, but the fruit flavors that do come into view are delicious; dried plum, Medjool date, and more of the dried tamarind. Sweetness rates very high (9.3!), and lays out complex flavors of pressed sugarcane juice, panela, unrefined cane sugar types. The cup is very 'fresh' in flavor, and while fruits are milder, they're most present in the cup, which is where we want them, right? Light roasts also have a dark black tea note that feeds in the finishing mouthfeel that is tannic with a pleasant bittering aspect. A sharp lemony accent note takes the light roasts to a level of vibrance that is uniquely Kenya!

This review was written by Tom Owens and colleagues at Sweet Maria's, which is one of many retail distributors of specialty green beans. We urge you to do a simple web search "green coffee beans for roasting" to get a sense for the astonishing variety of green beans available for purchase. Many types cost only about $6 per pound.

Why does one batch of green coffee beans taste different from another? Everything hinges on the unique chemical composition of the green beans, and how those molecules are altered during roasting and released during brewing. There are more than 1,000 uniquely identified molecules that give rise to the flavors present in coffee, and as mentioned above, minor changes in growing conditions and processing procedure can alter the relative composition. The roasting process can enhance or diminish different aspects of the bean's flavor profile. Moreover, many of the most subtle flavors (such as "Medjool date" or "dried tamarind") are highly volatile and transient. If you wait too long after roasting, the flavors dissipate… and you're left with the more bitter molecules. Most coffee aficionados recommend that you store roasted coffee in a sealed container and brew it about 2 to 7 days after roasting. You can still brew the coffee after longer delays, but it will be more difficult to catch the types of refined and varied flavors that are possible (as highlighted in the review above).

Of course, there is more to making coffee than simply brewing it within the right time period! The upcoming labs will help you think more scientifically about the process of roasting and brewing coffee, with the ultimate goal of brewing coffee with delightful flavors like those described here.

Part II

Analysis of Coffee

Lab 2 – Reverse Engineering a Drip Coffee Brewer

Objectives: In this lab we will overview and perform the process of brewing drip coffee, and learn about the important "brew ratio." We will partially disassemble a Mr. Coffee brewer to consider how it works from an engineering perspective.

Equipment:

☐ Mr. Coffee   ☐ Thermometer and thermocouple ☐ Screwdriver

Activities:

☐ Part A – one brew in the Mr. Coffee, to learn how to brew and to introduce R_{brew}

☐ Part B – partial disassembly of the Mr. Coffee to reverse engineer it

☐ Part C – one more brew with temperature measurements

Report:

☐ Labeled photos of the Mr. Coffee (inside and outside)

☐ Qualitative process flow diagram for brewing

☐ Scatter plot of temperature vs. time

☐ Paragraph discussing key questions about the lab

Background

There are two key components of engineering practice: *analysis* and *design*. Engineering *analysis* is the process of learning how a system of interest works, typically by combining experimental observations with theoretical interpretations. In contrast, engineering *design* refers to using that understanding to create or improve a process to accomplish some specific goal – for example, to make the best tasting coffee using the least amount of energy.

In this lab, we will be performing a specific type of engineering analysis called "reverse engineering," where we take a process that somebody else has already designed and figure out how it works. Specifically, we will reverse engineer a standard drip brewer, with a focus on the question, "What makes the water move?" Furthermore, as part of this process we will make a "process flow diagram." The picture at right shows a simplified and **incomplete** process flow diagram superimposed over a photo of a Mr. Coffee. Your goals in this lab are to (1) reverse engineer a Mr. Coffee and (2) make a qualitative process flow diagram for this brewing process. In Lab 3 you will make a more complete and quantitative process flow diagram that includes roasting.

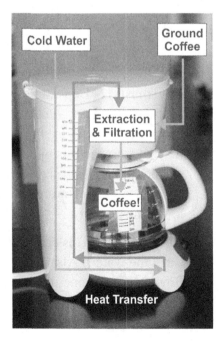

Background – Reverse Engineering a Drip Brewer

We could just tell you exactly how a drip brewer works, but that would be boring. Instead, we want you to figure it out! To help you along the way, here are some of the items you will discover as you inspect the brewer.

☐ **Spring valve** – The first thing you should identify before you even open up the brewer. When you push on the spring, the valve opens; when you stop pushing on it, the valve closes. This valve allows you to pull the carafe out before brewing is complete (without making a mess).

☐ **Power Switch** – This is how you turn it on. It's easy to find from the outside; what does it look like from the inside? How do you think it works?

☐ **Wires** – As soon as you open up the bottom of the brewer you will definitely see several electrical wires inside. As you examine them, consider these two questions. (i) Why are they coated in plastic? (ii) Why are there two wires connected to the heater? Why couldn't just one wire deliver the electricity to it? (This is a subtle question!) Hint: pretend you're an electron: what path would you follow through the circuitry? On some models, you will have even more wires headed to indicator lights or other features. In a simple 4-cup Mr. Coffee brewer, one set of wires is only used to illuminate the power switch; where does the remainder go?

☐ **Heating tube** – There will be a large metallic "u"-shaped tube inside. Why do you think it's made out of metal? Why not plastic or ceramic? What else does this heating tube keep hot beside the water inside of it?

☐ **Electrical heater** – When you make electricity flow through a "resistor," the resistor heats up. This is the same effect you see in an incandescent light bulb, where it heats up so much that it starts glowing.

☐ **Thermal Fuse** – A thermal fuse has a special type of thin wire inside of it that allows electrical currents to pass through, but if the temperature gets too high, the thin wire physically melts and breaks, stopping the current. (Why do you think you might want a thermal fuse, **or two**, inside a coffee maker?)

☐ **Thermostat** – Depending on the model of coffee maker, you might have a thermostat or "Klixon" that regulates the flow of electricity. If the temperature gets too high, the thermostat or Klixon simply cuts the electricity to the heater. More expensive brewers may have a "thermistor." A "resistor" resists the flow of electricity, making the current smaller (and thus the temperature smaller). A "thermistor" is a resistor whose resistance depends on temperature. The higher the temperature, the higher the resistance, and the lower the current.

☐ **Check valve** – This can be difficult to locate! (Look closely inside the plastic tubes that carry the water.) Also known as a "one-way" valve, a check valve only allows fluid to flow through it one direction. Typically, there is a flap or ball inside that opens when you push it one way but closes when you push it the other way.

Background – Process Flow Diagrams

As mentioned above, one goal of this lab is for you to construct a "process flow diagram" for the process of making coffee. You can think of a process flow diagram as a kind of map that shows how different materials move through different processes or pieces of equipment. Typically, the process flow diagram shows major pieces of equipment and omits minor details (such as piping). A process flow diagram for a large-scale operation, such as a petroleum refinery, can be extremely complicated – there can be thousands of pieces of equipment and distinct "unit operations." *A unit operation is any step in a process where a chemical or physical change takes place.* For example, a roaster induces a variety of chemical reactions to occur in the green beans; a grinder changes the average size of the roasted beans; a brewer extracts the hopefully tasty coffee molecules into the hot water. Each of these can be considered a "unit operation," but even within a single piece of equipment there can be multiple unit operations. A drip brewer combines the unit operations of heating, extraction, and filtration in one compact unit.

Here we start simple. Examine the figure below, which shows a simplified process flow diagram for a process you're probably familiar with: doing laundry! Note it includes both the obvious "material streams" that you handle personally (like the clothes) as well as the streams you probably don't think about (like the waste water). Importantly, conservation of mass (discussed in Lab 3) must be satisfied around each unit operation. Check that the mass going into the washer is equal to the mass exiting it. (In fact, can you figure out the mass of dirt on the dirty clothes? It's possible to calculate based on the given information.)

A coffee brewer is much simpler, but still requires thought. The most important thing is to think about "what goes in" and "what goes out" in each material stream. Specifically, there are two obvious streams of material that go into the coffee brewer – cold water and dry coffee grounds – but how many streams come out? There are at least three, and each one needs its own arrow. Keep this question in mind as you perform your first brews!

Example of a Process Flow Diagram: Doing your Laundry!

(Note that every material stream is shown entering or exiting the correct unit operatic

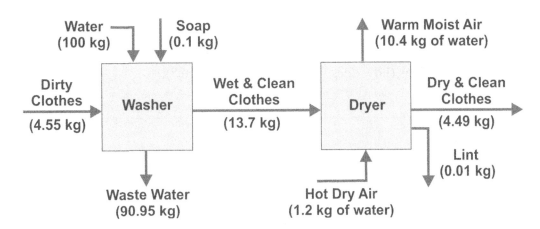

Part A – Your First Drip Brew

Time to brew! First, get some roasted coffee beans (about 40 grams), and place them in the grinder. For a drip brew, you want a "medium" grind, which is not a fine powder, but more like kosher salt or coarse beach sand. (On Baratza Encore grinders this is a grind size setting of about 18.) Place a weighed mass of coffee grounds into the basket. Then pour a known <u>mass</u> (not volume) of cold water into the back of the drip brewer. How much water? The metric that matters is known as the "brew ratio," defined as

$$R_{brew} = \frac{\text{mass of water}}{\text{mass of dry coffee grounds}}. \tag{1}$$

The brew ratio is a hugely important parameter for brewing, and as we shall discover it turns out that small changes in R_{brew} can yield large changes in taste. For this initial brew, you want to use R_{brew} somewhere between 14 and 19. As an example, if you put in 40 grams of coffee grounds and 600 grams of cold water, you would have a brew ratio of 15. Remember: **the higher the brew ratio, the weaker the coffee!** (Refer to Appendix B and Appendix C for a concise summary of brewing and useful conversion factors.)

Watch the brewer carefully as it operates. Most importantly, think about the movement of the water as it moves up from the reservoir and then onto the grounds. Keep this question in mind: what causes the water to move up? Pour your brew into cups and turn off and unplug the Mr. Coffee. Taste the resulting coffee. What are your qualitative impressions? Refer to the "coffee flavor wheel" – can you detect any specific flavor notes? (Refer back to Lab 1 for a guide to tasting coffee.)

Data for the First Brew

Coffee type_____

Mass of water:_____ grams   Mass of beans:_____ grams

Brew Ratio (mass of water per mass of ground beans):

$R_{brew} = $ _____ ÷ _____ = _____

Sensory Evaluations (how does the brew smell and taste?):

_____

_____

Hypothesis for why the water moves:

_____

_____

_____

Part B – Partial Disassembly of a Drip Brewer

Once the Mr. Coffee is cool enough to handle, you will partially disassemble it to figure out how it works. Refer to the instructions and the guided questions below.

1) Turn off and unplug the brewer. Remove the spent grounds and put the glass carafe somewhere to the side. After the Mr. Coffee maker is cool enough to safely handle, turn the Mr. Coffee upside and use the provided screwdriver to remove the rubber feet and 6 screws on the bottom. Don't lose the feet or screws! Put them into an empty coffee cup.

2) Remove the bottom plate, and carefully inspect the interior of the Mr. Coffee. Try to identify each of the components visible underneath. Discuss with your group mates what mechanism you think there is for making the water move up to the grounds. Take a look at the various tubes that connect the cold water reservoir to the upper basket where the ground coffee is placed. **IMPORTANT: Do not attempt to remove anything more or further disassemble the Mr. Coffee, this will likely break it.**

3) Take photos! While the Mr. Coffee is still opened up, have at least one person in your group take photos: one from the side, one from the top looking at the reservoir and grounds basket, and one looking at the inside from underneath (showing all the electrical components). These photos are necessary for your lab report.

4) After you are satisfied with your photos, review and answer the guided questions below. Work with your group to identify the key components listed on the checklist on page 28.

5) Reassemble the Mr. Coffee. Make sure that the wires are not pinched.

Reverse Engineering Guided Questions

After you remove the bottom cover of the drip brewer, carefully examine (and photograph) the interior. Recall all the important components are listed on page 28.

(i) First, trace the path of the water.

Are there any pumps or moving parts inside? _____

Look for a "check valve" inside of the rubber tubing. Which way does the check valve let the water flow?

_____

(ii) Next, let's examine the electrical circuitry.

Where is the electrical heater? _____

Why do you think it is located there, instead of where you pour the water in?

_____

Why are there wires connected to both sides of the heater? Why can't just one wire deliver the electricity?

_____

_____

There is at least one "fuse" between the heater and the wires leading to the electrical plug, and there likely is a "thermostat" attached to the heater. Why do you think the fuses and thermostat are there? What purposes do they serve?

_____

_____

(iii) After having looked at both the path of the water and the electrical components, what do you think forces the water to move up to the spray head? Do you think it boils and floats up as steam? How would you check this? If the water is not moving up as steam, what would make the hot water move up? (Think about what happens when bubbles expand... when you vaporize liquid water, it increases in volume by more than a factor of 500!) If the check valve wasn't there, what do you think would happen when you try to brew coffee?

_____

_____

_____

_____

Part C – Second Brew with Temperature Measurements

Finally, brew a second batch of coffee with two goals: measuring the masses of water, dry grounds, brew, and wet grounds carefully, and **testing any hypotheses your group generated regarding the mechanism for how the water moved up against gravity**. You will find a thermometer helpful! If the first brew was too "weak" or "strong" you may want to adjust your coffee to water ratio or the grind size to improve your second brew.

1) Carefully measure the mass of ground coffee you put into the Mr. Coffee, and carefully measure the mass of water you put in.

2) Measure the temperature in an appropriate location versus time during the entire brewing process. Hint: to understand why the water moves up to the spray nozzle, measure the temperature of the water dripping out of the spray nozzle. Recording every 15 seconds is recommended (see next page for template). What does the temperature tell you? (Recall the boiling point of water is 100°C.) After you're done brewing, measure the mass of coffee in the carafe. Also carefully weigh the moist "spent" grounds. Did the grounds gain or lose mass during the brewing? How much drinkable coffee did you get?

3) Does the second batch taste similar to the first? If not, why not? Again, refer to the coffee flavor wheel and the tasting guide in Lab 1.

Data and Tasting Notes for Second Brew

Coffee type:_____

Mass of empty carafe: _____ grams

Mass of water:_____ grams   Mass of beans:_____ grams R_{brew} :_____

Combined mass of plastic basket and filter paper: _____ grams

Mass of carafe with brewed coffee: _____ grams

Actual mass of brewed coffee = mass of carafe with brewed coffee – mass empty carafe

Actual mass of brewed coffee = _____ – _____ = _____ grams

Combined mass of plastic basket, filter paper and spent moist grounds: _____ grams

Actual mass of spent moist grounds: _____ – _____ = _____ grams

Sensory Evaluations: _____

_____

Temperature Data for Second Brew

Make sure the thermocouple is plugged in correctly into the meter. The big prong goes in the big hole. If the temperature goes down or negative, it is inserted backwards!

Time (seconds)	Temperature (°C)	Time (seconds)	Temperature (°C)
_____ (first drips)	_____	_____	_____
_____	_____	_____	_____
_____	_____	_____	_____
_____	_____	_____	_____
_____	_____	_____	_____
_____	_____	_____	_____
_____	_____	_____	_____
_____	_____	_____	_____
_____	_____	_____	_____

(Last time recorded should correspond to the last drips delivered.)

Lab Report

By your specified due date, each group will submit their lab report that includes four main required parts: (1) labeled photos of the Mr. Coffee, (2) a qualitative process flow diagram, (3) a labeled scatter plot of temperature versus time, and (4) a brief paragraph discussing the mechanism for moving the water up in a Mr. Coffee.

(1) Open a new file in PowerPoint, and then import your best three photos of the Mr. Coffee: one from the side, one from the top looking under the lid, and one looking at the inside from underneath. Next, label all of the components and different parts of the Mr. Coffee. Use bright red arrows and easily readable text. (Hint: important labels include "reservoir," "carafe," "heating plate," and "filter basket.") Make sure you label all the components listed on page 28. Underneath each label, put a brief description (one phrase or one sentence max) of the purpose of that component or part. Use a smaller but still legible font for the description. You should end up with about a dozen unique labels.

(2) Sketch a "process flow diagram" for the brewing of coffee. Start with roasted coffee beans, and end with a final carafe full of coffee. An example process flow diagram (for doing laundry) is on page 29. Each unit operation can simply be a labeled rectangle (e.g., "grinder", "filter", etc.), but more importantly include labeled arrows showing **all** material streams entering and leaving each unit operation. Don't forget waste streams (e.g., the spent moist grounds). Most importantly, record your measurements of the masses of ground coffee and water you put into the Mr. Coffee, and the masses of what came out (moist spent grounds and drinkable coffee). You will be doing this more carefully in Lab 3. Import your sketch into your PowerPoint.

(3) Review the section on "Data and Plotting" in Appendix A. Then, use Excel or Google Sheets to enter your measured temperature data, and generate a "scatter plot" of your temperature versus time. Make sure you label your axes and use proper units! For the title of the plot, indicate precisely where the temperature was measured. Copy your scatter plot into PowerPoint on a separate slide.

(4) On a final separate slide, insert a text box and write a brief paragraph (10 sentences max) that clearly answers the following questions: What causes the water to move upward? Why is there a check valve? What does your temperature data indicate regarding the mechanism? Why do you think the designers of the Mr. Coffee chose this approach for heating and moving the water?

Lab 2 Bonus Box – Caffeine the Wonder Drug

Coffee, tea, soda, chocolate - there are a lot of different ways to get your caffeine fix. But what is caffeine? In chemistry terms, it's an "organic" molecule composed of carbon, nitrogen, oxygen, and hydrogen, arranged in the molecular structure shown at right. Here we use the word "organic" in the chemistry sense that the compound contains carbon, not that it was a food grown without pesticides (as you find the word used in grocery stores). The chemical formula might look intimidating ($C_8H_{10}N_4O_2$), but caffeine is a natural substance: many different plants, including *Coffea arabica*, produce caffeine as a defense mechanism against insects – to them it is toxic. Happily, caffeine has positive psychoactive effects on mammals: reduced drowsiness, faster and clearer flow of thought, increased focus, better body coordination.

How much caffeine do you consume when you drink a cup of coffee? Well, each 8-ounce cup of coffee has between 75 to 175 milligrams (mg) of caffeine, depending mostly on the type of coffee and how it was brewed. The roast level doesn't really affect it, since the caffeine molecule doesn't break down during roasting (it is very stable). A rule of thumb is about 100 mg caffeine per cup of coffee. Caffeine is "generally regarded as safe," since the lethal dose for humans is about 10 grams. You would have to chug about 100 cups in a row to hit that dosage!

In comparison to coffee, a typical cola (diet or regular) has a meager 25 to 45 mg of caffeine. Black tea has about 50 mg, while green tea has about 25 mg (all based on 8 ounce cups). Typical dark chocolate, say 70%, has about 80 mg per 2 ounces, or a whopping 320 mg if you ate a full 8 ounces (which is a half-pound of chocolate!) Caffeine in chocolate comes from the amount of cocoa "bean" (still a seed like coffee beans) in the chocolate; the darker the chocolate, the higher the cocoa bean content and the greater the caffeine. The average adult consumes 300 mg of caffeine per day from all sources.

The range of caffeine levels in coffee stems partly from differences between the caffeine content in arabica vs. robusta coffee beans (another variety of *Coffea*). Specialty or gourmet coffees are typically arabica because it is considered to have a much better flavor profile, partially because arabica contains about half as much of caffeine and twice as much sucrose (sugar) compared to robusta. (The sucrose plays a key role in many of the roasting reactions that yield awesome flavors.) Robusta is definitely more "robust," with about 2.7% caffeine by mass to arabica's 1.5%. If you drink inexpensive instant coffee, it likely contains robusta. About 70% of coffee grown worldwide is arabica because of the better taste and higher price.

Now why is caffeine considered a "Wonder Drug"? Believe it or not, some of the most extensive research on the effects of caffeine was carried out by various branches of the armed forces. In a military situation, staying alert could be a life or death proposition. Compared to other stimulants, caffeine is considered one of the safest – it has extremely low incidences of abuse and adverse health effects, it is a substance most people have experience with, it is known to help alleviate sleep deprivation-induced cognitive impairment, and it even improves strength and endurance. When you drink a caffeinated beverage or take a capsule, it takes about 30 to 45 minutes to have the full effects. To overcome this delay Wrigley and the Walter Reed Army Institute of Research developed "Stay Alert" caffeinated chewing gum which reaches your system in 5 to 10 minutes – a significant advantage if you need a quick pick-me-up.

Lab 3 – Process Flow Diagram & Mass Balances for Coffee

Objectives: The overarching goal of this lab is to answer the question, "Where does the initial mass of green coffee beans ultimately end up when you make coffee?" To answer this question, we will carefully measure the mass of each material stream through both the roasting and brewing processes, to make a complete process flow diagram that includes all unit operations.

Equipment:

☐ Mr. Coffee ☐ Fresh Roast roaster ☐ Colander and brush ☐ Graduated cylinder

Activities:

☐ Part A – four brews in the Mr. Coffee, to determine mass balances and R_{abs}

☐ Part B – one roast in the Fresh Roast, to measure mass and volume changes

Report:

☐ Quantitative process flow diagram, with mass balances

☐ Summary of mass balance calculations

☐ Scatter plot of m_{brew} vs. $m_{grounds}$, with best fit slope for R_{abs}

☐ Photos of your roast showing volume change

☐ Paragraph discussing key questions about the lab

Background

As discussed in the previous lab, a "unit operation" is any step in a process where a chemical or physical change takes place. The process of making coffee involves many different unit operations. The roaster causes a variety of chemical reactions to occur in the green beans; the grinder physically alters the beans by changing their size; a brewer extracts the hopefully tasty coffee molecules into the hot water and then filters out the residual solids.

A fundamental aspect of every unit operation, regardless of how big or small, is that **mass must be conserved**. In other words, if we put 100 grams into a unit operation, ultimately we must get 100 grams out. This might sound very obvious. Things get tricky, however, if we have multiple streams of mass moving into and out of the same unit operation. For example, a drip coffee brewer has two streams moving into it – ground coffee and cold water – but three streams moving out of it – (1) coffee to drink, (2) moist spent grounds, and (3) volatile gasses (steam, carbon dioxide, and volatile organic compounds or VOCs, which are the molecules you smell in the air). The existence of these other two streams has a profound consequence: if we put in 300 grams of cold water into the brewer, we **don't** get 300 grams of coffee to drink! Some of the water is "lost" to the other waste streams.

So, if we want to design a process to make a large quantity of coffee (say 1 liter of coffee for the design competition), we must first analyze how mass flows through the system. The crucial question is: how much water and coffee grounds should we put in to get a certain amount of brewed coffee? Likewise, how much coffee should we roast?

Mass Balance for Water in Brewing

Let's focus first on the mass of water in the drip brewer. In words, our equation for conservation of mass is

$$Mass\ of\ Water\ In = Mass\ of\ Water\ Out. \tag{1}$$

Recognizing that we have one stream of water feed in, but three streams that contain water feed out, equation (1) means we have

$$m_{feed} = m_{brew} + m_{spent} + m_{evap}. \tag{2}$$

Here m_{feed} is the mass of cold water put into the brewer, m_{brew} is the mass of water in the brewed coffee, m_{spent} is the mass of <u>water</u> in the moist spent grounds, and m_{evap} is the mass of water lost as evaporated steam (water vapor) into the atmosphere. Importantly, in this balance each of these terms refers only to the mass of water in that stream, so m_{spent} is not the combined mass of solid coffee and water in the moist spent grounds – it's only the water mass.

Equation (2) isn't so useful yet, but it turns out we can make some very helpful **simplifying assumptions**. First, under most circumstances the mass lost to evaporation is pretty small, so we can neglect it. (You will test whether this is a good assumption in this lab.) Second, it turns out that brewed coffee is about 99% water, i.e., the coffee solids dissolved in the brew are only about 1% by mass. So for now, we will ignore the mass of coffee solids in the brew and just approximate it as all water mass. (As we shall see in Lab 6, another mass balance applies to the coffee solids, and we can determine the mass of coffee solids extracted into the brewed coffee.)

Third, and most importantly, we need to know how much water gets "left behind" in the spent grounds. The initially dry coffee grounds have a finite capacity to "absorb" water, in much the same way a paper towel can only absorb so much water. To a good approximation, the mass of water absorbed into the spent grounds is simply proportional to the initial mass of dry coffee grounds, i.e.,

$$m_{spent} = R_{abs} \times m_{grounds}. \tag{3}$$

Here R_{abs} is the "absorption ratio" that describes the ratio of how many grams of water are absorbed in the moistened grounds, per gram of initial dry coffee grounds, i.e.,

$$R_{abs} = \frac{\text{mass of water absorbed into the coffee grounds}}{\text{initial mass of dry coffee grounds}} \tag{4}$$

If we substitute Eq. (3) into Eq. (2), and neglect the mass lost to evaporation, we obtain the very useful prediction

$$m_{brew} = m_{feed} - (R_{abs} \times m_{grounds}). \tag{5}$$

In other words, if we want to know **how much drinkable coffee we're going to get**, we need to know three things:

      i)   how much cold water
      ii) how much dry coffee grounds
      iii) the numerical value of R_{abs}

A key goal of this lab is for you to measure R_{abs} experimentally. You can do this by systematically varying the mass of dry grounds but with a fixed amount of cold water. Instead of calculating R_{abs} for each individual brew, we will perform a more accurate procedure. Equation (5) is what's known as a "linear equation," of the form you likely studied in high school. A plot of how much drinkable coffee you get (m_{brew}) on the vertical axis versus how much dry grounds you used ($m_{grounds}$) on the horizontal axis will yield a straight line. The intercept of this plot will be m_{feed}, and the slope will be equal to $-R_{abs}$. (You can refer to Appendix A for tips and advice on plotting.) This procedure effectively yields what's known as a "best fit" value for R_{abs}.

Mass Balance for Roasting

To complete our process flow diagram, we also need to think about roasting. The principle of conservation of mass equally applies to roasting:

$$Mass\ of\ Coffee\ In = Mass\ of\ Coffee\ Out. \tag{6}$$

Just like for brewing, in roasting there are multiple streams that exit the roaster. Obviously, you have the roasted beans. As you will see during your first roast, you also have the "chaff," which is the paper-like outer skin of the green coffee beans that flakes off during roasting. In small home roasters, the chaff is usually trapped in a bin of some sort by a filter screen in the exhaust from the roaster (much like the lint screen in a clothes dryer). In large commercial roasters, chaff is caught in a "cyclone separator" that uses the swirling motion of the exhaust air to direct the chaff into a bin.

Finally, the least obvious stream of mass exiting the roaster is the escaping gasses. In our brewing mass balance we neglected the volatile gasses because they were so small. Roasting, in contrast, reaches much higher temperatures, and it turns out that a very significant fraction of mass is lost as water vapor, carbon dioxide, and other VOCs formed during the roasting reactions.

Putting everything together, equation (6) becomes

$$m_{green} = m_{roasted} + m_{chaff} + m_{gas}, \tag{7}$$

where m_{green} is the initial mass of green beans, $m_{roasted}$ is the mass of roasted beans afterwards, m_{chaff} is the mass of chaff collected during roasting, and m_{gas} is the collective mass of all the gasses that escaped during roasting.

The first three masses are easy to measure, but m_{gas} cannot be directly measured. That's ok – you will measure it indirectly in this lab!

Part A – Mass Balances for Brewing

1) First, weigh out about 65 grams of roasted coffee beans and then grind all of them together at the same time. This ensures a uniform grind size for all experiments in Part A.

2) Weigh the empty glass carafe and empty filter basket (with a dry filter paper inside of it). You will need these weights later.

3) Pour 300 grams of cold water into the Mr. Coffee, and place 20 grams of your ground coffee in the filter basket. (Set the other 45 grams to the side.) Before you begin brewing, however, weigh the entire Mr. Coffee and record the mass. **Make sure the electrical cord is unplugged and draped over the top of the Mr. Coffee**; otherwise your mass measurements will vary with how much tension is on the cord. You will eventually compare this initial mass to the mass after the brewing is done. What will these numbers tell you about the mass of lost gases (like steam)?

4) After the Mr. Coffee is done brewing, weigh the entire mass of the Mr. Coffee in the same fashion you did at the start (in step 3), and then separately weigh the glass carafe (with coffee) as well as the combined mass of the plastic basket (with moist spent grounds).

5) Go ahead and taste the coffee – how does it taste?

6) Repeat steps (3) and (5) for three more brews (no need to repeat step 4, unless you want to). Each time, use exactly 300 grams of cold water, but vary the mass of ground coffee beans. Recommended: second brew, use 30 grams; third brew, use 10 grams, fourth and final brew, use 5 grams. Make sure you carefully record the mass of brewed coffee each time. How does the brew ratio affect the taste?

Data for First Brew (and Flow Diagram)

Coffee type_____

Mass of empty glass carafe: _____ *grams*

Combined mass of plastic basket and filter paper: _____ *grams*

Mass of cold water:_____ *grams* Mass of beans:_____ *grams* R_{brew}=_____

Mass of entire Mr. Coffee (with water and grounds) **before** brewing: _____ *grams*

Mass of entire Mr. Coffee (with water and grounds) **after** brewing: _____ *grams*

Mass lost to evaporation: _____ – _____ = _____ *grams*

Mass of carafe with brewed coffee: _____ *grams*

Actual mass of brewed coffee: _____ – _____ = _____ *grams*

Combined mass of plastic basket, moist filter and spent moist grounds: _____ *grams*

Actual mass of spent moist grounds: _____ – _____ = _____ *grams*

Sensory Evaluations: _____

_____

Data for Second Brew

Mass of cold water: _____ *grams*   Mass of beans: _____ *grams* $R_{brew}=$_____

Mass of carafe with brewed coffee: _____ *grams*

Actual mass of brewed coffee: _____ − _____ = _____ *grams*

Sensory Evaluations: _____

_____

Data for Third Brew

Mass of cold water: _____ *grams*   Mass of beans: _____ *grams* $R_{brew}=$_____

Mass of carafe with brewed coffee: _____ *grams*

Actual mass of brewed coffee: _____ − _____ = _____ *grams*

Sensory Evaluations: _____

_____

Data for Fourth Brew

Mass of cold water: _____ *grams*   Mass of beans: _____ *grams* $R_{brew}=$_____

Mass of carafe with brewed coffee: _____ *grams*

Actual mass of brewed coffee: _____ − _____ = _____ *grams*

Sensory Evaluations: _____

_____

Part B – Mass Balances for Roasting

1) After you feel adequately caffeinated, it's time to turn to roasting. Review the safety guidelines for proper use of the roaster. Carefully weigh out 120 grams of green coffee beans, and place them in the graduated cylinder – what volume do they occupy? Take a picture of your green beans in the graduated cylinder, using a white piece of paper for background.

Safety note: Don't put too many green beans into the Fresh Roast roaster – and don't put too few! If you put in too many beans they will not circulate properly and they will catch on fire. Likewise, if you put in too few, they will get too hot too quickly and likely catch on fire. **The max is about 130 grams** of green coffee beans. Do not leave your roaster unattended for any reason. If you see lots of smoke, stop the roast! To stop it, press "Run/Cool."

2) Do a light roast, using the settings Fan 7, Power 7, Time 5.0 (for a Fresh Roast). The last three minutes of the roast is a cooling cycle, so the total time in the roaster is eight minutes. **Observe the beans as they roast!** Proper roast time is highly dependent on the beans' moisture and the specific electrical line voltage, which can vary considerably from one outlet to another. Try to listen for the first crack and **observe the color** – this will tell you more than the timer!

3) Next, measure the mass of an empty metal bowl. This is where you are going to collect the chaff. After the roast cooling cycle is complete, carefully remove the **hot** top of the Fresh Roast and place it in the metal bowl. Most of the chaff is inside. Carefully open the top, and brush the chaff into the bowl.

4) Next, dump the roasted beans into the metal mesh colander while holding it over the metal bowl to catch loose chaff. Important: for this lab you need to weigh all chaff! (In subsequent labs we won't collect the chaff; in fact, chaff is full of antioxidants that are good for human nutrition, so there is no need to remove it.) Carefully collect all the chaff, including any remaining loose chaff in the roasting chamber.

5) Weigh the collected chaff (subtract the empty bowl mass). Weigh the roasted coffee beans. Is the chaff weight appreciable or negligible? (Note many scales have a minimum weight tolerance – the chaff by itself won't register unless you use a heavy enough container.)

6) Pour the roasted beans back into the graduated cylinder. What volume do they now occupy? How much have they expanded? Take a picture of the roasted beans in the graduated cylinder. What type of roast would you characterize your beans as? Smell the roasted beans. The fragrance is likely not that strong yet, but it will develop over the next couple days. Feel free to taste one (they're edible.)

7) Once the roasted beans are completely cool, place them into a storage bag, and write your group's name, section number, and sample number on it. Warm beans can partially melt the bag causing unpleasant flavors – be patient!

Roasting Data

Coffee type_____

Mass of green beans:_____ grams   Volume of green beans:_____ mL

Roaster settings: _____ Time spent roasting: _____ minutes

Mass of roasted beans:_____ grams   Volume of roasted beans:_____ mL

Mass of empty metal bowl:_____ grams   Mass of bowl with chaff:_____ grams

Mass of chaff: _____ – _____ = _____ grams

Mass lost as volatile gasses: _____ – _____ – _____ = _____ grams

Note and observations: _____

_____

Lab Report

By your specified due date, each group will submit their lab report that includes (1) a quantitative process flow diagram that reflects **all** mass balances on the different material streams, (2) summary of mass balance calculations, (3) a scatter plot of m_{brew} vs. $m_{grounds}$, (4) labeled "before/after" photos of your roast, and (5) a brief paragraph discussing your group's observations.

(1) Open your qualitative "coffee process flow diagram" from last week, and make any modifications as necessary to it so that it is a complete diagram, including roasting (cf. the discussion and example process flow diagram on page 29). Using the data from your first brew, your group will then start inserting your quantitative mass measurements (numerical values). We will focus here only on the coffee solids and water streams – be sure to include waste streams. Make sure you include appropriate units (e.g., grams) with each number you insert! Start with green coffee beans, and end with a final cup of coffee. You will find that you roasted more beans than you could use in one brew, which is OK. Just indicate that the difference goes to "storage," so that your masses balance out. Even if you couldn't directly measure the mass of a stream, use conservation of mass and equations 2 and 7 to determine the mass.

(2) The second page should be your calculations to obtain the mass measurements. What you measured in lab should be clearly identified, and your calculations should be easy to follow. It is OK if you hand write this page and then scan or photograph it to insert into PowerPoint, but you will probably find it easier to use Excel (cf. step 3).

(3) In Excel, use your experimental data to generate a scatter plot of m_{brew} (on the vertical axis) versus $m_{grounds}$ (on the horizontal axis). Use the built-in line fitting to make a "best-fit" line and determine the slope. As discussed on page 38 the slope of this line is the negative of R_{abs}. (Refer to pages Appendix A for important Excel tips.)

(4) On the next page of your report, insert your "before/after" photos of the green and roasted beans. Make sure they're clearly labeled! What is the percent volume change?

(5) On a final separate slide, insert a text box and write a paragraph that clearly answers the following questions:

  (i)   What did your experiments tell you about the absorption ratio during brewing? What numerical value did you get for R_{abs}? As a specific example, if you start with 600 grams of cold water, how much drinkable coffee would you get if you used 50 grams of ground coffee?

  (ii) How much water was lost to steam or vapor during the brewing? Is the water lost to the gas phase a significant or negligible fraction of the overall water mass balance? In other words, how good was our first simplifying assumption on page 37?

  (iii) How much mass of initial green coffee beans do you "lose" during roasting? What fraction is the chaff? Where does the rest of the mass go? Do you think this answer will be the same for light and dark roasts?

Lab 3 Bonus Box – What happens to spent coffee grounds?

Every time you brew coffee, you are left with two things: hopefully the first is a great cup of coffee; the second is spent coffee grounds. We all know what to do with a great cup of coffee, but what can be done with spent coffee grounds? You definitely don't want to rebrew them, because you have already removed about 2/3 of the soluble coffee from the grounds (that's the 18 to 22% percent extraction that you will learn about in Lab 6). What's left behind are less desirable flavor molecules that take longer to extract and will not enhance your next brew.

If you go on-line, there are a wealth of resources and ideas for uses of spent coffee grounds. First, spent coffee grounds are a great fertilizer, especially if your soil is alkaline (pH>7). Most plants prefer soil pH to be between 6 to 7. Acid loving plants include cucumbers, eggplant, carrots, roses, and hydrangeas (which happen to be pH sensitive and turn a lovely purplish blue when fertilized with coffee). The grounds are also thought to keep some insects (ants, slugs, and snails) and even the neighbor's cat from using your garden as a litter box. Spent coffee grounds also can be used in your kitchen refrigerator or freezer as a deodorizer and are a handy way to keep worms alive for fishing or aid their digestion in the compost heap. But the uses don't stop there: spent grounds can even be part of your beauty regimen as an exfoliate (body scrub), face mask, or added to some shampoo to help remove styling product residue from hair.

These sorts of uses are great at the home scale where you might generate 100 grams of spent coffee grounds each day. Your local coffee house generates 10 to 50 pounds per day, though, and manufacturers can generate thousands of pounds of spent coffee grounds every day. For example, one medium size Bay Area cold brew coffee company we like produces 15,000 to 20,000 pounds of spent coffee grounds – per day! To put this on an even grander scale, Americans consume about 400 million cups of coffee per day, which corresponds to a staggering 24 million pounds of spent coffee grounds, each and every single day of the year.

Unfortunately, most of the spent grounds end up in landfills. Just as you might find it difficult to get every possible use out of your spent coffee grounds, coffee houses and companies have a difficult time, as well. That Bay Area manufacturer offers their spent coffee grounds for free to anyone who can find a way to use them. Unfortunately, few take them up on their offer.

This is a shame, because the spent coffee grounds contain useful chemicals not completely removed during brewing – such as remaining aromatic flavor compounds, lipids and fats, proteins, minerals, and phenolic antioxidants, which could be removed and used in other products. The bulk of the material, however, is cellulosic (plant cell walls). Cellulose and hemicellulose can be used as feedstocks for biorefineries, but with crude oil (petroleum) relatively inexpensive, biorefining of coffee grounds isn't profitable. Simply burning the spent grounds for energy is difficult as the grounds must be dry and burning them generates a lot of particulates, which are not good for air quality. The engineering challenge is to develop an environmentally sound and economically viable process. As more research is done, new treatments, processes, and uses may become available to improve the situation. Indeed, a completely integrated use/exploitation processing system where every valuable component is extracted and used optimally is possible with existing technology – and with further engineering work, should someday be economically viable.

Lab 4 – The pH of Coffee and Chemical Reactions

Objectives: In this lab, we will consider how the pH (the acidity) of brewed coffee depends on the roast level, and how the pH changes with time after brewing to estimate a "reaction rate." We will also do some more roasts to prepare for the next lab.

Equipment:

☐ Clever Coffee Dripper ☐ Electric kettle ☐ Mr. Coffee ☐ pH meter

☐ paper cups (or many small glasses) ☐ Fresh Roast roaster

Activities:

☐ Part A – Mr. Coffee brew with systematic sampling of pH over 60 minutes

☐ Part B – two Clever Coffee brews, to compare the pH of a commercial dark roast and your light roast from Lab 2

☐ Part C – two roasts in the Fresh Roast (one dark, one light) for the next lab

Report:

☐ Scatter plot of pH vs. time

☐ Estimate of the *rate* of the chemical reaction

☐ Tasting notes and pH of light roast vs. dark roast

☐ Paragraph discussing key questions about the lab

Background

Imagine that you carefully roast some high-quality green beans, and a few days later you carefully brew them. You taste it, and you think it's absolutely the best coffee you've ever made. Excited, you text your friend and invite them over. Half an hour later your friend arrives, but the response when they taste your coffee is a polite "I guess it's OK." Confused, you taste it again, and you agree… now it tastes mediocre. What happened?

A key thing to realize about coffee is that the taste of any given brew will change with time. The moment the hot water hits the coffee grounds, three processes start occurring. The first process is "mass transfer," which is the migration of the molecules out of the solid phase (ground beans) and into the liquid phase (water). This change is manifested as an obvious change in the color of the water, from transparent to dark. (We examine mass transfer in more detail in Lab 6.) This process stops once you separate the grounds from the brew.

Two other processes, however, continue to occur. The second process is the escape of volatile organic compounds (VOCs) from the liquid phase into the gas

phase. These VOCs comprise the wonderful aromas that you smell while brewing coffee; over 1000 unique different molecules have been identified as contributing to the aroma of coffee. As long as the coffee is exposed to the open atmosphere, the VOCs will continue to volatilize and escape. The VOCs in the brew are eventually depleted, so the wonderful coffee aroma disappears, and the taste stales and suffers.

The third process involves chemical reactions. This process is much less obvious, and most people have no idea it occurs. Even though it might look like your coffee pot is just sitting there with motionless coffee, in reality a bewildering variety of complicated reactions are taking place within the coffee. Some of these reactions generate new VOCs; others consume them. In particular, several chemical reactions release additional acidic molecules. Some acidity is good: coffee aficionados highly value coffees that yield a pleasant acidity, or "brightness," in their coffee. (Here the term "brightness" has nothing to do with how it looks visually!) Too much acidity, however, makes the coffee taste increasingly sour. These are the primary reasons that coffee sitting on a hot plate for a long time tastes "stale" and "sour."

Although the chemical reactions are complex, they have an easily measured effect on the brew: the pH of the brew changes with time. Recall that pH is a measure of the acid concentration in a solution, defined as

$$pH = -\log_{10}[H_3O^+], \tag{1}$$

where $[H_3O^+]$ is the concentration, in moles/liter, of "hydronium ions." A hydronium ion is basically a water molecule with an extra hydrogen atom attached to it, giving it a net positive charge. Note that the pH is a logarithmic scale. Distilled water has a pH of 7, which means the hydronium concentration is 10^{-7} mol/L. In contrast, the vinegar you buy at the store has a pH closer to 4, so the hydronium ion concentration is 10^{-4} mol/L. The difference between pH 4 and pH 7 might seem small numerically, but it's a logarithmic scale: the vinegar is $10^3 = 1000$ times more acidic.

As an example calculation, let's say you measure a coffee with pH = 5.2. The actual hydronium concentration is ten raised to the power of -5.2. In other words,

$$[H_3O^+] = 10^{\wedge(-5.2)} \frac{mol}{L} = 0.0000063 \frac{mol}{L} = 6.3 \times 10^{-6} \frac{mol}{L}. \tag{2}$$

Here the square brackets mean "concentration in moles per liter." Don't be fooled by the seemingly small number: the human tongue can definitely detect the acid associated with such small concentrations!

What sets the pH of coffee? The initial pH upon brewing will depend on several factors, including the variety of beans, how they were roasted (light vs. dark), as well as the initial pH and "alkalinity" of the water you use to brew. (We will explore alkalinity and water quality in more detail in Lab 7.) If the initial pH of the water is slightly basic (say around 8), then the initial pH of the brewed coffee might be around 6. With time, however, the chemical reactions keep generating more hydronium ions, and the pH will decrease, causing the coffee to taste increasingly sour. If it reaches a pH of 5, your coffee is now 10 times more acidic than when first brewed – with a very noticeable effect on taste! The main goal of Lab 4 is for you to measure the pH of a brew vs. time, and to compare your numerical pH measurements with corresponding sensory evaluations.

The pH changes because of a chemical reaction, so a natural question is, "How fast does the chemical reaction happen?" When we ask that question, what we really mean is "How many acid molecules per liter of brew are produced per minute?" The coffee pot is effectively what chemical engineers refer to as a "batch reactor," so you can use the pH data to get an estimate for the rate of reaction as

$$\text{rate} = \frac{d}{dt}[H_3O^+] \approx \frac{\Delta[H_3O^+]}{\Delta\ \text{time}} \approx \frac{\text{change in } [H_3O^+]}{\text{change in time}} \approx \frac{[H_3O^+]_{final} - [H_3O^+]_{init}}{t_{elapsed}}, \quad (3)$$

where "init" means the initial hydronium concentration (at $t = 0$), "final" means your final concentration, and $t_{elapsed}$ is the amount of time (in minutes) until your final measurement. Note that the rate has units of moles per liter per minute, i.e., mol/(L×min). Also note that the above expression is only a rough estimate (because we approximate the time derivative), but that's OK if we only need an estimate… we call it an "engineering approximation."

Part A – Measuring the pH versus time with dark roasted coffee

   Important: you need to multitask during this experiment – get part A started, and then simultaneously start working on part B then part C.

1) Get ready to make some coffee in the Mr. Coffee, <u>using some purchased **dark** roasted coffee</u>. The darker the better. If you use light or medium roasted coffee, the initial brew is so acidic that it is difficult to measure a change in pH. Make sure you use dark beans.

2) Prepare a large amount: use about 600 grams of water, and 40 grams of coffee ($R_{brew} = 15$). Measure the pH of the water that you put into the brewer.

3) As soon as it's done brewing (i.e., there are no more drips) make note of the time by starting a cell phone timer: the end of the brew is our $t = 0$. Pour out **small** samples to taste (about half an ounce max), and assess the perceived acidity (or "brightness") of the coffee. How does it taste?

4) Next, review the warnings below about proper usage of handheld pH meters. They typically only provide an accurate pH when the coffee is cool – don't try to measure the pH of steaming hot coffee! To do this, pour a little bit of coffee in a small paper cup or glass mug, let it cool down for a few minutes so that it is body temperature or less (i.e., not hot to the touch). Only then insert the pH probe (or alternatively, pour the cooled coffee into pH probe cap to measure). Wait until the reading stabilizes (about 10 seconds), then record the pH of the brew sample.

5) For the next 60 minutes, **keep the glass carafe on the hot plate, with the Mr. Coffee turned on,** and take a small sample for pH measurement every 5 minutes. (Keep your cell phone timer running.) You can taste every time if you like, but the changes will be gradual – instead focus on taking small tastes at the 30-minute and 60-minute marks. How has the perceived acidity changed with time compared to the initial brew?

Special warnings about handheld pH meters:
1) DO NOT push the "CAL" button (this changes the calibration!)
2) DO NOT submerge the buttons in coffee or water – only the tip!
3) Always measure room temperature coffee, less than body temp.
4) Rinse and gently blot dry the pH probe tip between readings.

pH versus Time Data

Coffee type_____

Mass of water:_____ *grams*   Mass of beans:_____ *grams* R_{brew}:_____

pH of tap water: _____

pH of coffee at end of brew: _____   (This is your pH at time=0.)

Time (minutes)	pH	Time (minutes)	pH
_____	_____	_____	_____
_____	_____	_____	_____
_____	_____	_____	_____
_____	_____	_____	_____
_____	_____	_____	_____
_____	_____	_____	_____
_____	_____	_____	_____

Sensory Evaluations at **t=0 (end of brew):**   pH = _____

_____

_____

Sensory Evaluations at **t=30 minutes:**   pH = _____

_____

_____

Sensory Evaluations at **t=60 minutes:**   pH = _____

_____

_____

Part B – Measuring the pH of your light roast vs. a dark roast

1) Our next task will be to do a head-to-head comparison of your light roast from Lab 3 vs. the same dark roast used in part A. We will use a new brewing technique – set up two Clever Coffee Drippers. Do your best to grind the light roast and the dark roast to the same grind size, and add equal masses to either brewer. Use the electric kettle to heat water to 94°C, and brew each for the same amount of time (about 5 minutes).

2) Measure the pH of each brew. How do they compare?

3) Do a "blind" taste of the two brews. Let somebody else pour them for you so that you don't know which is which. How do they taste? Which do you prefer?

Part C – Roasting a light and a dark roast

During the 60 minutes of your pH data acquisition, we will multi-task to also perform two roasts – a light roast and a dark roast, both with the same type of green beans. Use the exact same procedure as last week, but don't bother measuring the chaff or the volume change (those activities were only for Lab 3). Observe the beans as they roast! Recall, for a light roast use 120 grams of green coffee with the following settings: Fan 7, Power 7, Time 5.0 minutes. For the dark roast, try 100 grams of green coffee, Fan 5, Power 7, and Time 6 minutes. Note: you can always hit the Run/Cool button to stop heating and go to the cooling cycle early while roasting. Make sure you let the roaster cool for about five minutes between roasts. Label and store your beans for next week. Remember, only bag fully cooled beans.

If you like, you can taste the roasted beans (just pop one in your mouth and chew). Can you taste a difference between the light and dark roast?

---

pH Data for Light vs. Dark Roast

LIGHT ROAST   Type: _____

Mass of hot water: _____ *grams*   Mass of grounds: _____ *grams* R_{brew}:_____

Grind: _____   Extraction time: _____ *minutes*   Temperature water: _____ °C

pH of brew: _____   Sensory Evaluations:

_____

_____

DARK ROAST   Type: _____

Mass of hot water: _____ *grams*   Mass of grounds: _____ *grams* R_{brew}:_____

Grind: _____   Extraction time: _____ *minutes*   Temperature water: _____ °C

pH of brew: _____   Sensory Evaluations:

_____

_____

Roasting Data

Coffee type: _____

First Roast (Light)

Mass of green beans: _____ *grams*   Mass of roasted beans: _____ *grams*

Roaster settings: _____   Time spent roasting: _____ *minutes*

Second Roast (Dark)

Mass of green beans: _____ *grams*   Mass of roasted beans: _____ *grams*

Roaster settings: _____   Time spent roasting: _____ *minutes*

Lab Report

By your specified due date, each group will submit their lab report that includes (1) a plot of pH versus time, (2) an estimate of the reaction rate, (3) tasting notes and pH of light vs. dark roast, and (4) a brief paragraph discussing your group's observations.

(1) First, use Excel to generate a scatter plot of the pH versus time that you generated with the Mr. Coffee. (Put the pH on the vertical axis, and time on the horizontal axis.) What trends do you observe?

(2) Using equation (3), what is the estimated rate of reaction for generating hydronium ions? If you let the coffee sit on the hot plate for three times as long (say 3 hours instead of 60 minutes), and if we assume the rate stayed constant (a poor assumption since we also evaporate water from the brew!), what would the final pH be?

(3) Next, write down your tasting notes for your Clever Coffee brews of the light and dark roasts, and their pH values. Qualitative taste impressions are fine! You can type if you like, or just scan your handwritten notes. Which did each group member prefer, light or dark?

(4) On a final separate page, write a brief paragraph (10 sentences max) that clearly answers the following questions:

    (i) What was the pH of your light and dark roast brews? In absolute terms, what was the hydronium ion concentration in each brew?

    (ii) How did the taste of the coffee vary with time as it sat on the heating plate? Qualitative impressions are fine! Did you notice a correlation with pH?

    (iii) How much did the concentration (in mol/L) of hydronium ions change while the coffee was sitting around for 60 minutes?

Lab 4 Bonus Box – What Happens During a Roast?

Roasting is a critical step towards obtaining "nirvana in a cup" quality coffee. There is a myriad of physical and chemical changes that occur when you roast green coffee beans, all triggered by heating the beans. Initially, green beans contain about 12% water moisture, less if they have been stored for a long time. As the beans and water inside them heat up, the water vaporizes. At a certain point near 200°C, the vapor pressure in the bean, due to the expansion of gases with temperature, is so large that the beans actually crack open. An audible crack or popping noise can be heard in most roasters. The cracking and fissures in the beans allow the water vapor and other gases to escape and also cause a significant increase in the volume of the bean. In the image above it is possible to see some of these cracks.

The same type of cracking happens when you pop popcorn. The corn kernels contain water and gases that heat up, and once the pressure exceeds the strength of the corn kernel shell – they explode. The cell walls of coffee beans are just tougher and less continuous, so that explosive event is less dramatic. Moreover, have you ever noticed that old corn kernels don't pop up that much? The reason is simply that the kernels have dried out and there isn't enough water in the kernel to build sufficient pressure to pop the kernel. If you add some water to the old bag and let it sit overnight, those kernels will absorb the moisture and pop much better the next day. As you keep heating coffee beans they even crack a second time starting around 225°C. This further opens up the bean and plant cell walls. As a result, oils in the bean migrate to the surface and cause the bean to appear shiny or oily.

But pops and cracks aren't all that is happening. Just like baking or roasting other foods, there are a host of complex chemical reactions that also occur as the beans heat up. The most obvious changes are from "Maillard" reactions, which result in the brown color of the roasted bean. Maillard reactions occur between proteins and sugars – just like when you toast bread. The other main type of chemical reaction is "pyrolysis," which is a general term that means a reaction caused by heat in the absence of oxygen – which occurs inside the bean. Pyrolysis caramelizes sugars and carbohydrates, and changes the fats in the bean to aromatic oils. If you have cooked food, you have carried out both Maillard and pyrolysis reactions, but hopefully not too much combustion! Yes, if you go too far with your coffee roast, you can actually burn the coffee beans, just like wood in a fireplace. Combustion reactions are caused by heat as well, but in the presence of oxygen. Combustion is not good in coffee!

Another important aspect of green coffee beans is that they contain a lot of chlorogenic acids, which make up 4-9% of the green beans. Why focus on this one type of molecule? Well, chlorogenic acids are not found in a lot of plants, but they are incredible antioxidants. Drinking coffee is actually a great source of antioxidants! Roasting, however, actually breaks down chlorogenic acids; in fact, only about 40% of these molecules remain in a medium roast and really dark roasts are down below 10%. So, lighter roasts are "brighter" (more acidic) and may actually be healthier.

If all these changes that occur during roasting are confusing for you to follow, you are not alone. There are so many different possible reactions during roasting that scientists still don't have a full handle on all that is going on either. Moreover, the composition of the green beans varies like any natural crop, so a roast that gives you "nirvana in a cup" using one type of green bean may lead to brown swill with another. But all is not lost: try different roasting levels and explore what yields the best tasting brew.

Lab 5 – Measuring the Energy Used to Make Coffee

Objectives: The overarching goal of this lab is to answer the question, "How much energy does it take to make coffee?" We will measure the heat capacity of water, and compare the energy requirements for brewing, roasting, and grinding.

Equipment:

☐ Electric kettle   ☐ Kill-a-Watt meter   ☐ Hot-air popcorn roaster   ☐ Fresh Roast

☐ Clever Coffee Dripper

Activities:

☐ Part A – heating water in the electric kettle (twice), to determine C_p for water

☐ Part B – two brews using Clever Coffee Drippers

   ☐ Measure the average power used during grinding

   ☐ Blind taste test of dark versus light roast from Lab 4

☐ Part C – measuring the energy of roasting

   ☐ Practice roast, then fully measured roast in hot-air popcorn roaster

   ☐ Third roast in Fresh Roast for comparison

Report:

☐ Three scatter plots for heating water, of water temperature, energy, and time

☐ Table of calculations for C_p of water

☐ Two scatter plots for roasting, temperature vs. time and energy vs. time

☐ Column plot of energy per gram used by different unit operations

☐ Paragraphs discussing tasting notes and key questions about the lab

Background

Everybody has a qualitative idea of what "energy" means. When you are tired and sluggish after exercise, you say "I'm out of energy…" In contrast, when you move around quickly from task to task, you say "I have a lot of energy!" The idea of energy is clearly tied to motion, and indeed the most general definition of energy is "the ability to do work."

Energy exists in many different forms, all of which have a connection to motion or the ability to yield motion. For example, one kind of energy is "kinetic energy," which is the name we give to the energy of an object (say a baseball) moving through the air. Other kinds of energy have a

much more subtle connection to motion. For example, "heat" is also a kind of energy, but the motion isn't something you can observe like a baseball: instead the motion is the vibration of the molecules in whatever substance is holding the heat. A glass of cold water contains relatively little "heat" since the water molecules jiggle around sluggishly. In contrast, a glass of hot water contains more "heat" since the water molecules jiggle around vigorously.

A fundamental aspect of the universe is that energy is never created or destroyed. Instead, energy simply changes from one form to another. This idea, often referred to as "conservation of energy," means that we can precisely quantify how much energy is needed to accomplish certain goals, by transferring energy from one form to another. An example that is hugely important to modern society involves hydroelectric dams, where the kinetic energy of falling water is transferred to the kinetic energy of a spinning turbine; magnets inside the spinning turbine transfer the kinetic energy to electrical energy (i.e., electrons moving along a conducting wire). When you flip on a light switch in your home, the electrical energy is transferred yet again to light energy (which involves moving photons).

In each of these transferences of energy, the efficiency isn't 100%; typically some fraction of the energy is "lost" as heat energy to the surroundings. Think of old-style incandescent light bulbs, which put out light but also get quite hot. Nonetheless, conservation of energy is absolute. Much like our mass balances from Lab 3, the total energy put in to any system must ultimately be equal to the energy pulled out of the system.

The standard unit of energy is named the "joule," after James Prescott Joule, a 19th century physicist (and professional beer brewer) who helped elucidate the idea of conservation of energy. To see what a joule of energy is, first we need to define the force necessary to put things into motion. Specifically, imagine you have a mass of 1 kilogram sitting around somewhere, and you want to accelerate it to 1 meter per second. You could either slowly accelerate it (by nudging it gently) or you could quickly accelerate it (by pushing hard). If you push it precisely hard enough so that it reaches 1 meter per second within exactly one second, then you have applied 1 "newton" of force,

$$\text{Force:} \qquad 1 \text{ newton} = 1 \text{ N} = 1 \ \frac{\text{kg} \times \text{m}}{\text{s}^2}. \tag{1}$$

The newton is of course named after Sir Isaac Newton, who developed the famous Newton's Laws of Motion. One joule of energy, then, is defined as the energy transferred when applying a force of 1 newton over a distance of 1 meter, i.e.,

$$\text{Energy:} \qquad 1 \text{ joule} = 1 \text{ J} = 1 \text{ N} \times \text{m} = 1 \ \frac{\text{kg} \times \text{m}^2}{\text{s}^2}. \tag{2}$$

The *rate* at which you transfer energy is referred to as the "power," typically measured in watts, and is defined as how many joules you use per second,

$$\text{Power:} \qquad 1 \text{ watt} = 1 \text{ W} = 1 \text{ joule / second} = 1 \text{ J / s}. \tag{3}$$

The Watt is named after yet another famous engineer, Mr. James Watt, who helped develop the steam engines that powered the industrial revolution. In fact, Mr. Watt invented the idea of "horsepower," a still commonly used measure of power, since Watt's steam engines were replacing horses. We emphasize that the watt and horsepower are both a metric for describing a *rate* of energy per time, analogous to a metric for volumetric flow rate like gallons per second, or a mass flow rate like kilograms per second, or a rate of chemical reaction like moles per liter per minute (cf. Lab 4). Rates are always a measure of something per time!

What does all of this have to do with coffee? Well, energy is definitely required to convert green coffee beans into a drinkable beverage. For our purposes the most important type of energy transfer is of electrical energy to heat energy (since we need to heat the beans during roasting as well as heat the water for brewing). Electrical energy, like any other energy, is also measured in joules, and the power (or energy per time) is measured in watts.

If you go to a hardware store you might see that an incandescent light bulb for sale requires about 100 watts, which means it consumes 100 joules / second of electrical energy to operate. Let's say you buy the lightbulb, plug it in and leave the light on for ten hours. Since there are 3600 seconds in one hour, this means that over the course of the ten hours the light bulb has used

$$100 \, \frac{\text{joule}}{\text{second}} \times 36{,}000 \text{ seconds} = 3{,}600{,}000 \text{ joules.} \tag{4}$$

Although this number is correct, it's kind of inconvenient to keep multiplying everything by 3600 seconds per hour, so engineers came up with another measurement of energy, the "kilowatt hour." A kilowatt is 1000 watts (kilo is the SI prefix that means 1000). So the energy consumed by our 100 watt lightbulb over 10 hours could also be denoted as

$$100 \, \frac{\text{joule}}{\text{second}} \times 10 \text{ hours} \times \frac{1 \text{ kW}}{1000 \text{ J/s}} = 1 \text{ kW-hr.} \tag{5}$$

This is exactly the same amount of energy as 3,600,000 joules, just expressed in a different unit. It's kind of a funny unit: a kilowatt-hour is "energy per second times hours." If we did the same thing for volumetric flow rate, we might say "gallons per minute times hours," which of course is simply some number of gallons. Despite being an odd unit, the kW-hr is widely used because it's convenient for expressing energy consumption on an hour timescale.

Don't read "kW-hr" as "kilowatts *per* hour," that is a huge mistake. The power is not divided by time! It is multiplied by time, so it would be more accurate to say "kilowatts multiplied by hours." That sounds awkward, though, so everybody just says "kilowatt hours."

One last comment about lights is that the huge push to switch to use LEDs is all about energy. In terms of light output, a 10-watt LED bulb is equivalent to a 100-watt incandescent bulb. The LED needs 10 times less power to operate. Instead of using 1 kW-hr to operate for 10 hours, the LED would only need 0.1 kW-hr!

In regard to coffee, the primary focus for us here is transferring electrical energy to heat energy. When you plug in an electric hot water kettle, the energy of the moving electrons is transferred to heat through a "resistive element." Essentially, the moving electrons generate some heat each time they collide with a molecule inside the resistor that doesn't allow them to move so easily. The higher the electrical current (i.e., how many electrons per second), the more collisions occur, and more energy is transferred to heat. The "resistive element" in the automatic drip coffee maker in Lab 2 was a copper wire.

How much actual energy is required to heat the water? A key physical concept is that every kind of matter has a "specific heat capacity," which is defined as the amount of energy required to raise 1 gram by 1 degree Celsius. If we denote the specific heat capacity as C_p, then the energy required to heat a given mass m of some material by a temperature difference $\Delta T = T_{final} - T_{initial}$ is

$$\text{Energy} = m \times C_p \times \Delta T. \tag{6}$$

Hopefully this expression is intuitive. (Check the units on the right-hand side of the equation and make sure after multiplying through you have units of energy.) If you try to heat a larger mass, more energy is needed; if you try to raise the temperature by a lot, then more energy is needed. Precisely how much energy depends on the specific heat capacity of that material, which varies with the chemical composition of the material. Many metals (like copper or gold) have pretty low specific heat capacities, around 0.3 J/(g × °C). Water actually has a very large specific heat capacity, around 4.2 J/(g × °C), which means a large amount of energy is required to heat it up. You don't have to take our word for it, however: you'll be measuring C_p for water yourself in this lab.

Part A – The Energy to Heat Water

1) First, review the below instructions on use of the electric water kettle for heating water, and set the kettle for 95°C. Don't start it yet!

2) Add a known mass of water to the kettle (about half full); make sure you record the mass of water! Plug in the kettle through a zeroed Kill-a-Watt meter, but still don't turn it on yet. You zero a Kill-a-Watt meter simply by unplugging it from the outlet and then plugging it back in.

3) Below and on the next page, you will record the time, the water temperature, and the cumulative kW-hrs of energy.

4) Once you're all set, turn on the kettle, and begin recording the instantaneous water temperature and time. Every time the energy reading of the Kill-a-Watt meter increases by 0.01 kW-hr, record the time at which it changes, and the corresponding temperature and energy.

Temperature vs. Time Data

Mass of water in **HALF-FULL** kettle: _____ *grams*

Time (sec)	Temp. (°C)	Energy (kW-hr)	Time (sec)	Temp. (°C)	Energy (kW-hr)

Temperature vs. Time Data (continued)

Mass of water in **ALMOST-FULL** kettle: _____ *grams*

Time (sec)	Temp. (°C)	Energy (kW-hr)	Time (sec)	Temp. (°C)	Energy (kW-hr)
_____	_____	_____	_____	_____	_____
_____	_____	_____	_____	_____	_____
_____	_____	_____	_____	_____	_____
_____	_____	_____	_____	_____	_____
_____	_____	_____	_____	_____	_____
_____	_____	_____	_____	_____	_____
_____	_____	_____	_____	_____	_____
_____	_____	_____	_____	_____	_____
_____	_____	_____	_____	_____	_____
_____	_____	_____	_____	_____	_____
_____	_____	_____	_____	_____	_____

5) Discard the hot water, then repeat the measurements one more time. Use a different mass of water, with the kettle almost full (record this new mass). Make sure you zero your Kill-a-Watt meter and let the temperature settle before turning on the kettle (the water will heat up a bit as the kettle is hot). Again, once you are set, record the time, temperature and energy at every change in 0.01 kW-hr. Later you will graph and analyze these data, but discuss with your lab mates – qualitatively how does the energy usage vary with temperature and time?

6) Don't discard the full kettle of hot water – you're going to use that water in part B.

Part B – Taste Comparisons of Light and Dark Roasts

1) Set the electric kettle to the side momentarily. It is now time to use the Clever Coffee Dripper, again, for two head-to-head brews with your roasts from Lab 4.

2) Set up two Clever Coffee Drippers to brew. You will be doing a taste comparison, so try your best to prepare the beans from the two roasts identically: grind equal masses, and try to grind them equivalently (so the particulates are similar in size).

3) For at least one of your roasts, use the meter to measure the energy usage of grinding. Put in a known mass of roasted coffee beans to grind. You can't measure the energy directly in kW-hr, since the grinder uses so little energy. You can estimate it, however, using the Kill-a-Watt meter's instantaneous measure of the power (in watts) being drawn by the device. The power in watts will fluctuate a bit as you grind, so do your best to record the average power. Also measure how much time you spent grinding. What do you multiply electrical power by to get energy?

Energy Data for Grinder

Mass of roasted beans: _____ *grams*

Average power output during grinding: _____ *watts = joules/second*

Time spent grinding: _____ *seconds*

Energy usage: _____ *watts* $\times$ _____ *seconds* = _____ *joules*

Energy usage in kW-hr: _____ *joules* $\times \dfrac{1\ kw-hr}{3.6 \times 10^6\ Joules}$ = _____ *kW-hr*

4) Decide the brew ratio and water temperature you will use for your light vs. dark roast comparison. Use the same brew ratio, grind size, and extraction time. Brew both coffees and make sure you have correctly recorded all the pertinent data below.

5) Now, time for a blind taste test! Have one person in your group be the server and have the other(s) turn around and/or close their eyes. Serve out samples to your groupmates into two different small cups, but don't let them know which is which. Taste each one. Can you determine which is your light roast and which is your dark roast? Refer to the coffee flavor wheel – what flavor notes do you detect? Which one tastes "best"? Write down your sensory impressions of each brew.

Data for Brewing Blind Taste Test

Grind size: _____   Water temperature: _____ $°C$

Mass of hot water: _____ *grams*   Mass of beans: _____ *grams* R_{brew}: _____

Extraction time: _____ *minutes*

Coffee type and roast level: _____

Sensory Evaluations / Blind tasting notes: _____

_____

_____

Coffee type and Roast level: _____

Sensory Evaluations / Blind tasting notes: _____

_____

_____

Special warnings about hot air popcorn roasters

1) Don't put in too much – if you do, the beans won't move and the ones on the bottom will catch on fire.
2) Don't put in too few – if you do, they might fly out of the popper.
3) As soon as you turn it on, **immediately** check to make sure the beans are swirling... if not, you will start a fire!
4) A damp paper towel in a bowl is a good way to catch the chaff.

Part C – The Energy of Roasting

1) The next activity is to roast some beans using your popcorn roaster. You will do this twice – once to get a feel for the roasting process and once where you measure temperature and energy consumption as a function of roast time. Do not roast for longer than approximately 6 minutes; many (but not all) popcorn poppers have thermal regulators that prevent the temperature from increasing past a certain point.

2) To do the first roast, add just enough green beans to cover the air vents. The exact mass of beans depends on the type of popcorn roaster and on the density of the beans. Roughly speaking this amount can be anywhere from 50 to 100 grams (for Air Crazy use 60 grams). The important thing is to confirm that you have the right amount by checking to see if the beans immediately begin moving when you turn on the popper. The amount of beans can be varied, but there are rules of thumb; too much and the beans will not be "fluidized" sufficiently leading to an uneven roast and possibly a fire; too few and some will actually fly out of the popper. Typically, when you first turn on the popcorn roaster, the mass of beans should be moving slowly. As the roast continues, the beans become less dense and move more rapidly.

3) To catch the chaff, direct the outflow of the popcorn roaster towards a wet paper towel in a bowl. At all times be extremely careful – the roaster and all plastic and metal parts become very hot during the roasting process.

4) A roast time of around 5 minutes usually yields a good medium roast. During the roast, keep track of time and carefully note when you hear the "first crack". **Stop your roast about 1 minute after first crack starts!** Also note the color of the roast, the kW-hr, etc. During the second roast, you will measure the temperature and energy consumption. Record the mass of the green beans and resulting roasted beans.

5) Dump the roasted beans into the metal colander to cool. Record their mass, then bag and label (after they're cool!) to taste in next week's lab.

6) During the second roast, repeat the process but measure and record the temperature and the energy consumption (in kW-hrs) every 20 seconds for the duration of the roast. (Reset the Kill-a-Watt meter before you start!) Be even more careful not to burn yourself when you are measuring the temperature in the roaster. The thermocouple will become very hot, greater than 200°C. Use the oven mitts when handling all parts of the roaster. Record the volume and masses of the green beans and roasted beans.

7) Perform one more roast, but use the Fresh Roast. Remember that the minimum mass of green beans in the Fresh Roast is about 100 grams (compared to a smaller amount in the popcorn popper). Determine the energy usage as well for this roast. Measure the mass of green beans and roasted beans. You will be comparing the energy usage of the roasters on a mass basis, i.e., how many kW-hr used per gram of green beans.

Energy Data with Hot Air Popcorn Roaster

1st roast Coffee type: _____

Mass of green beans: _____ *grams*   Mass of roasted beans: _____ *grams*

Time of first crack: _____ *minutes*

Time spent roasting: _____ *minutes*   Energy usage: _____ *kW-hr*

2nd roast Coffee type: _____

Mass of green beans: _____ *grams*   Mass of roasted beans: _____ *grams*

Time of first crack: _____ *minutes*

Time spent roasting: _____ *minutes*   Energy usage: _____ *kW-hr*

Time (sec)	Temp. (°C)	Energy (kW-hr)	Time (sec)	Temp. (°C)	Energy (kW-hr)
_____	_____	_____	_____	_____	_____
_____	_____	_____	_____	_____	_____
_____	_____	_____	_____	_____	_____
_____	_____	_____	_____	_____	_____
_____	_____	_____	_____	_____	_____
_____	_____	_____	_____	_____	_____
_____	_____	_____	_____	_____	_____
_____	_____	_____	_____	_____	_____
_____	_____	_____	_____	_____	_____

Energy Data with Fresh Roast

3rd roast Coffee type: _____

Mass of green beans: _____ *grams*   Mass of roasted beans: _____ *grams*

Roaster settings: _____

Time of first crack: _____ *minutes*   (might be hard to hear!)

Time spent roasting: _____ *minutes*   Energy usage: _____ *kW-hr*

Lab Report

By your due date, each group will submit their lab report that includes the following: (1) three scatter plots for heating water: temperature vs. time, energy vs. time, and temperature vs. energy; (2) a spreadsheet table of your C_p calculations for water; (3) a scatter plot of your roasting temperature profile and energy usage; (4) a column plot (or bar plot) showing the energy per mass for each unit operation; and (5) brief paragraphs discussing your results.

(1) Enter your electric water kettle data (the time/energy/temperature measurements) into Excel, and prepare the following three scatter plots, each with two curves: (i) temperature vs. time, (ii) cumulative energy (in kW-hr) vs. time, and (iii) cumulative energy versus temperature. Make sure you use good practices in spreadsheet analysis. Each of the three scatter plots will have two distinct curves, for both of the two masses of water that you heated. Make sure each scatter plot has a legend that specifies which set of points corresponds to which mass of water. What trends do you observe?

(2) Next, prepare a table in Excel that has 4 columns: mass, overall ΔT, overall total energy, and C_p. Here "overall" refers to the change between the beginning and end of the trial. Enter the two sets of data (one for each mass), and then calculate C_p in the fourth column using an appropriate formula. (Which is what? Examine equation 6...) Report your measured heat capacity in terms of J/(g × °C). How closely do your calculated values correspond to the established specific heat capacity for water?

(3) Now, for the roasting. Prepare a plot of your roast profile, i.e., your temperature versus time, for the hot-air roaster. Also prepare a plot of the energy (in kW-hr) versus time.

(4) Prepare a column plot that compares the energy usage for the four different pieces of equipment you measured: the kettle, the hot air roaster, the Fresh Roast roaster, and the grinder. A column plot is similar to a scatter plot except the points are columns instead of discrete markers; make sure you use good plotting practices (cf. Appendix A). Important: each of these pieces of equipment works on a different mass of material, so normalize your energy usage on a mass basis. In other words, calculate how much energy per gram of water for the kettle, how much energy per gram of green coffee beans for the roasters, and how much energy per gram of roasted coffee for the grinder. Make sure your column plot is clearly labeled.

(5) On a final separate page, write clear answers to the following questions using no more than a few sentences each:

   (i) What trends do you see in your temperature & energy measurements versus time for heating water? How does the slope of the temperature or energy vs. time depend on the mass of water? How did your measured specific heat capacity for water compare to the established value? Be quantitative – what percent difference is there? What might account for any discrepancy?

   (ii) What qualitative impressions (tasting notes) did you have about the light roast compared to the dark roast? How did the brews prepared in the Clever Coffee Dripper compare to those you've made previously in the Mr. Coffee?

   (iii) At what time and temperature did first crack occur? Add any additional notes on how the roast color changed as a function of time.

   (iv) Which roaster used "more" energy? Think carefully about this: which roaster used more energy per mass of green beans?

Lab 5 Bonus Box – Water: The Fluid of Life (and Coffee)

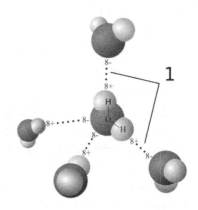

Water: the fluid of life? Yes, water is pretty unique, and frankly special. Water is one of the most important fluids on the planet – and the universe. First, and most obviously, we couldn't survive without water. In the context of coffee, water is almost 99% of what we are drinking in the cup. But that is just the starting point for why water is so interesting.

In terms of its chemical structure, water is H_2O – two hydrogen atoms bonded to an oxygen atom. The figure at right shows the sort of structure or orientation of water molecules relative to each other in ice, where the dark sphere represents oxygen and the lighter spheres are the hydrogens. Because oxygen has what's known as "lone pair electrons" and is very "electronegative" (which simply means that it attracts electrons), each water molecule can form "hydrogen bonds" with surrounding water molecules (as depicted by the dashed lines). All the details of this are pretty cool, but the main aspect of this (if you aren't interested in the details) is that water forms hydrogen bonds with itself and consequently has structure. Why do we care? Well, because of this structure, when you freeze water the molecules are able to make those hydrogen bonds really well – so that each water molecule is hydrogen bonded to 4 other water molecules – and they, therefore, make a nice crystal structure. This ordered crystal formation is why we have the beauty of snowflakes like the one shown here.

In liquid water, the molecules can move around more so there are actually less than 4 hydrogen bonds per water molecule. As a result, the water molecules can actually be a little closer. These differences in packing are why ice floats on liquid water – ice is less dense than liquid water because the hydrogen bonds keep the molecules a little further apart on average. The lower density of ice also means that the water actually expands upon freezing. Most liquids contract or decrease in volume when they freeze or solidify. Pretty cool, but a note of caution – this is why you shouldn't freeze water in a sealed bottle or container. If you put a can of soda in the freezer, the can will bulge and potentially burst, leaving a slushy mess.

In terms of life, ice being less dense than liquid water is pretty important if you think about bodies of water like oceans or lakes. If ice were denser than liquid water, lakes would freeze from the bottom and then continue freezing all the way up, killing the plant life and beaching the animal life on a giant, solid ice cube; less plants, less fish, less animals, less life.

Another interesting point regarding the need for each water molecule in ice to make 4 hydrogen bonds is that this can't happen at the very surface of ice. At the surface there isn't water surrounding all of the molecules, but air on one side. Air can't hydrogen bond. Because of this, the surface molecules of water are not as strongly bound and are fluid, which enables you to ski, snow board, and ice skate. The slipperiness of that thin liquid water layer at the surface enables your skies, board, or skates to easily slide due to the fact that you are actually skidding along liquid water. In fact, the surface layer of ice doesn't actually freeze until about -10°C or 14°F. At this point you actually are on solid ice and the friction goes up dramatically. Of course, not too many people are interested in trying to ski, snow board, or skate when it's that cold (brrrrr!)

These changes from solid to liquid are captured in the "phase diagram" of water, which tells you at what temperature and pressure water is in its various phases like solid (ice), liquid (water), and gas (vapor). The large arrow shows what happens at 1 atmosphere (that's normal atmospheric pressure at sea level). The horizontal dashed line is 1 atmosphere pressure and the vertical lines show the melting or freezing point and the boiling point of water. As you move horizontally to the right along that dashed line, below 0°C, water is in the form of ice, as you heat and move to the right the water melts at 0°C turning into liquid water, and if you keep heating it will start to boil at 100°C.

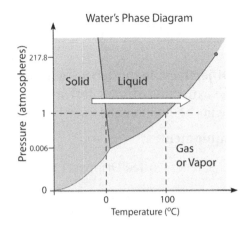

If you like to go hiking up in the mountains or live near Denver, you might have noticed some differences when you cook. A big reason for these changes can be understood from the phase diagram of water. As you go up in elevation, atmospheric pressure decreases – that's what makes it harder to breath. At an elevation of 8000 feet (1.5 miles above sea level) the pressure is only about 0.75 atmospheres, or 25% lower than the pressure at sea level. Now, if you look back at our phase diagram, the lower pressure means that water actually freezes at a slightly higher temperature and water boils at a lower temperature - about 92°C instead of 100°C. That's why you have to cook pasta longer when you are backpacking (the boiling water is not as hot up there), and the instructions for baking a cake are different at high elevations vs. at sea level. At the top of Mount Everest (with elevation of 29029 feet or 5.5 miles) the pressure is only 0.33 atmospheres and water boils at a little above 70°C.

How does this matter for coffee? Well, another cool thing is that below a certain pressure – around 0.006 atmospheres, which you can reach pretty easily reach with a vacuum pump – when you heat ice it doesn't actually melt to a liquid. Instead, it goes directly from the solid phase to the gas phase. This process of going from a solid directly to a gas is called "sublimation," and is easy to observe with dry ice (made of solid frozen carbon dioxide). If a material (like coffee) has water in it, then the sublimation process removes the water without melting it. You can freeze the coffee then put it under vacuum, sucking all the moisture out as water vapor. This "freeze drying" process is used not only to make instant coffee but also to process and store various pharmaceuticals that would degrade if they were left in liquid water. Almost half of the instant coffee sold in the United States is freeze dried. Spray drying is used for the rest where small coffee droplets are sprayed and allowed to come in contact with heated air to evaporate the water. Freeze drying is a little more expensive than spray drying but is thought to better preserve the aroma and flavor molecules. To make both methods more economical, the brewed coffee is first concentrated using a variety of techniques before drying. (This point is discussed more in the Lab 12 Bonus Box.)

Many coffee aficionados look down on instant coffee, and it is true that instant coffee is not as popular in the United States. Around the world, however, instant coffee is actually about 40% of the global coffee market – which is a lot of coffee, made possible by the phase diagram of water!

Lab 6 – Mass Transfer and "Flux" in Brewing

Objectives: In this lab we will study the concepts of mass transfer and flux as applied to the extraction of solid coffee grounds into water. We will compare quantitative measurements of "total dissolved solids" with qualitative sensory evaluations of the taste.

Equipment:

☐ Clever Coffee Drippers ☐ Electric kettle ☐ Digital refractometer

☐ Kill-a-Watt meter ☐ Roaster ☐ Paper cups ☐ Pestle and mortar

Activities:

☐ Part A – measuring TDS and PE with several Clever Coffee brews

    ☐ Three brews at different grind sizes

    ☐ Two brews at different temperatures

    ☐ Two brews, with periodic samples to get TDS vs. extraction time

☐ Part B – one or two roasts to have beans for next time

Report:

☐ Labeled column plot of TDS vs. brew condition

☐ Labeled column plot of PE vs. brew condition

☐ Scatter plot of TDS vs. extraction time

☐ Paragraphs discussing tasting notes and key questions about the lab

Background – Mass Transfer

In chemical engineering, a crucial question one often has to consider is "How do we get the chemicals from over here to over there?" This question applies at large length scales (such as in large pipelines), but even more importantly at small molecular length scales. This consideration can be seen very clearly in the case of coffee. Getting the organic flavor molecules and caffeine from the solid coffee grounds into the hot water is a pivotal step that often determines the overall quality of the brewed coffee.

In this lab, we will consider two key ideas in regard to mass transfer at the molecular scale. The first is the idea of "flux," which to engineers has a very specific meaning:

$$\text{Flux} = \text{"amount of stuff" per unit area per unit time} = \frac{\text{moles}}{\text{m}^2 \times \text{s}} \qquad (1)$$

The flux is thus a measure of how much stuff (i.e., how many moles of molecules) are moving through a particular area per unit time. If, as is often the case, you are interested in how many total molecules have transferred, you would integrate over the total area and the total time. With regard to coffee, this concept thus has two key implications: (1) The more surface area of the solid particulates, the more area you have for flux, the more molecules you'll get, and (2) the longer you expose it for, the more molecules you'll get. In the lab, we will directly compare grind size and extraction time on how much "coffee stuff" you extract into the water during brewing.

The second key idea is that the magnitude of the flux is proportional to the "concentration difference." One representation of this famous observation is

$$\text{Flux} = k \times (C_s - C_b). \tag{2}$$

Here C_s is the concentration of some molecule (say caffeine) at the surface of the solid particulates (coffee grounds), while C_b is the concentration of that molecule in the bulk of the fluid further away from the solid. The parameter k is known as a "mass transfer coefficient" and is a measure of how easily a molecule can move around. Big molecules are slow and cumbersome, while small molecules bounce around quickly. Importantly, k depends on temperature: the higher the temperature, the higher the mass transfer coefficient. Furthermore, k depends on whether the molecules get any help moving around because the liquid itself is moving. If you stir the mixture, then k is larger and you get a higher flux.

The concentration difference $(C_s - C_b)$ provides the "driving force" for mass transfer. You'll get the highest driving force, and hence the highest flux, if the concentration in the water (C_b) is initially zero. As time progresses, C_s decreases (because the molecules in the solid particles are being depleted), while C_b increases. Eventually the water is saturated with the molecule and you won't get any more mass transfer because you've reached the solubility limit (e.g., you can only dissolve so much sugar or salt into water). Equivalently, the driving force for mass transfer goes to zero because $C_s = C_b$. This is why it's usually a terrible idea to use already brewed coffee to extract from fresh grounds: all you're doing is extracting the larger bitter molecules that weren't fully extracted the first time around.

Background – Brew Strength & Extraction

What do you do if you brew coffee that is too "weak" or too "strong"? We intuitively know that if the brew is too strong we should increase the brew ratio or grind the coffee beans a little coarser. If you have a brewing method where you control the time for brewing, you might decrease the extraction time. This laboratory will provide a fundamental understanding of mass transfer and why these sorts of adjustments dramatically alter the quality and "strength" of the brew. Because there are so many different types of molecules in brewed coffee, it is challenging to measure the concentration of any specific molecule. Instead, we measure the cumulative concentration of *all* the different molecules that move from the solid coffee grounds to the liquid. This cumulative concentration is known as the Total Dissolved Solids (TDS), and is often expressed as a mass percentage. In brewed coffee, a typical TDS is about 1%, which means that 1% by mass is dissolved solids, and close to 99% is water (with the remainder as trace emulsified oils and gasses).

Usually when people refer qualitatively to how "strong" a particular cup of coffee is, they are responding to their perception of the TDS. It is easy to visualize that 'weak,' mostly translucent coffee has a relatively small TDS, while 'strong', extremely dark coffee has a large

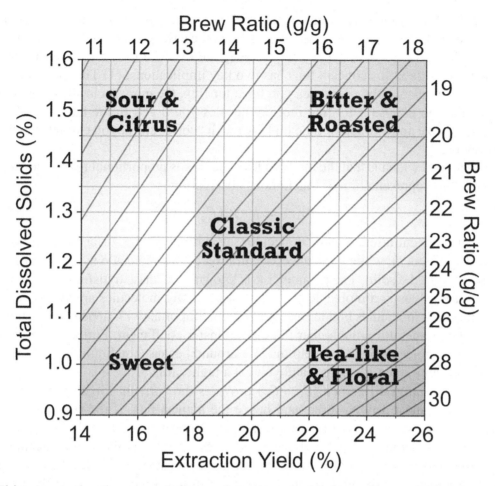

TDS. This perspective, however, is incomplete. A second independent variable governing the quality of the brew is the "percent extraction" (PE), which refers to the percent weight of solids originally in the coffee grounds that were transferred to the liquid phase. (The PE is also known as the "yield" or "extraction yield.") In other words, the PE is how much of the solid coffee mass is <u>removed</u> from the grounds to the water. Typical coffee grounds are composed of about 70% cellulose-like materials and other compounds that simply won't dissolve in water. The maximum possible PE is thus about 30%.

It is undesirable, however, to extract all 30% of the soluble compounds. Taste tests have consistently found that coffee extracted to the full 30% is unpleasantly bitter. In contrast, 'under-extracted' coffee at less than about 15% PE is unpleasantly sour and vegetal. The broad consensus is that coffee should be extracted to within the range 18% < PE < 22%, with a TDS somewhere near 1.2 to 1.3% (this is the region labeled "Classic Standard" above). These results are summarized qualitatively in the "coffee brewing control chart" shown above, which relates the TDS (on the vertical axis), the PE (on the horizontal axis), and the brew ratio (on the diagonal lines) with sensory aspects of the brewed coffee.

Note that the sensory attributes in the corners of the control chart indicate where careful sensory descriptive analysis indicates that those attributes are *maximized*. For example, coffee has perceptible bitterness across the entire range of values in the chart, but if you want to maximize bitterness, you want a high TDS and a high PE (the upper right corner of the chart). In contrast, if you want to maximize perceptible sweetness, then you should aim for lower TDS and lower PE values (the lower left corner). The coffee will still have perceptible bitterness and sourness in that corner, but there should be more perceptible sweetness compared to the other regions of the chart. (See the "Further Reading" in the appendices for more details regarding how the chart shown here was developed.)

Given that the flavor depends sensitively on the PE, a natural question is: how do you measure the PE? There is no easy way of directly measuring PE, but you can calculate it indirectly using the same sort of mass balance that we discussed in Lab 3. The main idea is the same: the mass of coffee molecules fed into a unit operation must be equal to the mass of coffee molecules that exits the unit operation, i.e.,

$$Mass\ of\ Coffee\ Solids\ In = Mass\ of\ Coffee\ Solids\ Out. \quad (3)$$

Recognizing that we have one stream of coffee solids moving in, but two streams that contain solids moving out, equation (3) means we have

$$m_{dry\ grounds} = m_{spent\ grounds} + m_{coffee\ solids\ in\ brew}. \quad (4)$$

We emphasize that each of the terms in equation 4 represents the mass of solids in that stream, so $m_{coffee\ solids\ in\ brew}$ is just the mass of solids in the brew, while $m_{spent\ grounds}$ represents *just* the mass of solids remaining in the spent grounds (*not* the combined mass of water and solids in the spent grounds). Accordingly,

$$TDS\ in\ \% = \frac{m_{coffee\ solids\ in\ brew}}{m_{brew}} \times 100, \quad (5)$$

and the percent extraction is defined as "how much of the original solids were removed into the liquid,"

$$PE\ in\ \% = \frac{m_{coffee\ solids\ in\ brew}}{m_{dry\ grounds}} \times 100. \quad (6)$$

Combining, we obtain

$$PE = TDS \times \frac{m_{brew}}{m_{dry\ grounds}}. \quad (7)$$

Note that because TDS and PE are usually expressed as a percentage, we multiply by 100 in equations 5 and 6 to convert them from mass fractions. Equation 7 works either way as long as you use consistently use either mass fractions or percentage values for **both** TDS and PE (if TDS in %, you find PE in %). Note that we can also derive equation 7 from equation 4, but the process is a little less obvious. In this case, using mass fractions we note the mass of coffee solids in the brew is obtained by measuring the TDS where $m_{coffee\ solids\ in\ brew} = TDS \times m_{brew}$ and $m_{spent\ grounds} = (1 - PE) \times m_{dry\ grounds}$. Substitution into equation 4 again yields equation 7.

Hopefully the expression in Equation 7 is intuitive: the higher the TDS in the brew, the higher the extraction from the solid phase must have been. The important point is that measurement of the brew TDS, along with weighing the dry grounds and the brew, gives an estimate of the percent extraction – and a useful measure of whether you are under- or over-extracting your coffee.

Part A – Exploration of Mass Transfer & Extraction

Our primary experiments today will focus on comparing different mass transfer or extraction protocols to assess their effects on the final taste and amount of "coffee stuff" extracted into the brew. We will use the Clever Coffee Drippers to set up several extraction

PROPER USAGE OF THE REFRACTOMETERS

- **Let the coffee cool!** The meters will give error messages at high T. To cool it quickly, pipette a little bit into a cup, let it cool off for a few minutes, then pipette just a bit into the sample well of the refractometer.
- Only pipette enough to cover the glass sensor - don't add too much.
- Don't push the "menu" button… you don't need to change any settings.
- After you're done **use only a Kimwipe** (not a paper towel) to clean the sensor.
- Don't move the refractometers… please be patient and wait for your turn.

tests. For each brew we will measure the TDS in the brewed coffee with a digital refractometer, calculate the corresponding PE, and perform sensory evaluations.

0) First, measure the TDS of plain tap water. A normal reading will be somewhere around 0.01% to about 0.05% (compared to coffee, which is around 1.25%). Repeat at least two more times during the lab session. One reason to do this is to get a standard deviation, i.e., a measure of reproducibility. Another reason is to make sure that the refractometer is still calibrated properly and that the sample well isn't dirty.

1) Next, perform three simultaneous brews in the Clever Coffee Drippers to assess the impact of **Surface Area**. Use the same brew ratio, water temperature (~94°C), and extraction time (4 to 5 min), and compare 3 different grind sizes:

      i. Coarsely ground (as coarse as you can make it, or even whole bean if you like)
      ii. Medium ground (a 'normal' grind)
      iii. Finely ground (as fine as you can make it)

If you have a pestle and mortar, it is fun to make the coarsely ground sample with that (but you can use a coarse setting on a cone-and-burr grinder). Make sure you taste each brew, record your sensory impressions, and measure the TDS as well as the mass of the brewed coffee (which you get from the difference in mass of the full cup and the empty cup). You will need both the mass and TDS to calculate the PE.

2) The next goal is to assess the impact of **Temperature.** Perform two more brews, using the same brew ratio and extraction time as before, and a medium grind size. Compare two different temperatures:

      i. Moderate temperature (~70 °C)
      ii. Very hot temperature (around 99 °C).

Again, make sure you taste and record your sensory impressions, and measure both the mass of the final brew and the TDS. Be careful when you taste the very hot one!

3) The final goal is to quantify the effect of **Extraction Time**. Prepare two more brews, again using the same brew ratio, medium grind size, and ~94°C temperature. Compare two different extraction times:

      i. Short time (1 minute)
      ii. Long time (10 minutes, with small samples every minute)

For the ten-minute trial, dispense a very small sample into a paper cup or Eppendorf tube once every minute. You can do this by tapping up on the bottom of the Clever Coffee Dripper to open the check valve very briefly. Before you dispense, give the contents of the Clever Coffee a gentle stir to mix everything up, and then dispense only a very small amount (enough to get a TDS reading in the refractometer). As before, weigh the mass of the brews, and taste.

TDS Data for Impact of Surface Area

Coffee type_____

Mass of hot water: _____ *grams*   Mass of grounds:_____ *grams* R_{brew}:_____

Temperature of hot water: _____ °C   Extraction time: _____ *minutes*

Grind size: <u>COARSE</u>

Mass of empty cup: _____ *grams*   Mass of filled cup: _____ *grams*

Mass of brew: _____ – _____ = _____ *grams*

TDS: _____ %   PE: _____ × _____ ÷ _____ = _____ %

                                            TDS   × m_{brew} ÷ $m_{grounds}$

Sensory Evaluations:

_____

_____

Grind size: <u>MEDIUM</u>

Mass of empty cup: _____ *grams*   Mass of filled cup: _____ *grams*

Mass of brew: _____ – _____ = _____ *grams*

TDS: _____ %   PE: _____ × _____ ÷ _____ = _____ %

Sensory Evaluations:

_____

_____

Grind size: <u>FINE</u>

Mass of empty cup: _____ *grams*   Mass of filled cup: _____ *grams*

Mass of brew: _____ – _____ = _____ *grams*

TDS: _____ %   PE: _____ × _____ ÷ _____ = _____ %

Sensory Evaluations:

_____

_____

TDS Data for Plain Water

1st measurement: _____ % 2nd measurement: _____ % 3rd measurement: _____ %

TDS Data for Impact of Temperature

Coffee type_____

Mass of hot water: _____ *grams*   Mass of grounds: _____ *grams* R_{brew}:_____

Grind type: _____   Extraction time: _____ *minutes*

Temperature: <u>**MODERATE TEMPERATURE**</u>

Temperature of water: _____ °C

Mass of empty cup: _____ *grams*   Mass of filled cup: _____ *grams*

Mass of brew: _____ – _____ = _____ *grams*

TDS: _____ %   PE: _____ × _____ ÷ _____ = _____ %

Sensory Evaluations:

_____

_____

_____

Temperature: <u>**VERY HOT**</u>

Temperature of hot water: _____ °C

Mass of empty cup: _____ *grams*   Mass of filled cup: _____ *grams*

Mass of brew: _____ – _____ = _____ *grams*

TDS: _____ %   PE: _____ × _____ ÷ _____ = _____ %

Sensory Evaluations:

_____

_____

_____

TDS Data for Impact of Extraction Time

Coffee type_____

Mass of hot water: _____ *grams*   Mass of grounds: _____ *grams* R_{brew}:_____

Grind type: _____   Temperature of hot water: _____ °C

Extraction Time: <u>**VERY SHORT**</u>

Extraction time: _____ *minutes*

Mass of empty cup: _____ *grams*   Mass of filled cup: _____ *grams*

Mass of brew: _____ – _____ = _____ *grams*

TDS: _____ %   PE: _____ × _____ ÷ _____ = _____ %

Sensory Evaluations:

_____

_____

Extraction Time: <u>**VERY LONG**</u>

Mass of empty cup: _____ *grams*   Mass of filled cup: _____ *grams*

Mass of brew: _____ – _____ = _____ *grams*

Time (minutes)	TDS	Time (minutes)	TDS
_____	_____	_____	_____
_____	_____	_____	_____
_____	_____	_____	_____
_____	_____	_____	_____
_____	_____	_____	_____

Sensory Evaluations:

_____

_____

Roasting Data

Coffee type: _____ Roaster settings: _____

Mass of green beans: _____ *grams*   Mass of roasted beans: _____ *grams*

Time spent roasting: _____ *minutes*   Energy usage: _____ *kW-hr*

Notes: _____

Coffee type: _____ Roaster settings: _____

Mass of green beans: _____ *grams*   Mass of roasted beans: _____ *grams*

Time spent roasting: _____ *minutes*   Energy usage: _____ *kW-hr*

Notes: _____

Part B – Roasting

Do two roasts for next time so that you have fresh beans ready to brew. Try different beans and roast levels to try to optimize the roast profile for your beans.

Note an important point: the settings from previous labs were not optimized for roasting. They were designed to obtain particular roast levels for comparison. Depending on the beans, excellent tasting roasts easily last eight or more minutes, not five! Here are some tips – higher Fan speeds increase the time required to roast in the Fresh Roast roaster. However, don't drop the Fan speed below 5, because the beans will likely get scorched. You can simply switch the bean type and do a similar roast as before, but we strongly urge you to start exploring how the roast profile (temperature versus time) alters the flavors.

The Fan speed, Power level, and Time remaining can all be altered during the roast. To change the Fan speed, Power level, or Time remaining you have to first press down the control knob and toggle through the different positions of Fan, Power, and Time, to the setting you want to change (flashing). Then, turn the knob to the desired value. **At any time, if you want to stop roasting (but still have time remaining), hit the Run/Cool button to switch from roasting to cooling.** To help keep track of the roast time, start your cell phone timer when you start the roast. Seeing "time remaining" can get confusing, especially if you change it! Another important tip is that you can see the temperature of the entering air into the roaster by turning the control knob 90 degrees.

Generally speaking every roast needs to keep the beans moving at the start (i.e. a Fan speed of 9), so that the beans don't get scorched at the bottom where the heated air enters the glass roast chamber. As the beans lose water and become less dense, they move more easily, and you can decrease the fan speed (e.g. 5-8) to drive more heat into the beans. You can also change the Power level during the roast. As a rule of thumb, you can aim to achieve a nice light/medium roast at 8-9 minutes or a dark roast at 9-10 minutes. Coffee beans vary wildly, however, so you will need to optimize your roast around your particular beans.

Lab Report

Each group will submit (1) a labeled column plot that shows the TDS value for each of your 7 brews, (2) a labeled column plot that shows the PE for each of your 7 brews, (3) a scatter plot of TDS vs. extraction time, and (4) a paragraph answering the questions below. On the column plots each column should be properly labeled, and you can use "insert text" to put some abbreviated tasting notes next to each column. (Choose one chart or the other to put the tasting notes on.) Then, on a separate page answer the following questions:

(1) What is the TDS of tap water? Do you think the number you obtained is reasonable? Why or why not? What is the TDS in PPM? (See the Lab 6 bonus box.)

(2) Which variable (grind size, temperature, or extraction time) had the most pronounced effect on TDS? Why do you think this was the case? (Hint: see equation 1.) Did it also have the most pronounced effect on qualitative taste? If not, why not?

(3) Likewise, which variable (grind size, temperature, or extraction time) had the most pronounced effect on PE? Did you see any differences in trends with PE when compared to the trends in TDS? If so, what might account for these differences?

(4) Recall the ideal extraction is typically considered to be about 20%, with a TDS near 1.3%. Which of your brewing conditions yielded a brew closest to those ideals? Did you think this was the best tasting coffee you brewed? How did it taste compared to the others? (Remember that the best measuring device for coffee taste isn't the TDS meter... it's your palate!) What is the TDS of your best brew in PPM?

(5) Describe how the TDS varied with extraction time. Why do you think it behaved like this? Do you think you would have obtained different results if you hadn't stirred the coffee before dispensing the small samples? What do you think would have happened to the TDS and PE if you let it brew for 20 minutes?

Lab 6 Bonus Box – What the Heck is "ppm"?

When the concentration of something is really, really small, one of the units that might be used is "parts per million," or ppm. For example, the amounts of certain naturally occurring chemicals in drinking water that are desirable (like sodium, magnesium, fluoride) or undesirable (like lead and arsenic) are often listed in ppm. Most cities issue water quality reports if you are interested in what your tap water contains. If you use tap water for your coffee brewing, then ulti-

Liquid	Approximate Dissolved solids
Distilled water	1 ppm
Bottled water	250 ppm
"Hard" tap water	450 ppm
Brackish water	3,000 ppm
Black coffee	13,000 ppm
Sea water	35,000 ppm

mately your coffee also has those chemicals! For example, in Davis, California the average level of sodium is 85 ppm, chloride is 21 ppm, and fluoride is 0.3 ppm. Some levels are so low that parts per billion (ppb) are used, like for lead which is less than 5 ppb.

So what exactly does ppm mean? If we use fluoride (F) as an example, 0.3 ppm means that there are 0.3 grams of fluoride per 1,000,000 grams of tap water. The units of measure here are grams, but any unit of measure can be used as long as they are the same for both quantities – like pounds or kilograms.

$$1 \text{ ppm F} = \frac{1 \text{ gram of F}}{1,000,000 \text{ grams of water}}, \text{ or in general, } 1 \text{ ppm} = \frac{1 \text{ unit of stuff}}{1,000,000 \text{ units of water}}$$

Fluoride is interesting because unlike Davis, most cities and towns supplement their water with fluoride to reach the level of 0.7 ppm recommended by the federal government's Health and Human Services Department to help prevent dental tooth decay. Too much fluoride in your water, however, results in dental fluorosis – a permanent change in the appearance of the tooth enamel from white spots in mild forms to staining or even pitting in severe cases. Fortunately, dental fluorosis is only really a concern when your teeth are developing, which is why children are taught to spit out tooth paste and rinse after brushing.

But what do ppm and different chemicals in water have to do with coffee? Well, coffee contains a cornucopia of different chemical molecules extracted from the roasted coffee beans in the ppm level. When you are measuring TDS to quantify all of the stuff in the brewed coffee, the ideal is around 1.3% TDS, which if you convert to ppm is

$$1.3\% \text{ TDS} = \frac{1.3 \text{ grams of solids}}{100 \text{ grams of water}} = \frac{1.3 \text{ grams of solids}}{100 \text{ grams of water}} \times \left(\frac{10^6 \text{ grams of water}}{10^6 \text{ grams of water}}\right)$$

$$= \frac{\left(1.3 \times 10^6 / 100\right) \text{ grams of solids}}{10^6 \text{ grams of water}} = \frac{13,000 \text{ grams of solids}}{10^6 \text{ grams of water}} = 13,000 \text{ ppm}.$$

That might sound like a lot, but many of the individual and important flavor molecules are in the 10 to 100 ppm range or lower (remember there are about 1000 different molecules that contribute to the flavor of coffee!) The low levels of all sorts of different chemicals in the coffee is part of what makes it so darn difficult to optimize brewed coffee through chemical analysis. The myriad of chemical reactions that occur during roasting are too complex to fully analyze, and the low concentrations makes it hard to quantify their effect on the brew's taste profile. Moreover, people's sensitivity to the various flavor molecules varies. Add the fact that the chemical content of the starting water is also variable based on the water source, and all in all the analysis and optimization of coffee becomes a very difficult scientific problem. Of course, you should use all the analytical tools you have available, but at the end of the day, the best measuring devices are your own taste buds.

Lab 7 – Water Chemistry and its Effect on Brewing

Objectives: The overarching goal of this lab is to answer the question, "What is the best water to use when I brew coffee?" We will discuss various measures of water chemistry, and compare measurements of pH and TDS with qualitative sensory evaluations of the taste.

Equipment:

☐ Clever Coffee ☐ Electric kettle ☐ pH meter ☐ Refractometer ☐ Roaster

☐ Distilled water ☐ Epsom salt ☐ Baking Soda

Activities:

☐ Part A – Prepare and taste five waters with different compositions

☐ Part B – Brew coffee with different waters and do a taste test comparison

    ☐ Four Clever Coffee brews of the same coffee with different waters

    ☐ Two more brews with custom waters for best tasting coffee possible

☐ Part C – two roasts for the next lab

Report:

☐ Column plots of pH and TDS versus water type

☐ Column plot of brewed coffee pH versus water alkalinity

☐ Column plot of brewed coffee TDS versus water total hardness

☐ Paragraphs discussing tasting notes and key questions about the lab

Background

Imagine that you carefully roast some high quality green beans, and a few days later you carefully brew them at home. You taste it, and you think it's absolutely the best coffee you've ever made. You've already learned in Lab 4 that you can't brew coffee and expect it to taste the same an hour later. This time you decide you will truly amaze your friend with your coffee brewing prowess. You call your friend and arrange to go to their place and make them nirvana in a cup! You bring your beans, grinder and brewing  equipment. You duplicate your process from home and make coffee. Your friend tastes the coffee and you once again hear "I guess it's OK." Confused, you taste it, and you agree… now it tastes only "OK". Argh! What happened this time?

Brewed coffee is almost 99% water. Not surprisingly, the quality of the water is a critical aspect of brewing an excellent cup of coffee. It's entirely possible that the quality of the tap water at your friend's house was very different than at yours. That's not a hypothetical concern: the people who run chains of coffeehouses know that water quality varies from city to city, or even neighborhood to neighborhood, and they take great pains to make sure they prepare their water in each location to their desired specifications. But, what should those specifications be? What makes for good brewing water?

One might think using distilled water would make the best brew, since it is pure water, but that is not the case. "Distilled water" is water that was boiled into steam, and then condensed back into liquid in a different container. All the ions and minerals that were originally present in the water are left behind, so the distilled water is very pure. If you ever taste distilled water, you'll see that it doesn't really taste that good – the missing ions and dissolved minerals help it taste good. Water for coffee likewise needs the right amount of ions and minerals to "taste good" and to make a great brew.

The Specialty Coffee Association has spent a lot of time trying to figure out what water makes a good cup of coffee. According to their "Water Standards", the water should smell clean and fresh, be free of odors, and be clear/colorless. This sounds really reasonable. (Who would want to drink water that smelled funny or was discolored?) The water specifications, however, go much further. Specifically, there are four chemical quantities that define the quality of water for coffee brewing:

- pH
- Sodium
- Total hardness
- Alkalinity

In chemistry terms, each of these is a concentration (amount per volume) of particular chemical species. The SCA "Water Standards" provides targets and acceptable ranges for each concentration, as shown in the table on the next page. As you can see, brewing coffee with tap water (at least in Davis, CA) is definitely outside of the standards. Does it matter? This lab will let you explore how the properties of the brewed coffee change as a function of the brewing water's characteristics! But first, let's discuss what each of these water qualities means.

pH — You should already be familiar with pH from Lab 4. Again, pH is a measure of the acid concentration in solution, $pH = -\log_{10}[H_3O^+]$, where the square brackets indicate "concentration in moles per liter." Perfectly distilled water is pH 7, but upon exposure to the air, the carbon dioxide naturally present in the atmosphere will absorb into the water and turn into carbonic acid, decreasing the pH slightly to about 5.8. The pH matters greatly for brewing coffee. If you use water with too low a pH, the brewed coffee will be too sour and acidic. Some acidity is good, though; if you use water with too high a pH, the brewed coffee will taste "flat" and boring because the acids from the coffee will be neutralized. The pH should be in the range of 6 to 8, with a target of around pH 7. (As discussed below, the alkalinity also affects the acidity of the brew!)

Sodium — This quantity is the concentration of sodium ions, Na^+, present in the water. Recall that "sodium chloride," which has the chemical formula NaCl, is simply table salt. So, you can think of the sodium level as affecting the "saltiness" of the water. Obviously too much salt tastes bad, but too little also leaves the water tasting dull and lifeless. The desired range is 10 mg/L, and should be less than 30 mg/L. (For comparison, seawater is about 30 grams/L, a thousand times saltier. Don't use seawater to brew your coffee!)

SCA Standards for Brewing Water					
Water Parameter	Target Value	Acceptable Range	Well Water, UC Davis[1]	Spring water, Crystal Geyser[2]	Distilled water
pH	7	6 – 8	8.3	7.2 – 7.3	5.5 to 6
Hardness	68 mg/L	50 – 175 mg/L	120 mg/L	26 – 38 mg/L	0
Alkalinity[3]	40 mg/L	40 – 75 mg/L	210 mg/L	45 – 57 mg/L	0
Sodium	10 mg/L	< 30 mg/L	72 mg/L	10 – 12 mg/L	0

[1] The Environmental Protection Agency (EPA) requires community water systems (usually cities) to issue water quality reports. Just search your city's name and "water quality report" to find out what's in your tap water. These numbers for UC Davis are from ground water wells Jan – Dec, 2019. Starting July 2017, the University began to integrate treated surface water from the Sacramento River to the drinking water system, which softened the water. Coffee brewed with campus tap water did noticeably improve!

[2] It's also easy to look up the water analysis reports for commercial bottled waters. Crystal Geyser Alpine Spring Water is frequently recommended for home espresso machines where the lower hardness is considered best for maintaining espresso equipment.

[3] Other species contribute to alkalinity but are summed here as equivalents of $CaCO_3$. Note that 1 mg/L is equivalent to 1 part per million (ppm). See also page 72.

Total hardness — This is a trickier concept, so we go into some detail. Total hardness is primarily a measure of the calcium (Ca^{2+}) and magnesium (Mg^{2+}) ion concentration in the water. Originally, water hardness referred to how easy or difficult it was to make soap lather. With hard water you had to work extra hard to form a lather. Soft water is much easier to lather and when you shower everything feels slicker – the friction of your hand on your skin is lower. With hard water, the friction is high and likely resulted in the phrase "squeaky clean".

To be more exact, water hardness refers to the concentration of polyvalent, positively charged ions in water. What exactly does that mean? Well think of adding table salt, NaCl, to water when you make pasta. The small amount of salt readily dissolves in the water so that you have Na^+ and Cl^- ions to help flavor the pasta while it is cooking. Both Na^+ and Cl^- are monovalent ions (+1 and −1). In the case of polyvalent cations like Ca^{2+} and Mg^{2+}, which each have two positive charges, these ions can react with soap and result in the precipitation of metals and salts. This makes it harder to form a lather, makes friction higher, and results in that soap scum ring in the bathtub. Both calcium and magnesium are divalent (+2) metallic ions, but your water might also contain some other polyvalent metallic ions like aluminum, barium, iron, manganese, and zinc. In Davis, California these other ions are below the detection limit.

So what defines hard and soft water? This is where things get a little tricky. A chemical engineer, or the folks who measure water quality for cities like Davis, simply tell you the actual concentrations of what exactly is in your water (in mol/L or mg/L). Unfortunately, water hardness is an old term and definitely much more confusing. Water hardness is most commonly expressed as *milligrams of calcium carbonate CaCO3 equivalent per liter*. That includes all the other polyvalent metallic ions, but put into the same scale as if they were from $CaCO_3$. That is why water hardness is sometimes described by carbonate (temporary) and non-carbonate (permanent) hardness. Temporary refers to hardness from $CaCO_3$ and permanent hardness from other polyvalent cations. For example, if we had MgSO4 (molecular weight = 120 g/mol) dissolved in water (Mg^{+2} and SO_4^{-2}) at 12 mg/L the concentration in moles per liter would be

$$\left(\frac{0.012g}{L}\right)\left(\frac{mol}{120g}\right) = 0.00010\frac{mol}{L}$$

There would be 0.0001 moles of Mg^{2+} and 0.0001 moles of SO_4^{2-} in the water. If we wanted that as equivalent milligrams of $CaCO_3$, we would convert the moles of Mg^{2+} to equivalent moles of Ca^{2+} as if they came from $CaCO_3$ (molecular weight = 100 g/mol). In other words:

$$\left(0.00010\frac{mol}{L}\right)\left(\frac{100g}{mol}\right) = 0.010\frac{g}{L} = 10\frac{mg}{L}$$

Don't worry about this craziness – we are thinking like chemical engineers and will therefore stick to actual concentrations of ions in the water.

How do these calcium or magnesium ions get into water? Lots of rocks, minerals, and soil contain calcium and magnesium, which can dissolve into water. Calcium carbonate (also known as lime stone) is the active ingredient in Tums™, which neutralizes stomach acids. Below is the reaction of calcium carbonate with acetic acid from vinegar, which yields calcium acetate, water, and carbon dioxide.

$$CaCO_3 + CH_3COOH \rightarrow Ca(CH_3COOH)_2 + H_2O + CO_2$$

Similar reactions happen with magnesium. Both affect the actual taste of the water – think distilled vs. alpine spring water. They taste different because the alpine spring water has minerals and salts.

Finally, what is considered soft and hard water? Now that we know that water hardness is a measure of dissolved polyvalent metallic ions expressed as *milligrams of calcium carbonate equivalent per liter*, soft water is generally from 60–120 mg/L, moderately hard from 120–180 mg/L, and hard water has more than 180 mg/L. The use of $CaCO_3$ makes a tiny bit more sense as we can readily convert this to actual moles of polyvalent metallic ions in the water by dividing by 100, the molecular weight of $CaCO_3$. For moderately hard water with 150 mg/L:

$$\left(\frac{0.150g}{L}\right)\left(\frac{mol}{100g}\right) = 0.0015\frac{mol}{L}$$

As a final note about water hardness, you might also see references to "grains per gallon of hardness." One grain is defined as 65 mg per gallon of water. Thus, the SCA target water hardness of 68 mg/L is equivalent to about 4 grains per gallon.

How does the hardness affect brewed coffee? This is a complicated question, and still an active area of research. The main idea, however, is that the concentration of polyvalent cations plays a key role in the dissolution of the solid coffee grounds into the water. In other words, the relative amounts of Ca^{2+} and Mg^{2+} affect how easy or difficult it is for different chemical species to dissolve into the brew, thus affecting the flavors. Not enough ions, less mass transfer; too many ions, more mass transfer. Whether the coffee flavor is affected positively or negatively in either case depends on the individual coffee, so the SCA guidelines are a general rule of thumb.

Alkalinity — Unfortunately, alkalinity is another old and odd measure of water quality. It is essentially a measure of the water's ability to neutralize acids, described in terms of the concentration of the compounds carbonate CO_3^{-2}, bicarbonate HCO_3^-, and hydroxides OH^- in the water, but it is represented again in *milligrams of calcium carbonate equivalent per liter*. Each of these compounds CO_3^{2-}, HCO_3^-, and OH^- can bind/react with H_3O^+ ions and thereby neutralize the acid. Recall pH is a measure of the H_3O^+ or H^+ concentration of the water; in contrast, total alkalinity measures the water's ability to resist a change in pH by neutralizing the acids.

Total alkalinity is determined by measuring the amount of acid (e.g. sulfuric acid) needed to bring the water to a pH of 4.2. Why pH 4.2? At pH 4.5, all carbonate and bicarbonate are converted to carbonic acid H_2CO_3, as the hydroxide reacts to form water. Below this pH (i.e. from pH 4.5 to 4.2), the water and compounds in it are unable to neutralize the sulfuric acid and there is a linear relationship between the amount of sulfuric acid added to the sample and the change in the pH of the sample. Why sulfuric acid? That is how the Environmental Protection Agency (EPA) determines the alkalinity of water!

$$2H^+ + CO_3^{2-} \rightarrow H_2CO_3$$

Some of the focus on *calcium carbonate equivalent per liter* should be a little clearer now that we see how important it is for understanding and quantifying water quality, and that other compounds or species behave similarly to it. For the most part, chemical engineers would not bother will all this reference to $CaCO_3$ and simply state what exactly is in the water. The downside of this approach is that determining individual species concentrations would require more careful and expensive measurements.

Sample Calculations

As an example, we compare Davis city water directly to the ideal brewing conditions recommended by the SCA. Later we will show an easy way to mix distilled water with Davis city water to obtain more ideal brewing water. What we do here should also be a reasonable example for comparing your own city's water to SCA recommendations. Just search your city's name and "water quality report" to find out what's in your tap water.

First, we have to convert the mg/L of Ca^{2+} and Mg^{2+} in Davis water to *milligrams of calcium carbonate $CaCO_3$ equivalent per liter*. Diving deeper into the City of Davis water report, we find that the total hardness is composed of 17 mg/L calcium and 12 mg/L magnesium (yielding the reported total hardness of 29 mg/L). So, we need to (1) determine the moles of Ca^{2+} and Mg^{2+}; (2) assume we have equivalently the same number of moles of $CaCO_3$; and (3) convert the moles of $CaCO_3$ to mass. We will then have the *milligrams of calcium carbonate $CaCO_3$ equivalent per liter* based on the actual amount of Ca^{2+} and Mg^{2+} in the Davis water.

1. We convert the mg/L of Ca^{2+} to moles per liter. The molecular weight of Ca is 40 g/mol.

$$\left(\frac{17\ mg\ Ca^{2+}}{L}\right)\left(\frac{1g}{1000mg}\right)\left(\frac{mol}{40\ g}\right) = 0.00043\ \frac{mol\ Ca^{2+}}{L}$$

2. We have 0.00043 moles/L of Ca^{2+} and we assume we have the same number of moles of equivalent $CaCO_3$.

$$0.00043 \frac{mol \ Ca^{2+}}{L} = 0.00043 \frac{mols \ equiv \ CaCO_3}{L}$$

3. Next, we convert the moles of equivalent CaCO₃ to mass based on the molecular weight of CaCO₃ = 100 g/mol to find the *milligrams of calcium carbonate CaCO₃*.

$$0.00043 \frac{mols \ equiv \ CaCO_3}{L} \left(\frac{100 \ g \ CaCO_3}{mol}\right) \left(\frac{1000 mg}{g}\right) = 43 \frac{mg \ CaCO_3 \ equiv}{L}$$

The process is repeated for the 12 mg/L of Mg^{2+}, which has molecular weight 24.3 g/mol.

$$\left(\frac{12 \ mg \ Mg^{2+}}{L}\right) \left(\frac{1g}{1000mg}\right) \left(\frac{mol}{24.3 \ g}\right)$$
$$= 0.00049 \frac{mol \ Mg^{2+}}{L} \ or \ 0.00049 \frac{mols \ equiv \ CaCO_3}{L}$$

and

$$0.00049 \frac{mols \ equiv \ CaCO_3}{L} \left(\frac{100 \ g \ CaCO_3}{mol}\right) \left(\frac{1000mg}{g}\right) = 49 \frac{mg \ CaCO_3 \ equiv}{L}$$

Adding the *milligrams of calcium carbonate CaCO₃ equivalent per liter* for Ca^{2+} and Mg^{2+} we get 43 + 49 = 92 mg/L, and we see that Davis water is higher than the SCA recommendation of 68 mg/L, but still in the acceptable range of 50 – 170 mg/L. Yeah!

The alkalinity, however, is much too high at 170 mg/L compared to the acceptable range of 40 – 75 mg/L. How could we correct this? Well, one easy method to get reasonably close would be to dilute Davis water with distilled water. If we made a 50:50 mixture of Davis water and distilled water we would have:

$$\text{Total hardness} = 92 \ mg/L \div 2 = 46 \ mg/L$$

$$\text{Alkalinity} = 170 \ mg/L \div 2 = 85 \ mg/L$$

This gets us pretty close to the acceptable ranges; 10% too low on total hardness and 10% too high on alkalinity. This 50:50 mixture is straightforward and worth trying to see if the taste of your brew improves! (Note we ignored the change in pH for simplicity.)   If you are extra industrious and want to hit the **ideal** SCA brewing water guidelines, you would have to dilute further with distilled water to obtain the ideal alkalinity of 40 (a ratio of 3.25 distilled water to 1 of Davis water). However, if we diluted the water that much, our hardness would only be 21 mg/L. That is much lower than the 68 mg/L for ideal brewing water. To adjust the hardness without changing the alkalinity, we can add Epsom salt ($MgSO_4$, molecular weight = 120 g/mol). Adding Epsom salt will increase the hardness through the addition of Mg^{2+} ions, but will not change the alkalinity. Unfortunately, you would have to add only 22 mg/L of Epson salt to hit a total hardness of 68 mg/L. That's a mighty small number.

Let's do this in an easier manner that we can handle with simple kitchen tools. If we dumped out a quarter of a gallon of distilled water and replaced that amount with Davis city water, we would have about the right alkalinity 42 mg/L. However, our total hardness would only be 23 mg/L. We would then have to add some Epsom salt to bring up our total hardness.

To work with more measurable amounts, let's dissolve ¾ of a teaspoon of Epson salt (10 grams) in a cup of water. A cup of water is about 225 grams. If we added a teaspoon (5 grams) of this Epsom salt water solution to our gallon container of 25% Davis water and 75% distilled water, we would have a total hardness of 72 mg/L – again pretty close to ideal brewing water!

Finally, if you are doing commercial brewing – especially espresso – there are additional considerations to prevent scaling and corrosion. Here, we are focused on how the characteristics of the brewing water impact the quality of the extracted coffee for personal, home brewing. There are some rules of thumb to help in this regard.

Brewing water rules of thumb:

- Always make sure you are using fresh, clean water!

- The higher the alkalinity of the brewing water, the higher the acid neutralization capacity of the water. As a result the brewed coffee will be less acidic (less bright). So, beans that you light roast and find to be too bright, might benefit from brewing with higher alkalinity water. Conversely, you could brighten a dark roast with lower alkalinity brewing water.

- The higher the hardness of the water, the higher the extraction efficiency. In sensory evaluation some clear differences were detected in aroma and flavor, but more precise information from careful research is still lacking.

- Check out your city's water quality report and see what is in your water. You can easily dilute with distilled water and/or a mineral spring water to obtain the total hardness and alkalinity that falls within the recommended brewing water range. See if that improves your sensory evaluation of the brewed coffee.

Part A – Prepare and taste five waters with different composition

Get ready to drink some water! Our first task is to prepare several different water samples. Specifically, you will compare: (i) distilled water, (ii) tap water, (iii) hard water, and (iv) "ideal" brewing water.

1) First, we will make a 'super salty' stock solution, which we will then dilute to the appropriate amounts to make hard water and ideal water. (If you have access to a high-precision scale with 0.01 gram resolution, you don't need to do this.) Important: you don't have to taste the super salty solution! (It won't hurt you, but it will taste pretty salty.) Gather your salts, a clean container, the distilled water, and some large (1 liter) containers. Then follow this recipe to prepare the "super salty" solution:

    a. Pour in 500 grams of distilled water into a clean container (e.g. empty water bottle or graduated cylinder).

    b. Add 6 grams of food-grade baking soda $NaHCO_3$.   ($NaHCO_3$ 1200 mg / L)

    c. Add 15.5 grams of food-grade Epsom salt.   ($MgSO_4$ 3100 mg / L)

    d. Mix thoroughly until both salts are dissolved.

2) With your "super salty stock" solution prepared, now we need to dilute it to the appropriate amount. Prepare two solutions as follows, stirring to ensure they are well mixed:

    a. Hard water – 950 grams of distilled water, 50 grams of super salty water.

    b. Ideal water – 990 grams of distilled water, 10 grams of super salty water.

Label each container to make sure you don't get them confused.

3) Prepare samples of the four waters to taste (distilled, tap, hard, ideal). Perform a blind tasting of each of the different waters, and record your sensory impressions of each. First, compare head to head distilled and ideal brewing water. Could you detect a difference between the waters? What was different? Next, compare ideal brewing water to hard water. Finally, compare tap water to distilled water and ideal brewing water. Which do you think will make better tasting coffee.

4) Next, measure the pH and TDS of all five water samples (including the super-salty). Is the measured TDS consistent with your expectations based on the known dilutions? Optional: if you have access to a hand-held water conductivity meter, use that to compare to readings from the refractometer. A conductivity meter actually measures the electrical conductivity of the water and is thus highly sensitive to the salt concentration. The units here are in ppm, parts per million. (See the Bonus Box for Lab 6 for more on ppm.)

Water Quality and Taste

Distilled Water   pH = _____   TDS: _____ %

Sensory Evaluations: _____

_____

Tap Water   pH = _____   TDS: _____ %

Sensory Evaluations: _____

_____

Hard Water   pH = _____   TDS: _____ %

Sensory Evaluations: _____

_____

Ideal Water   pH = _____   TDS: _____ %

Sensory Evaluations: _____

_____

Super Salty Water   pH = _____   TDS: _____ %   *(sensory optional)*

Sensory Evaluations: _____

_____

Part B – Brew coffee with different waters and do a taste test comparison

1) Finally… it's time to brew some coffee! This experiment is easier if you have at least two kettles available, so that you can heat up two different types of water simultaneously. If not, perform the following experiments sequentially. In either case, thoroughly rinse out the kettle with a bit of the water of that type before you pour in and heat the rest, to avoid contamination or dilution.

2) Prepare two Clever Coffee brews to assess the impact of water chemistry. We will start with the most extreme difference: distilled water versus hard water. Get the waters heating, prepare the Clever Coffees. Use the same coffee grounds, same brew ratio, same water temperature (91 to 94°C), and same extraction time (4 minutes), and brew the coffees.

3) When the coffees are done brewing, smell them carefully… can you tell even by aroma whether there is a difference? Measure the TDS and pH of each brew.

4) Taste each brew and record your sensory evaluation of the brewed coffee. Could you taste a difference between the brews? Which tasted better? Could you detect a difference in the brightness (i.e., the acidity) of the different brews? Which was the brightest?

5) Repeat the experiment, but this time compare tap water versus the "ideal" water. Remember to rinse out the kettle(s) with the respective water. Use the same coffee grounds and all brewing parameters. Measure the TDS and pH of both brews, then record your sensory impressions. Was there a difference? Can you relate the difference in pH to the sensory perception of the coffee brightness?

6) Next, you will do two more brews using custom waters of your choice. Review your sensory impressions of the first four brews, then discuss with your group what types of water you think are worth trying in more detail. You can change the water recipe, to try softer or harder water, or more or less alkaline water, by preparing either new dilutions or completely new "super salty water" with a different composition. Record your water recipes, and the rationale for why you want to test them in particular. What improvements are you trying to make? Taste the custom waters and record your sensory impressions; measure and record their pH and TDS.

7) Finally, brew two more Clever Coffee brews using your two custom waters. When brewing the coffee, as before remember to keep the brewing conditions (other than the different water) identical. Taste each brew and record your sensory evaluation of the brewed coffee. Could you taste a difference between the two brews? Which tasted better? Hypothesize why. Record the pH and TDS of the brewed coffee. Was there a difference? Can you relate the difference in pH and TDS to the sensory perception of the coffee? What effect on the coffee taste, pH, TDS did you expect and why? Did you observe those changes?

Part C – Roasting

Do at least two roasts for next time so that you have fresh beans ready to brew. Try different beans and roast levels to try to optimize the roast profile for your beans.

Data for Clever Coffee Experiments – Comparing Distilled vs. Hard Water

Coffee type_____

Mass of hot water: _____ *grams*   Mass of grounds: _____ *grams* R_{brew}: _____

Temperature of hot water: _____ °C   Grind size: _____

Initial extraction time: _____ *minutes*

Distilled Water

Mass of brew: _____ – _____ = _____ *grams*   (filled cup – empty cup)

TDS: _____ %   PE: _____ × _____ ÷ _____ = _____ %

pH = _____

Sensory Evaluations:_____

_____

_____

_____

Hard Water

Mass of brew: _____ – _____ = _____ *grams*   (filled cup – empty cup)

TDS: _____ %   PE: _____ × _____ ÷ _____ = _____ %

pH = _____

Sensory Evaluations:_____

_____

_____

_____

Data for Clever Coffee Experiments – Comparing Tap vs. Ideal Water

Coffee type_____

Mass of hot water: _____ *grams*   Mass of grounds: _____ *grams* R_{brew}: _____

Temperature of hot water: _____ °C   Grind size: _____

Initial extraction time: _____ *minutes*

<u>Tap Water</u>

Mass of brew: _____ – _____ = _____ *grams*   (filled cup – empty cup)

TDS: _____ %   PE: _____ × _____ ÷ _____ = _____ %

pH = _____

Sensory Evaluations:_____

_____

_____

_____

<u>Ideal Water</u>

Mass of brew: _____ – _____ = _____ *grams*   (filled cup – empty cup)

TDS: _____ %   PE: _____ × _____ ÷ _____ = _____ %

pH = _____

Sensory Evaluations:_____

_____

_____

_____

Data for Clever Coffee Experiments – Comparing Custom Water Types

(Use same coffee type and brewing parameters as previously.)

Water Type 1: _____ pH = _____ TDS: _____ %

Recipe & rationale: _____

_____

Water Sensory Evaluations: _____

_____

Mass of brew: _____ – _____ = _____ *grams* (filled cup – empty cup)

TDS: _____ % PE: _____ × _____ ÷ _____ = _____ % pH = _____

Brew Sensory Evaluations: _____

_____

_____

Water Type 1: _____ pH = _____ TDS: _____ %

Recipe & rationale: _____

_____

Water Sensory Evaluations: _____

_____

Mass of brew: _____ – _____ = _____ *grams* (filled cup – empty cup)

TDS: _____ % PE: _____ × _____ ÷ _____ = _____ % pH = _____

Brew Sensory Evaluations: _____

_____

_____

Roasting Data

Coffee type: _____ Roaster settings: _____

Mass of green beans: _____ *grams*   Mass of roasted beans: _____ *grams*

Time spent roasting: _____ *minutes* Energy usage: _____ *kW-hr*

Notes: _____

Coffee type: _____ Roaster settings: _____

Mass of green beans: _____ *grams*   Mass of roasted beans: _____ *grams*

Time spent roasting: _____ *minutes* Energy usage: _____ *kW-hr*

Notes: _____

Lab Report

By your specified due date, each group will submit their lab report that includes (1) column plots of the pH and TDS of the different water types you brewed with, (2) a scatter plot of brewed coffee pH versus the brewing water alkalinity, (3) a scatter plot of brewed coffee TDS versus the brewing water total hardness, (4) your tasting notes and assessment, and (5) a paragraph discussing your group's observations in the ideal and optimized brewing cases.

(1) First, use Excel to generate column plots of the TDS and pH of the different water samples. Are the values consistent with what you anticipate based on your dilutions of the super-salty water, and the water quality report for your tap water?

(2) Next, prepare separate scatter plots of the pH and TDS for the brewed coffee versus, respectively, the brewing water alkalinity and total hardness. Calculate the hardness and alkalinity of each sample (or look up the value for the tap water). Put the pH or TDS of the brewed on the vertical axis, and brewing water alkalinity or hardness on the horizontal axis.) Add text boxes so the water type is clearly identified. What trends do you observe?

(3) Summarize your tasting notes for the different waters. Could you detect a difference between the waters? What was different? Which water did each of your group members prefer? Next, summarize your tasting notes for your Clever Coffee brews comparing waters. Qualitative taste impressions are fine! Which did each group member prefer?

(4) On a final separate page, write a few sentences for each item below that clearly answer the following questions:

(iv) In comparing the "ideal brewing water" to distilled, tap, or hard water, which was better and why? Try to use information about the alkalinity, pH, hardness and TDS to inform your answers.

(v) Which coffee did you perceive as the "brightest"? Did the pH measurement correlate with your perception of the coffee acidity? Did the hard water have a higher TDS?

(vi) For the custom water brew comparison, how did you change the brew and why? Did the sensory evaluation, pH, and/or TDS measurement of the brewed coffee accords with your expectations?

Lab 7 Bonus Box – DIY Ideal Brewing Water!

Ok, so the previous lab went into great detail about water hardness and alkalinity, and used some archaic definitions based on the *milligrams of calcium carbonate CaCO3 equivalent per liter*. We also learned that the SCA considers ideal brewing water to have "ideal" values for these quantities. In this bonus box, we offer another "do it yourself" (DIY) for how to change distilled water into ideal brewing water. The main difference here is we get the hardness from calcium instead of magnesium by using calcium citrate ($Ca_3(C_6 H_5O_7)_2$). Give it a try and see if your coffee tastes better. Food grade calcium citrate is inexpensive, about $8 per pound, and easily purchased online.

Recipe with calcium citrate: We will make a 5x stock solution (that is, it's too strong by a factor of five), then dilute it five-fold to get ideal brewing water.

1. If you have an accurate scale, you can make a liter of 5x stock solution by adding 2.1 grams of calcium citrate and 0.6 grams of baking soda to 1 liter of distilled water.
2. If you have a less accurate scale, make a 5x stock solution by adding 8 grams of calcium citrate and 2.4 grams of baking soda to 1 gallon of distilled water.
3. Leave the stock solution for at least a day with periodic shaking to make sure all the salt dissolves before using.
4. Finally, add 200 mL of the 5x solution to 800 mL of distilled water. This is now ideal.

The alkalinity and hardness of the 5x solution is 5 times that of ideal brewing water, just like the hard water made using Epsom salt (with magnesium) in Lab 7. You can therefore use these two "stock" solutions (one using magnesium, one using calcium) to make variations in the amount of Ca and Mg to see if you have a personal preference. For example, if you want water with hardness derived 50% from magnesium and 50% from calcium, then add 100 mL of each solution to 800 of distilled water to obtain a new "ideal" brewing water to test!

Why are we only making a 5x stock solution rather than 100x stock solution as in Lab 7? Moreover, why don't we just use calcium carbonate, $CaCO_3$, since hardness is measured in terms of that? The answer is each of these compounds has a different solubility in water. In fact, $CaCO_3$ is only sparingly soluble in water, only 13 mg/L at 25°C. Just adding $CaCO_3$ would yield water that has both a low hardness and alkalinity compared to ideal brewing water. In general, most sulfate salts like $MgSO_4$ are soluble in water, while most carbonate salts like $CaCO_3$ are not. The table here shows the solubility in water of the various salts used for modifying "water quality" for brewing. The reason why salts generally dissolve in water goes back to the saying "like dissolves like." Salts are made of positively and negatively charged ions, so water can often dissolve various salts because the negative part of water molecules (oxygen) attracts the positive salt ions, while the positive part of the water molecules (hydrogen) attracts the negative salt ions. In the case of $CaCO_3$, however, the calcium and carbonate form a really strong electrostatic bond. Their attraction is much stronger than the attraction to water molecules, so water cannot pull them apart and the $CaCO_3$ remains solid

Compound	Solubility (25°C)
Baking soda, $NaHCO_3$	105 mg/L
Epsom salt, $MgSO_4$	376 mg/L
Table salt, NaCl	361 mg/L
Calcium citrate, $Ca_3(C_6 H_5O_7)_2$	950 mg/L
Calcium carbonate, $CaCO_3$	13 mg/L

Lab 8 – Pressure Driven Flow through Coffee Grounds

Objectives: In this lab we will study "fluid mechanics" as applied to the motion of water through coffee grounds. We will relate the concepts of pressure and flow rate using an equation known as "Darcy's Law," and we will assess how the flow rate affects the strength and quality of the brewed coffee.

Equipment:

☐ AeroPress ☐ Electric kettle ☐ Digital refractometer ☐ Bathroom scale

☐ Ruler ☐ Kill-a-Watt meter ☐ Roaster

Activities:

☐ Part A – four brews with the AeroPress, to examine Darcy's law & pressure

    ☐ **Review safety guidelines!** Then a practice brew to gauge your applied pressure

    ☐ Three brews at different applied pressures

☐ Part B – four more brews with the AeroPress, to examine permeability

    ☐ Two brews at same pressure but different grind sizes

    ☐ Two brews at same pressure and grind, but different masses of grounds

☐ Part C – two or more roasts to have beans for the next lab

Report:

☐ Scatter plot of flow rate versus the applied pressure gradient

☐ Scatter plot of TDS versus flow rate

☐ Paragraph discussing tasting notes and key questions about the lab

Background – Fluid Mechanics

We have learned in previous labs that the "extraction time" is a critical parameter that affects the final taste of the coffee: too short of a time yields sour and "under-extracted" coffee, but too long of a time yields bitter and "over-extracted" coffee. In most methods of brewing coffee, the extraction time is controlled by how quickly the hot water moves past the coffee grounds. In other words, the fluid velocity is a key parameter, so understanding 'fluid mechanics' is necessary.

The motion of fluids, like all other forms of matter, is governed by Newton's second law, i.e., $F = ma$ (where F is the sum of the forces acting on the fluid, m is the mass, and a is the acceleration). Unlike the rigid objects (like cannonballs etc.) you might have studied previously in physics courses, a key difference for fluids is that they are deformable. This difference tremendously complicates interpretation of the forces acting on fluids, so there are entire courses in engineering curricula dedicated just to fluid mechanics.

For the purpose of this lab, we will focus on how liquids move through "porous media," in this case coffee grounds. Specifically, we will use an AeroPress brewing apparatus (pictured on the previous page), where we apply a pressure by hand and measure the resulting flow rate. We will assess the observations in terms of an empirical equation known as Darcy's Law, which is a mathematical description of the observation that "the harder you push on the fluid, the faster it will flow." Specifically, Darcy's law states that the flow rate Q of the liquid (e.g., in cm^3/s) is proportional to the pressure difference across the porous medium:

$$Q = \frac{\kappa}{\mu} \times A \times \frac{\Delta P}{L} = \frac{\kappa}{\mu} \times A \times \frac{(P_{top} - P_{bot})}{L}. \tag{1}$$

There are several terms here, so let's define them. The "viscosity" μ of the fluid characterizes how easy it is for it to deform or to "shear". Water has a low viscosity, whereas honey has a very high viscosity. The area A is the cross-sectional area of the porous media through which the flow moves. The "permeability" κ characterizes how much open space there is in the porous medium versus solid surface area: the higher the surface area to volume ratio, the more surface area is available to "slow" down the fluid. As a result, finely ground coffee has a higher surface-area-to-volume ratio and smaller permeability than coarsely ground coffee. (Think of a single, whole Rubik's cube representing a coarsely ground coffee particle vs. each small cube of the Rubik's cube as a separate element, where each individual element is a finely ground particle). The surface-area-to-volume ratio is also a great way to think about how grind level affected flux in Lab 6 – there is much larger surface area with smaller particle sizes so the rate of mass transfer is much faster.

Finally, the pressure difference ΔP (which you read aloud as "delta P") is the driving force for the fluid flow. Recall that pressure is force per area. The quantity ΔP is how much the pressure changes over the thickness L of the porous medium (where the thickness is measured in the direction of flow). When you use the Mr. Coffee or a pour-over technique, the pressure difference is provided by gravity acting on the weight of the water. Other devices, however, provide more control over the pressure difference (most famously in espresso machines). The applied pressure P_{top} is the pressure you apply by hand plus the atmospheric pressure, while the pressure P_{bot} is the pressure in the air outside the bottom of the AeroPress, which is just the atmospheric pressure. In other words, the pressure difference is

$$\Delta P = P_{top} - P_{bot} = \left(P_{applied} + P_{atm}\right) - P_{atm} = P_{applied}. \tag{2}$$

Note the atmospheric pressure cancels out because it pushes on both the top and bottom.

How do we measure the applied pressure? In this lab, we will use a standard bathroom scale (what you typically use to measure your body weight). When you put the AeroPress on the scale and push on it, you can see how many pounds of force you apply by reading the scale. The force will naturally fluctuate a little bit, but with some practice you can keep the applied force approximately constant during the AeroPress brew. Say you apply 20 pounds of force. The corresponding pressure is this force divided by the cross-sectional area of the plunger in the AeroPress, which is about 1.6 inches in radius. The area is $A = \pi r^2$. Thus,

$$P_{applied} = \frac{F_{applied}}{Area} = \frac{20 \; lbf}{3.14 \times (1.6 \; inch)^2} = 2.5 \; \frac{lbf}{in^2} = 2.5 \; \text{psi}. \tag{3}$$

Here *lbf* means "pounds force" and psi stands for "pounds per square inch." One "atmosphere" of pressure is 14.7 psi. If you applied 200 pounds of force (don't try this!) you would have 1.7 atmospheres of pressure. Espresso machines apply about 9 atmospheres of pressure.

A key goal for this lab is to gain a semi-quantitative appreciation for Darcy's law and how quickly fluid flows through the porous coffee grounds and affects the taste of the resulting cup. The lower the applied pressure, the longer the effective extraction time will be – with a corresponding impact on the mass transfer and ultimate sensory qualities of the brew. Likewise, you can use a much finer grind size and therefore a shorter brewing time. Which approach is better? In this lab you get to test for yourself!

DANGER OF BURNS! PROPER USE OF THE AEROPRESS

Be very careful with the AeroPress – it is easy to burn yourself if careless!

- The maximum capacity is about 200 grams of water.
- **DO NOT ADJUST THE AEROPRESS AFTER YOU PUT HOT WATER IN IT.** You likely will spill hot water and burn yourself.
- Before dispensing, **double-check that the filter cap is hand-tight** and secure. If it is loose, the brew will fall out onto your hand and burn you badly when you invert it. If it is crooked, brew will leak out the side.
- Hold the AeroPress steady with one hand as you apply an evenly applied pressure straight down. Avoid pushing it sideways or at an angle.
- Don't forget the filter paper – otherwise the brew will rush out, and you'll get a gritty mess.

Part A – Pressure driven flow in the AeroPress

We will perform eight brews using the AeroPress to get a feel for Darcy's law. First, we will review the safety guidelines, then do a practice brew (without any measurements) to get a sense for how the brewer works. Then, we will systematically measure the flow rate and corresponding TDS for different applied pressures, different grind sizes (which changes the permeability κ), and different masses of coffee grounds (which alters the distance L). In each case we will measure the time required for the water to move through the grounds.

1) Before doing anything, review the safety guidelines for the AeroPress in the box above.

2) To brew with the AeroPress, follow this procedure.

   i. Position the plunger at line "4" if there are markings. If there are no markings, adjust the plunger so that it is fully seated at the bottom of the reservoir with all the rubber inside, with the hexagonal rim on the opposite, open side.

   ii. Place the AeroPress on a counter or study table so that the plunger is down, and the open cylinder portion with the hexagon is up.

   iii. Add your ground coffee. Then, carefully add a pre-measured amount of hot water, making sure to wet all the grounds and stir the mixture briefly.

   iv. Place a filter in the cap. Secure the cap on top snugly, then wait for the desired amount of extraction time.

   v. Finally, doublecheck that the filter cap is on securely, then quickly and carefully invert the AeroPress onto a large glass mug or measuring cup, ideally on a bathroom scale placed on a counter so that you can measure the applied force.

    vi. Carefully press down until you finish pushing out the brewed coffee (you will feel it change when it starts pushing air through the coffee grounds). Keep an eye on the bathroom scale to assess how much force you are applying.

3) We will perform the first four trials all at the same grind size. Prepare enough ground coffee for the four brews in the AeroPress (about 60 grams). Heat water in the kettle.

4) For the first practice brew, don't worry about using the bathroom scale. Put 15 grams of coffee grounds inside the AeroPress, and then add hot water. Give a quick stir and wait 2 to 4 minutes to provide some extraction time. Then, invert the AeroPress over a ceramic or glass cup on the bathroom scale and apply a "gentle" pressure. Do your best to maintain the same force while dispensing.

5) Taste the brew. What are your sensory impressions?

6) For the second trial, repeat the process with everything identical, but this time be prepared to take more measurements. Place the cup and AeroPress on the bathroom scale, and prepare a cell phone timer to measure how much time it takes to dispense the brew. When dispensing, do your best apply a "gentle" continuous pressure, and record the average pounds of force on the bathroom scale. Record the time $t_{dispense}$ required to dispense the fluid, which is the time from when you first start pushing until you feel it change to pushing air through the compacted coffee grounds. (Don't discard the spent grounds yet until after step 7!)

7) Weigh the mass m of brewed coffee in the cup. If we approximate the density of brewed coffee as $\rho = 1$ gram / cm^3 (close to that of water), then the volume delivered is estimated as $V = m/\rho$. The average flowrate is then calculated as $Q = V / t_{dispense}$. Calculate and record this flowrate.

8) Carefully uncap the AeroPress and fully extend the plunger while holding it vertically. Use a ruler to measure the thickness L of the "puck" of spent coffee grounds. Then measure the TDS and taste the brew. What are your sensory impressions? Discard the puck, rinse and prepare for the next brew.

9) Repeat this process for two more brews, but increasing the applied force each time: first a "moderate" force, and then a "strong" force. (There is no prize for being too strong! If you apply too much force, the filter paper can rip or fluid can leak out the side of the filter cap). Each time, record the dispensing time, the mass of fluid delivered and corresponding flow rate, the applied force, the thickness L of the spent coffee grounds, and the resulting TDS and sensory qualities.

Part B – Permeability and path length in the AeroPress

In this part, our procedure is almost exactly the same as in Part A, except here we will focus on the effect of permeability and path length via the grind size and total mass of grounds.

1) Next, compare the effect of grind size. Grind 15 grams of coffee as fine as possible, and another 15 grams as coarse as possible. Perform an AeroPress brews with the fine grind, using the same "moderate" force to the best of your ability, then repeat with coarse grind, again with the same force. For both brews record all measurements.

2) Finally, compare the effect of the path length L. Grind a final 30 grams of coffee to medium grind size. Repeat two final AeroPress brews, one using just 10 grams of coffee, and the other using 20 grams. Using the same "moderate" force to the best of your ability, and record all measurements.

Data for Pressure Experiments

Keep the following parameters the same for all brews here unless otherwise specified.

Coffee type_____

Mass of hot water: _____ *grams*   Mass of grounds: _____ *grams* R_{brew}: _____

Temperature of hot water: _____ °C   Grind size: _____

Initial extraction time: _____ *minutes*

Gentle Pressure

Mass of brew: _____ – _____ = _____ *grams*   (filled cup – empty cup)

Applied force: _____ *pounds*   Thickness of spent coffee grounds: _____ *cm*

Total dispensing time with pressure applied: _____ *seconds*

Flowrate: _____ *cm³* ÷ _____ *seconds* = _____ *cm³ / second*

TDS: _____ %   PE: _____ × _____ ÷ _____ = _____ %

Sensory Evaluations: _____

_____

Medium Pressure

Mass of brew: _____ – _____ = _____ *grams*   (filled cup – empty cup)

Applied force: _____ *pounds*   Thickness of spent coffee grounds: _____ *cm*

Total dispensing time with pressure applied: _____ *seconds*

Flowrate: _____ *cm³* ÷ _____ *seconds* = _____ *cm³ / second*

TDS: _____ %   PE: _____ × _____ ÷ _____ = _____ %

Sensory Evaluations: _____

_____

Strong Pressure

Mass of brew: _____ – _____ = _____ *grams*   (filled cup – empty cup)

Applied force: _____ *pounds*   Thickness of spent coffee grounds: _____ *cm*

Total dispensing time with pressure applied: _____ *seconds*

Flowrate: _____ *cm³* ÷ _____ *seconds* = _____ *cm³ / second*

TDS: _____ %   PE: _____ × _____ ÷ _____ = _____ %

Sensory Evaluations: _____

_____

Data for Grind Size Experiments

Moderate Pressure, Coarse Grind

Grind size: _____

Mass of brew: _____ − _____ = _____ *grams*   (filled cup − empty cup)

Applied force: _____ *pounds*   Thickness of spent coffee grounds: _____ *cm*

Total dispensing time with pressure applied: _____ *seconds*

Flowrate: _____ *cm³* ÷ _____ *seconds* = _____ *cm³ / second*

TDS: _____ %   PE: _____ × _____ ÷ _____ = _____ %

Sensory Evaluations: _____

_____

_____

Moderate Pressure, Fine Grind

Grind size: _____

Mass of brew: _____ − _____ = _____ *grams*   (filled cup − empty cup)

Applied force: _____ *pounds*   Thickness of spent coffee grounds: _____ *cm*

Total dispensing time with pressure applied: _____ *seconds*

Flowrate: _____ *cm³* ÷ _____ *seconds* = _____ *cm³ / second*

TDS: _____ %   PE: _____ × _____ ÷ _____ = _____ %

Sensory Evaluations: _____

_____

_____

Data for Coffee Mass / Path Length Experiments

Moderate Pressure, Small Mass

Mass of grounds: _____ *grams*

Mass of brew: _____ − _____ = _____ *grams* (filled cup – empty cup)

Applied force: _____ *pounds* Thickness of spent coffee grounds: _____ *cm*

Total dispensing time with pressure applied: _____ *seconds*

Flowrate: _____ *cm³* ÷ _____ *seconds* = _____ *cm³ / second*

TDS: _____ % PE: _____ × _____ ÷ _____ = _____ %

Sensory Evaluations: _____

_____

Moderate Pressure, Large Mass

Mass of grounds: _____ *grams*

Mass of brew: _____ − _____ = _____ *grams* (filled cup – empty cup)

Applied force: _____ *pounds* Thickness of spent coffee grounds: _____ *cm*

Total dispensing time with pressure applied: _____ *seconds*

Flowrate: _____ *cm³* ÷ _____ *seconds* = _____ *cm³ / second*

TDS: _____ % PE: _____ × _____ ÷ _____ = _____ %

Sensory Evaluations: _____

_____

Optional extra calculation: Your data collected here allows you to calculate the permeability, in units of cm². To do this, solve equation (1) for the permeability κ, then insert your experimental values for Q and $P_{applied}/L$. Estimate the viscosity as simply that of water near 80°C, which is $\mu \approx 0.35 \times 10^{-3}$ Pa·s. Here Pa·s is read as "Pascal second," where the Pascal is a unit of pressure equal to 1 Newton per square meter. There are 6895 Pascals in 1 psi. How much does your calculated permeability vary with grind size?

Roasting Data

Coffee type: _____ Roaster settings: _____

Mass of green beans: _____ *grams*   Mass of roasted beans: _____ *grams*

Time spent roasting: _____ *minutes*   Energy usage: _____ *kW-hr*

Notes: _____

Coffee type: _____ Roaster settings: _____

Mass of green beans: _____ *grams*   Mass of roasted beans: _____ *grams*

Time spent roasting: _____ *minutes*   Energy usage: _____ *kW-hr*

Notes: _____

Part C - Roasting

Finally, do two or more roasts for next time. Keep track of your energy usage! The design competition is fast approaching, so optimizing your roasting will be a critical aspect. Have you found a roast profile for the available green beans that you like?

Lab Report

By your specified due date, each group will submit their lab report that includes (1) a scatter plot of the flow rate versus the pressure gradient, (2) a scatter plot of TDS versus flow rate and (3) a paragraph answering the questions below..

(1) Prepare a scatter plot of the flow rate versus the pressure gradient, i.e., a plot of Q in cm^3/s on the vertical axis versus the ratio $P_{applied}/L$ on the horizontal axis. If you did both parts A and B, there should be at least 7 data points on your plot; use different marker colors and/or shapes to delineate which experiments were performed with different grind sizes. Insert text boxes near each point to identify what grind size you used.

(2) Prepare a scatter plot of the TDS of each brew versus the flowrate. Use the same marker colors and shapes as your previous scatter plot, and insert text boxes to identify the grind sizes. What trends do you observe? Does TDS increase or decrease with flowrate? Or does it not change appreciably?

(3) A brief paragraph answering the following questions:

   (i) How accurately did Darcy's law describe the flow rate through the coffee grounds? Did you obtain a linear trend between Q and $P_{applied}/L$ for your medium grind?

   (ii) Why did your coarse and medium grind flow rates not fall on the same line as the medium grind? In terms of Darcy's law, which parameter differs with grind size?

   (iii) How did the TDS vary with the flowrate? What trends did you observe? In general, does the flowrate serve as a good predictor for what the TDS will be?

   (iv) How did the different flow rates and conditions affect the taste of the coffee?

Lab 8 Bonus Box – What Makes Espresso Different?

If you walk into a modern coffeehouse, you are likely to be presented with a long menu of different coffee based beverages. Lattes, cappuccinos, macchiatos, mochas, flat whites, Americanos, and red eyes are all typically available even at the smallest hole-in-the-wall café. Although these drinks feature different amounts of milk or other ingredients, they all share something in common: specifically, they all feature "espresso" as a central ingredient.

What is espresso? Some people mistakenly think of espresso as a different type of roast, but espresso is really a brewing method. In fact, espresso is very similar to brewing coffee with an Aero-Press, except with *very* high applied pressures. With your hand on the AeroPress, you're probably able to apply up to around 60 pounds of force, equivalent to about 7 psi (or 0.5 atmospheres). In contrast, the hot water inside an espresso machine is typically pressurized to around 130 psi, which is equivalent to about 9 atmospheres!

How does the espresso machine generate such a high pressure? Espresso was invented in Italy in the early 1900s, and many of these earliest espresso machines actually had a large lever that the barista would pull downward by hand to pressurize the water. This is why you often hear people talk about "pulling a shot" of espresso, even though modern baristas don't actually pull on anything. (Those early hand-lever espresso machines were quite dangerous: if your hand slipped, the lever would fly back up and potentially break your jaw!) Instead of a lever, many modern espresso machines use the "boiler," an enclosed chamber inside the machine, to boil the water and pressurize the steam up to 9 atmospheres. More expensive machines feature "positive displacement pumps" that provide precise control of the pressure.

With all this pressure available, very high flow rates through the coffee grounds become possible. In fact the name "espresso" alludes to the idea that this is a fast or "express" brewing technique. When you watch a shot being pulled, though, it might look like it's coming out pretty slowly, filling up only a small espresso cup in 30 or so seconds. Just like the AeroPress, the flow rate for espresso is governed by Darcy's law. Unlike the AeroPress, the coffee beans for espresso are typically ground extremely fine, which maximizes the surface area to volume ratio to maximize the rate of mass transfer (think back to Lab 6). At the same time, though, the very small grind size for espresso also decreases the permeability κ significantly. As a result, a typical shot of espresso has a small flowrate despite the huge applied pressure.

The role of the permeability helps give us insight on why baristas have to practice their technique to pull a good shot. Minor changes in the grind size have a big impact on the permeability, and hence the flow rate and corresponding mass transfer – resulting in a big change in the flavor. Baristas spend a lot of time "dialing in" their grind size. Furthermore, they need to perfect their "tamping" technique, where they use a heavy metal tamp to squish the dry coffee grounds into a nice, well-packed and level puck inside the "portafilter" that gets clamped into the espresso machine.

All this effort is worth it, however, because a good shot of espresso will be sweet, syrupy, and have a beautiful "crema" of foam on top resulting from the carbon dioxide released rapidly from the coffee beans. An espresso by itself should be drunk as soon as possible so that you can enjoy the crema before it dissipates. Of course, if you prefer milky drinks like lattes or cappuccinos, then the highly concentrated shot of espresso adds the desired intense coffee flavor. Whichever you prefer, thanks Darcy's law for making it possible!

Lab 9 – Coffee as a Colloidal Fluid & the Effect of Filtration

Objectives: In this lab we will examine the "colloidal particles" present in the coffee using optical microscopy, and assess how the filtration method affects the quantity of colloids and the mouthfeel of the coffee.

Equipment:

☐ AeroPress ☐ French press ☐ Clever Coffee ☐ Metal filter ☐ Electric kettle

☐ Microscope & slides ☐ Digital refractometer ☐ Kill-a-Watt meter ☐ Roaster

Activities:

☐ Part A – probing the effect of filtration

    ☐ Two AeroPress brews, comparing paper and metal filters

    ☐ Two French press brews, comparing grind sizes

    ☐ Two Clever coffee brews, comparing pre-wetting vs. dry filters

☐ Part B – Microscope observations to see the brew colloids and oil droplets

☐ Part C – one or two roasts to have beans for next time

Report:

☐ Column plot of TDS for different filtration methods

☐ Column plot of number of colloids per image for different filtration methods

☐ Photos and descriptions of microscopy observations

☐ Paragraphs discussing tasting notes and key questions about the lab

Background – Colloidal Dispersions

In the past few labs we have measured the "Total Dissolved Solids" (TDS) in the brew. By "dissolved," we mean that each individual molecule (such as caffeine or citric acid) is completely surrounded by water molecules. Not all of the mass that is extracted from the grounds are dissolved organic molecules. There are three other types of matter extracted from the solid grounds and in the brew that you drink.

First, there are gasses, primarily carbon dioxide and VOCs. The concentration of CO_2 is especially high in freshly roasted beans (because the CO_2 hasn't had sufficient time to leak away). When you pour hot water over freshly ground coffee that still has a large enough amount of CO_2 in it, you'll actually see bubbles rising up to the top of the slurry. This is exactly the same type of bubble formation and flotation that

happens with beer or soda, except that the CO_2 concentration isn't as high in coffee. Nonetheless the bubble formation is a good indication that you're dealing with freshly roasted coffee.

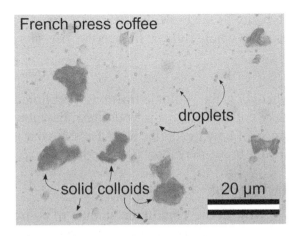

French press coffee

droplets

solid colloids

20 μm

Second, some amount of "non-dissolved solids" makes it past the filter and into the brew. Ideally during grinding you would make coffee particles all the same size, but this never happens. Instead there is a distribution of sizes, with some larger particles, many intermediate particles, and some very small ones. Any particles smaller than the average pore size in the filter are carried into the brew for you to consume. These small particles are referred to as "colloidal particles," where colloidal is the scientific term that simply means "microscopically dispersed and insoluble." Colloids are typically in the range of 1 to 10,000 nanometers, i.e., up to about 10 microns. (The unit for micron is μm, using the Greek letter mu. There are 1000 nanometers in 1 micron, and 1000 microns in 1 millimeter.) In comparison, the average diameter of an individual human hair is about 70 microns, and the naked eye is able to resolve objects about 30 microns or larger. That means these colloids in coffee are too small to see by eye!

Third, there are "emulsified oils" in the brew. The term "emulsion" simply means a colloidal suspension made of liquid droplets rather than solid; the classic example is well-shaken oil-in-vinegar salad dressing. Roasting coffee releases a variety of oils, which are especially evident in very dark roasts. As with the solid colloids, the emulsified oil droplets also affect the mouthfeel by altering the viscosity. The oil drops tend to be more 'potent,' however, because many of the more bitter tasting molecules tend to be more oil soluble than water soluble – which means the oil drops tend to impart a more bitter flavor to the brew. Typically, a little bit of oil is desired for good mouthfeel, but not too much for bitterness.

A key characteristic of colloids, both solid particulates and oil droplets, is that they undergo what's known as "Brownian motion." If you watch a micron-scale colloid under the microscope, you will see it jiggle around randomly. In the 1800s, people thought the jiggling must mean that the colloids were alive (because they were moving, and moving implies life!) Albert Einstein actually figured out the real reason. He showed that the jiggling motion is because of the surrounding water molecules: the surrounding molecules are continuously bumping into the colloid, and frequently more water molecules will bounce into one side of the colloid than the other, so the colloid lurches off in that direction. Each momentary imbalance in water molecule collisions causes the colloid to lurch off in some random direction. Einstein showed that the amount of jiggling for an isolated colloid is inversely proportional to the radius R of the colloid, such that

$$\text{speed of Brownian motion} \propto \frac{T}{\mu_w R}, \tag{1}$$

where T is the temperature and μ_w is the viscosity of the water. In other words, the hotter the fluid and the smaller the colloid, the faster it will jiggle around randomly.

Even though the individual colloids are too small for your tongue to detect them individually, the presence of these jiggling colloids nonetheless has a big impact on how the coffee tastes. Specifically, the colloids strongly affect the "body" (the mouthfeel) by altering the viscosity of the brew. Einstein also showed that the more colloids are present, the more viscous the whole fluid is. In fact, the viscosity of the brew follows the equation

$$\mu_{coffee} = \mu_w\left(1 + \tfrac{5}{2}\phi\right), \tag{2}$$

where ϕ is the "volume fraction" of colloids in the coffee, i.e., $\phi = V_{colloids}/V_{water}$. So, the more colloids present in your brew, the more viscous it will be, which affects the tactile sensation of how the coffee brew feels in your mouth. In other words, the more colloids present in your brew, the more "body" it has.

Background – Filtration

How do we control the amount of colloids present in the brew? The short answer is filtration. Both the colloids and the emulsified oil are strongly affected by the type of filtration. The average size of the pores in the filter directly control the size of the colloids that make it into your brew. If you use a very coarse filter with big pores, obviously you let more colloids into your brew.

There is surprisingly little data in the open literature on the pore size of typical paper coffee filters, with unreferenced websites stating between 5 and 100 microns (0.1mm). This is a huge range. If you look at filter paper under a microscope like the images shown on the next page, you will see a range of various shaped pores with sizes from 5-30 microns, but it also depends on where you look and the manufacturer of the paper as to the typical pore size. Filter paper is composed of lignocellulosic fibrous material, which is simply wood pulp primarily from fast growing trees like bamboo. The paper is crêped so that the coffee can more easily flow through the layers of fibers. The filter paper also varies based on whether the filter is conical or flat bottom in shape. Specialty Chemex filters are reportedly thicker with smaller pores. In comparison, metal or mesh filters are much more uniform as can be seen from the table and images on the right.

Differences in pore sizes and their quantity (i.e., percentage of surface area) affect the amount of ground coffee particles that make their way into your cup, as well as the water draining rate for gravity brewing methods. A typical automatic drip method usually uses 500-800 micron ground coffee particles. However, even when using a nice cone and burr grinder, you end up with a range of coffee particle sizes from about 10 microns to almost 1000 microns (where 1000 microns = 1 mm). This is also a huge range! It is analogous to grade distributions on an exam where the mean grade might be a "B", but all grades are represented across the class. The more uniform the grind size, the more uniform the extraction. Because of the coarser filtration and leakage around the sides of the filter with the French press, a typical grind size for this method is 800 – 1200 microns. In comparison, espresso grinds are around 200 microns.

Although the geometry of the filter clearly matters, the chemical composition of the filter also matters tremendously. Paper filters are made of cellulosic fibers, and cellulose is both hydrophobic (water-fearing) and oleophilic (oil-loving). In other words, paper filters will preferentially absorb the emulsified oil, so that little of it ends up in your brew. Filter paper

Filter Type	Pore Shape	Pore Size (microns)
Paper	woven	5-100
AeroPress Paper	woven	5-30
Aero Metal (Fine)	round	200
Aero Metal (Coarse)	round	250
Gold Tone Mesh	square	150
Nylon Mesh	square	250
French Press	rectangle	180-230

both adsorbs and absorbs the oil. Adsorption refers to the oil actually sticking to the paper fibers while absorption is the same phenomena as a sponge soaking up a liquid into the spaces of the sponge. If you look closely at coffee from an AeroPress with filter paper, you still get a significant amount of oil into the brewed coffee because the pressure you apply squeezes out a lot of the oil absorbed into the filter paper.

In contrast, metal filters are oleophobic (oil-fearing). They will let the oil droplets pass through uninterrupted, because the oil drops cannot absorb into the metal or adsorb onto the metal. Thus, using a metal filter will maximize the amount of emulsified oil droplets in your brew. These oil droplets affect the viscosity (and hence mouthfeel) similar to the solid colloids. They also strongly affect the flavor, because many of the bitter molecules present in coffee are more oil soluble than water soluble. In other words, the oil droplets often contribute to more perceivable bitterness.

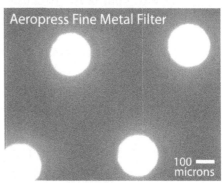

A final comment is that some coffee experts claim that you have to pre-wet your paper filter before you brew. Why would this be important? There are at least two possible reasons. First, some people can detect a "papery" flavor contributed by microscopic bits of paper that detach from the filter and make it into your brew. Pre-wetting washes these loose bits away. Second, if the filter paper is already fully wet, then it won't as easily absorb the first drips of coffee that might be packed with the most readily extractable flavor molecules. In other words, an initially dry filter paper will retain some of the initial

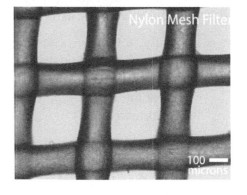

drips of coffee, while a pre-wet filter won't. But does this matter? We will do our own taste tests to find out!

Part A – Colloids and Filtration

We will perform three sets of head-to-head comparisons, focusing on the effect of filtration on the colloids and emulsified oils that end up in the brew. If possible, use the same coffee for all six brews.

1) First, set up two AeroPresses with identical conditions (same grind size, same mass of coffee same mass of water), except use a paper filter in one and a metallic filter in the other. Perform the brews with the same extraction time (two to four minutes) and same applied pressure.

PROPER USAGE OF THE REFRACTOMETERS

Be aware that the presence of any large particulates or oil droplets in your sample on the refractometer will give rise to large errors in the reading (because the relatively large objects alter the light path). Pipette your coffee from near the top of your sample, not the bottom! Avoid putting samples with visible particulates or oil films, and make sure the refractometer is cleaned using a **Kimwipe** before you measure your sample.

2) Measure the TDS of each, and taste the brews. What are your sensory impressions? Can you detect a difference in body / mouthfeel? Oils tend to accumulate at the surface of your brew (because oil is less dense than water)... can you see any oil?

3) Save small samples of each AeroPress brew, to perform microscopy on in Part B.

4) Next, set up two small French presses. For one of them, use identical conditions as you used with the AeroPress (same brew ratio, same water temperature, and same grind size). For the other, use all the same conditions except use a much smaller grind size. At the four-minute mark use the press to push down and filter out the grounds, then dispense the coffee.

5) Measure the TDS (but first see the warning above) and taste the brews – how do they compare to the AeroPress? How did the smaller grind size affect the flavor and mouthfeel for the French press brew? Does the finer grind brew feel more viscous? Again, save some samples for microscopy.

6) Finally, set up two Clever Coffee brewers with filter papers. Before you put in the coffee grounds, though, for one of the brewers pre-wet the filter paper by pouring hot water over it. Use enough to completely wet the filter paper; this amount will vary depending on the type of paper and your pouring technique. Leave the filter in the other brewer dry.

7) Smell and taste the water that was used to pre-wet the filter paper (i.e., the "filtrate" that ended up in the cup). Can you tell any difference from regular water? Measure the TDS of the filtrate... is it different than that of plain water? Keep a sample of the water that passed through the filter (the filtrate) for microscopy, then discard the rest.

8) Perform two identical brews in the Clever Coffees, using identical conditions as your AeroPress brews. After brewing, measure the TDS, and keep samples for microscopy. When tasting, make sure you do it blind – have your partner hand you the drink without letting you know which is which. Can you detect a difference from pre-wetting the filter? Or do they taste the same?

Data for AeroPress Experiments – Comparing Paper vs. Metal Filter

Coffee type_____

Mass of hot water: _____ *grams*   Mass of grounds: _____ *grams* R_{brew}: _____

Temperature of hot water: _____ °C   Grind size: _____

Initial extraction time: _____ *minutes*

AeroPress, Paper Filter

Mass of brew: _____ – _____ = _____ *grams*   (filled cup – empty cup)

Applied force: _____ *pounds*

Total dispensing time with pressure applied: _____ *seconds*

Flowrate: _____ *cm³* ÷ _____ *seconds* = _____ *cm³ / second*

TDS: _____ %   PE: _____ × _____ ÷ _____ = _____ %

Sensory Evaluations:_____

_____

_____

AeroPress, Metal Filter

Mass of brew: _____ – _____ = _____ *grams*   (filled cup – empty cup)

Applied force: _____ *pounds*

Total dispensing time with pressure applied: _____ *seconds*

Flowrate: _____ *cm³* ÷ _____ *seconds* = _____ *cm³ / second*

TDS: _____ %   PE: _____ × _____ ÷ _____ = _____ %

Sensory Evaluations:_____

_____

_____

Data for French Press Experiments – Comparing Grind Size

Coffee type_____

Mass of hot water: _____ *grams*   Mass of grounds: _____ *grams* R_{brew}: _____

Temperature of hot water: _____ °C   Initial extraction time: _____ *minutes*

French Press, Coarse Grind

Grind size: _____

Mass of brew: _____ – _____ = _____ *grams*   (filled cup – empty cup)

TDS: _____ %   PE: _____ × _____ ÷ _____ = _____ %

Sensory Evaluations:_____

_____

_____

_____

French Press, Fine Grind

Grind size: _____

Mass of brew: _____ – _____ = _____ *grams*   (filled cup – empty cup)

TDS: _____ %   PE: _____ × _____ ÷ _____ = _____ %

Sensory Evaluations:_____

_____

_____

_____

Data for Clever Coffee Experiments – Comparing Filter Pre-Wetting

Coffee type_____

Mass of hot water: _____ *grams*   Mass of grounds: _____ *grams* R_{brew}: _____

Temperature of hot water: _____ °C   Grind size: _____

Initial extraction time: _____ *minutes*

Clever Coffee, Dry Filter Paper

Mass of brew: _____ – _____ = _____ *grams*   (filled cup – empty cup)

TDS: _____ %   PE: _____ × _____ ÷ _____ = _____ %

Sensory Evaluations:_____

_____

_____

Clever Coffee, Pre-Wetted Filter Paper

TDS of plain water: _____ %   TDS of filtrate (after wetting filter): _____ %

Sensory evaluations of water filtrate:_____

_____

Mass of brew: _____ – _____ = _____ *grams*   (filled cup – empty cup)

TDS: _____ %   PE: _____ × _____ ÷ _____ = _____ %

Sensory Evaluations:_____

_____

_____

_____

Part B – Microscopy Observations of Brewed Coffee

1) Now that you're caffeinated, let's do some microscopy. The first order of business is to get a sense of the scale and magnification available on your microscope. You might have objects or calibration references of known size to put in the microscope – but if not, have you or your partner donate a little piece of hair (half a centimeter long is fine). Hair varies in size from about 50 to 150 microns in diameter depending on the person, so this is very crude – but it will give you a semi-quantitative basis for comparison of the coffee colloids. Place the hair (or object of known size) on a microscope slide, put it in the microscope, and adjust the focus and lighting until you have a nice image. Keep this approximate size in mind.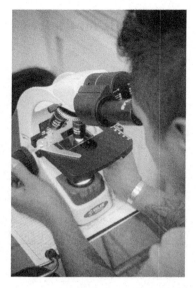

2) Pipette out a little bit of coffee from one of your French press brews onto a clean microscope slide, and then cover it with a cover slip. Avoid trapping air bubbles under the cover slip. Put it in the microscope and adjust the focus and light intensity until you can clearly see the coffee colloids. Look somewhere near the center of the sample (away from the edges, where evaporation of the water can cause motion).

3) The solid colloids will be irregular in shape, while oil droplets will be spherical. Approximately how large are they? Do you see any evidence of Brownian motion? If the particles are "stuck" to the glass slide, they will be stationary – look for particles that are actively moving. Track the motion of a large colloid versus a smaller one... does the jiggling velocity of large versus small colloids obey equation (1)? In other words, do the smaller colloids jiggle more rapidly than the larger colloids?

4) If possible, on your microscope take a photo of the colloids, and then count the number of colloids present in the field of view. If you can't save an image, then count or estimate the number of particles while the sample is still in the microscope.

5) Prepare slides for your other samples. For each, take a picture (if possible). What differences do you observe for the different brewing methods? Record your general impressions regarding the relative amounts of oil droplets, the number and size of coffee particles, and any other relevant observations. Do you see anything present at all for the filtrate from pre-wetting the filter?

Part C - Roasting

Finally, do two or more roasts for next time. Keep track of your energy usage! The remaining laboratory experiments will focus on the design competition, so optimizing roasting will be critical. Have you found a roast profile for the available green beans that you like?

Microscopy Observations

<u>French Press, Coarse</u>   Number of particles in field of view: _____

Observations and Notes: _____

_____

<u>French Press, Fine</u>   Number of particles in field of view: _____

Observations and Notes: _____

_____

<u>AeroPress, Paper</u>   Number of particles in field of view: _____

Observations and Notes: _____

_____

<u>AeroPress, Metal</u>   Number of particles in field of view: _____

Observations and Notes: _____

_____

<u>Clever Coffee, Dry</u>   Number of particles in field of view: _____

Observations and Notes: _____

_____

<u>Clever Coffee, Pre-Wet</u>   Number of particles in field of view: _____

Observations and Notes: _____

_____

<u>Pre-Wetting Filtrate</u>   Number of particles in field of view: _____

Observations and Notes: _____

_____

Roasting Data

Coffee type: _____ Roaster settings: _____

Mass of green beans: _____ *grams*   Mass of roasted beans: _____ *grams*

Time spent roasting: _____ *minutes* Energy usage: _____ *kW-hr*

Notes: _____

Coffee type: _____ Roaster settings: _____

Mass of green beans: _____ *grams*   Mass of roasted beans: _____ *grams*

Time spent roasting: _____ *minutes* Energy usage: _____ *kW-hr*

Notes: _____

Lab Report

By your specified due date, each group will submit their lab report that includes (1) a column plot of TDS versus the brewing filtration method, (2) if applicable labeled photos of the brews, (3) a column plot of particle numbers for the brews and (4) a paragraph answering the questions below.

(1) A column plot that shows the TDS versus the brewing and filtration method, and a column plot of the PE versus the brewing and filtration method. There should be 6 data points for each. Make sure you label everything clearly. What trends do you observe?

(2) If applicable (because you had the capability to record photos), labeled photos of your microscopy observations for each brewing/filtration technique.

(3) A column plot that shows the approximate number of colloids in each representative microscopy image versus your brewing and filtration method. Clearly label each column. If you were unable to photograph images to count colloids in them later, instead make a table simply arranging from highest to lowest which brewing and filtration methods had more particles. What technique yielded the most colloids? The least?

(4) A brief paragraph answering the following questions:

    (i)   Did the composition of the filter, paper versus metal, appreciably alter the flavor of the brew? Was any taste difference correlated with a difference in TDS?

    (ii) How did the grind size affect the French press brews? How much did the TDS change? How did the flavor change?

    (iii) Did pre-wetting the filter have any impact on anything? Were you able to taste or measure anything in the filtrate?

    (iv) In a few sentences, describe what you saw in the coffee samples under the microscope. Which brews had the most particles? Did any brews have more oil droplets than the others? How was the particle count correlated with your sensory impressions? In general, which brewing and filtration technique did you prefer?

Lab 9 Bonus Box – Turkish Coffee and Cowboy Coffee

Most coffee brewing methods have some sort of filtration step. Automatic drip, French press, AeroPress, Chemex, vacuum brewers, old-school percolators and even espresso makers all have some sort of filtration. But, **why** do we filter the brew – is it just to keep the sludge from the bottom of your cup? Do we need to filter?

The answer is: absolutely not! Millions of people around the world enjoy different types of unfiltered coffee. A famous example is Turkish coffee (also known as Arabic coffee, or in Israel as "botz" or "mud" coffee). In Turkish coffee, the beans are ground into an extremely fine powder (around 100 microns on average), and then they are put into a special brewing pot called a *cezve* in Turkish (known as an *ibrik* in English). The water and coffee grounds are then brought to a boil, allowed to cool, and brought to a boil again a couple times to increase the foam. It is then poured into individual cups, without any filtration. Often sugar and cardamom pods or other spices are added to sweeten the brew and add delicious flavors. Because there is no filtration, a lot of particles and colloids end up in the brew. Although the larger coffee particles settle by gravity, the smaller ones stay in suspension and make the beverage very viscous. Turkish people often joke that the coffee isn't properly made unless a spoon is able to stand straight up by itself when inserted in the cup.

You don't need to travel to the Middle East to experience unfiltered coffee, though. In fact, there's a tradition right here in North America of "cowboy coffee." That's the official name for throwing some coarsely ground coffee into water, heating it to a rolling boil (usually over a campfire) and then pouring the brew into a cup for consumption. If done properly, a good cup of coffee can result, but cowboy coffee in general has a reputation for being overly bitter and sour. The reason for cowboy coffee's bad reputation is twofold: the uncontrolled extraction, and the difficulty in controlling the heat so that the coffee isn't degraded. Recall Lab 4: leaving the coffee heating on the campfire further degrades the quality through those chemical reactions that decrease pH.

Even if you were able to control the temperature on the campfire, you'll still have difficulty controlling the extraction. Recall our ideal brew is 18-22% extraction. Since 26-30% of the mass of a roasted coffee bean is extractable, that means we want to leave some of the extractable coffee stuff behind. The idea behind this is that different flavor components have different solubilities in water, and those last few percent that take longer to extract are associated with bitter characteristics. Over extraction is normally avoided by filtering, which stops the extraction (i.e., ends the contact time) simply by removing the grounds. Furthermore, most coffee aficionados identify a 91 to 94°C brewing temperature as ideal for limiting the extraction of "bitter" flavor compounds, so most brewing methods and extraction times are based on this temperature range. Boiling at 100°C causes all of those bitter compounds to extract.

To make a much better cup of cowboy coffee, just heat the water first (if the water is brought to a boil, allow it to cool for a few minutes), then throw in the coffee. This will give you much better control over the water temperature and the extraction. After 4-6 minutes, it should be ready. Some cowboys then add a bit of cold water on top. The cold water will sink (due to its higher density) and carry the coffee solids down to the bottom. Then simply pour yourself and the other "cowboys or cowgirls" a cup of pretty good brew. No filtration needed!

Lab 10 – High Pressure Extraction & Viscosity of Espresso

Objectives: In this lab, we will explore espresso, with a focus on its viscosity. If you have an espresso maker that is great, if not use an AeroPress at very low brew ratios to make pseudo espresso. We will use a glass "Canon-Fenske" viscometer to measure viscosity.

Equipment:

☐ AeroPress ☐ Electric kettle ☐ Digital refractometer ☐ Espresso Machine (optional)

☐ Canon-Fenske viscometer size 50 ☐ Graduated cylinder, 100 mL

☐ Kill-a-Watt meter ☐ Roaster

Activities:

☐ Part A – pulling multiple shots with an espresso machine

    ☐ Practice shots to "dial in" the appropriate grind size

    ☐ Pull three shots (short, medium, long) and measure viscosity of each

☐ Part B – six brews with the AeroPress to make pseudo espresso

    ☐ Three brews at small but different brew ratios to approximate espresso

    ☐ Three more brews to optimize taste and measure viscosity

☐ Part C – two or more roasts to have beans for next time

Report:

☐ Scatter plot of measured viscosity versus the duration of the espresso shot

☐ Scatter plot of measured viscosity versus brew ratio with AeroPress

☐ Scatter plot of all measured viscosities versus measured TDS values

☐ Paragraph discussing tasting notes and key questions about the lab

Background – Espresso

First, what exactly is espresso? Most of us associate espresso with very dark, espresso roast coffee that your favorite coffee shop uses to make a very concentrated shot of espresso. Actually, any roasted coffee from light to dark can be used to make espresso. What makes espresso special isn't that it requires a special coffee roast, but that it is made to order and uses fairly complicated equipment capable of applying a large pressure to brew the espresso – or "pull" the espresso shot.

The Specialty Coffee Association (SCA) has a strict definition of an espresso: "a 25 to 35mL beverage

prepared from 7 to 9 grams of coffee through which clean water of 92° to 95°C has been forced at 9 to 10 atmospheres of pressure, and where the grind of the coffee is such that the brewing 'flow' time is approximately 20-30 seconds."

This definition is for what is commonly referred to as a "single shot" of espresso. An interesting aspect is that the definition is almost exactly the same for a double shot of espresso. A double shot uses twice the amount of coffee and yields twice the volume of espresso – but the brewing time of 20 to 30 seconds remains exactly the same. Let's think about this in reference to Lab 8 where we learned how Darcy's law relates the liquid flow rate to the pressure difference across the porous medium (the ground coffee):

$$Q = \frac{\kappa}{\mu} \times A \times \frac{(P_{applied})}{L}. \tag{1}$$

In an espresso maker, the $P_{applied}$ is set by the machine at 9 to 10 atmospheres. That's quite a bit of pressure! The viscosity μ of the fluid is essentially that of water at 92° to 95°C, and is the same for either a single or double shot. You might think the L changes – we have twice the amount of coffee, but as you see in the filter cup images below, the single and double shot filter cups for the coffee have about the same depth (the single is about 10% smaller L than the double). For our purposes here, let's assume that L is the same for a single or double shot ($L_s = L_d$). However, there is a very large difference in the area A for flow. The single shot filter cup has about half of the area for flow compared to the double shot ($2A_s = A_d$). If we keep the grind size the same for a single and double shot, the permeability κ is also the same. Plugging these values in shows that just the change in the area for flow can enable a doubling of the volume of coffee and espresso yield.

$$Q_s = \frac{\kappa}{\mu} \times A_s \times \frac{(P_{applied})}{L}. \tag{2}$$

$$Q_d = \frac{\kappa}{\mu} \times 2A_s \times \frac{(P_{applied})}{L} = 2Q_s. \tag{3}$$

In other words, we would obtain twice the volumetric flow rate just from the larger area of the double filter cup while keeping the other parameters (aside from the mass of coffee grounds to fill that area) exactly the same – and get double the amount of beverage. Note that most coffee shops only make double espressos. Instead of making small adjustments to the grind size (and thereby κ) to obtain the desired flowrate, baristas typically dial in the grind size that they think yields the best tasting espresso double shot. Also note that just because there is an SCA definition for espresso, it does not mean you have to color within the lines. Many home and professional baristas develop their own protocols and recipes for what they think makes the best tasting espresso.

For that reason, we prefer a broader definition of an espresso – a concentrated coffee beverage brewed to order with heated water at a pressure of 9 to 10 atmospheres. The unique aspect of espresso brewing is the use of high-pressure water for the extraction. So, how does that compare to our AeroPress experiments in Lab 8? To apply 9 atmospheres of pressure in the Aero-Press, we would have to apply over a 1000 pounds of force during the plunging phase. Obviously, this is not

Espresso filter cups

single   double

physically possible by hand! Moreover, the AeroPress itself isn't designed for such high pressures – it would likely shatter. Please don't try loading an AeroPress with multiple weights.

Espresso is so delicious, however, that it is worth thinking about how to approximate it even without an expensive espresso machine. To get a handle on why high-pressure extraction makes such a difference, look at the espresso image on the first page of this lab. The fluid is much darker and viscous than a typical brewed coffee, and at the top is a thick rich layer of foam called crema. The TDS of a typical espresso is around 5% to reportedly as high as 12%, much higher than regularly brewed coffee. A large part of this is the brew ratio of 2 to 4 used in espresso. The pressurized water also is better at extracting the oils (mainly triglycerides, diterpenes, and lipids) in the ground coffee. These oils become emulsified (small oil droplets in the liquid phase).

As a result, the viscosity of espresso can almost double that of regular coffee. This gives espresso a heavier mouthfeel and a certain silkiness. Those oils don't just add body and mouthfeel, but also carry oil soluble molecules from the ground coffee that enhance the taste.

As with all coffee brewing, water contact time with the ground coffee is essential to extract coffee yumminess into the cup. To ensure that that the high-pressure water doesn't flow too fast through the bed of ground coffee, a fine grind is used for espresso. The grind size correlates directly to the permeability of the ground coffee. The finer the grind, the more resistance to flow. To make an espresso in 20 to 30 seconds and obtain 25 to 35 mL of beverage with essentially the same water temperature, pressure, and filter cup means the main way to control flow rate, and thus extraction time, is through the grind size and resulting permeability. There are also tamps to compress the grounds into the filter cup, but the role of tamping has gotten blown out of proportion. It isn't that critical as studies have shown little difference when a hydraulic ram was used to apply really high even pressure versus very gentle pressure during tamping. Rather, the pressure of the water going through the grounds seems to do a fine job of tamping. In fact, most commercial espresso makers actually ramp the pressure to 9 atmospheres to "tamp" the grounds. That ramping of the pressure is commonly called "pre-infusion" and helps ensure that the water flows uniformly through the coffee and does not channel. Still, the grind size, the levelness of the bed of ground coffee in the filter cup, and the elimination of voids in the ground coffee that allow water to channel through, are all critical. Tamping is essential to achieve even levelness and compression of the ground coffee to eliminate any voids.

It is not just the liquid portion that is different. A well-made espresso should be about 10% foam or crema on the top. That foam, however, is fleeting. It starts to degrade as soon as the espresso is made. If you recall Lab 3 where you measured the mass lost when roasting green beans, you know that the bulk of the lost mass is water vapor, with some volatile organic compounds also released (you can smell changes as the coffee roasts due to the release of these VOCs). Although you can't smell it, another important gas that is formed and partially released during roasting is carbon dioxide, CO_2. The amount of CO_2 in freshly roasted coffee is actually about 2% of the total mass. The CO_2 is partially trapped in the roasted bean, but it slowly escapes over days and weeks after roasting. Conversely, the CO_2 can easily escape when you grind the coffee, resulting in the "coffee bloom" that you see when you pour hot water on freshly ground coffee during brewing. The oils that you extract from the ground coffee during espresso brewing are not only emulsified in the liquid phase but also help stabilize the small CO_2 bubbles in the crema. Gas is less dense than liquid so the crema sits on top. Finally, the eruption of foam is further augmented by the change in pressure from 9 to 10 atmospheres to 1 atmosphere as the espresso enters the cup.

These descriptions designate some of the properties of espresso, but the art and science for excellent espresso is better captured by Illycaffé - "*Italian espresso is a polyphasic beverage, prepared from roast and ground coffee and water alone, constituted by a foam layer of small bubbles with a particular tiger-tail pattern, on top of an emulsion of microscopic oil droplets in an aqueous solution of sugars, acids, protein-like material and caffeine, with dispersed gas bubbles and solids.*"

Background – Viscosity

As mentioned above, one of the key aspects of espresso is its wonderful mouthfeel, which is directly related to its *viscosity*. In this lab is that we will measure the viscosity of the different brews and correlate these quantitative measurements to our qualitative sensory evaluation of mouthfeel.

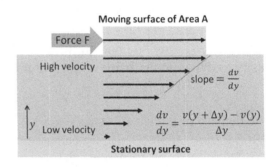

Recall in Lab 8, the "viscosity" μ of the fluid characterizes how easy it is for it to deform or to "shear". Qualitatively, "thinner" fluids, like water, have low viscosity and flow more easily than "thicker" fluids, like honey. Literally, there is more friction between layers of honey molecules moving relatively to each other and less friction between neighboring water molecules in motion. The fact that there is friction implies that a force is required to displace the fluid.

Sir Isaac Newton was the first to work out a mathematical model for viscosity. He determined that the force F to displace a fluid was proportional to the surface area A and the shear rate. The shear rate is the change in the velocity v of the fluid as depicted by the black arrows in the figure above. The shear rate is therefore the slope $= \frac{dv}{dy}$. Newton's law of viscosity is

$$F = \mu A \frac{dv}{dy}. \tag{4}$$

Fluids that obey this relationship, such as coffee and espresso, are called Newtonian fluids. The equation is more commonly shown as the shear stress $\frac{F}{A}$ is proportional to the shear rate $\frac{dv}{dy}$. The proportionality constant is the viscosity μ.

$$\tau = \frac{F}{A} = \mu \frac{dv}{dy}. \tag{5}$$

The viscosity has units of Newton-seconds per square meter (N·s/m²), which is equivalent to a Pascal second (Pa·s). Viscosity can also be given with units of grams per second per centimeter (also known as centipoise or cP). Pure water has a viscosity of about 0.001 Pa·s or 1 cP.

As discussed in Lab 9, a fluid's viscosity is impacted by the volume of colloids in the coffee. In Lab 9 those colloids were primarily coffee particle colloids. With espresso, we have a lot more coffee colloids as well as a lot more oil droplets along, with much higher concentrations of dissolved solids. These all combine to increase the viscosity of espresso by up to a factor of 2 or so over regularly brewed coffee. The viscosity tells you how easily the fluid particles slide past each other where the coffee and oil colloids add more resistance to flow. We can use our viscosity measurement to therefore estimate the volume of colloids in the espresso.

We can obtain a qualitative measurement of viscosity from the body or mouthfeel of the brew. In this lab, we will quantitatively measure the brew viscosity. To do this we will use a simple glass device called a Canon-Fenske viscometer (see figure below). This apparatus works by measuring the time for a fluid to flow by gravity through a glass capillary; the more viscous the fluid, the more time it takes to drain. The measured time (in seconds) is multiplied by the viscometer constant (often denoted as C), which accounts for the surface area of the viscometer tube, to give the viscosity of the fluid. For low viscosity fluids (like espresso) we will use a size 50 Canon-Fenske viscometer. This size is appropriate to measure viscosities between about 1 to 4 centistokes, where water is about 1 centistoke. More viscous fluids use larger-diameter capillaries so it doesn't take too long. Expensive Canon-Fenske viscometers are calibrated and provide the exact constant.

But what is a "centistoke"? The units might seem a little strange; Canon-Fenske viscometers measure the "kinematic viscosity," often denoted as v (the Greek letter nu), and which has units of area per time. This might seem confusing: up to this point we've been using the "dynamic viscosity" μ (also known as the absolute viscosity). To convert from kinematic viscosity to dynamic viscosity we just multiply by the fluid density ρ, so that

$$\mu = \rho \times v \tag{6}$$

The density of water only changes a little with temperature, from 0.997 g/cm^3 at 25 °C to 0.965 g/cm^3 at 90 °C. So, we can assume the density of the brews are all about 1 g/cm^3.

To measure and calculate the viscosity of your espresso, you measure the time t_{drain} required to drain in the viscometer. You multiply this time by the time constant C, which is already known for your viscometer and provided by the manufacturer. (Typical values of C are around 0.004 centistokes per second.) Then you multiply by the density of water, which here you can approximate as 1 g/cm^3. Thus, the viscosity is

$$\mu = \rho \times t_{drain} \times C. \tag{7}$$

If your viscometer constant is given to you in centistokes per second (cSt/s), then your dynamic viscosity will have units of centipoise (centigrams per centimeter per second).

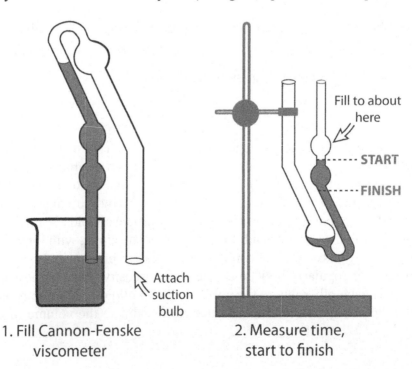

Fill to about here

START

FINISH

Attach suction bulb

1. Fill Cannon-Fenske viscometer

2. Measure time, start to finish

Unlike density, the viscosity of most fluids is very sensitive to temperature. The viscosity of water drops by about a factor of 6 as the temperature increases from 0 to 100 °C. This might seem like a lot, but the viscosity of 5W-30 motor oil decreases by a factor of 60 over the same temperature range. The main point here is that we want to keep the temperature constant when we measure the viscosity of the different brews. Make sure you allow your espresso shots and brewed coffee to cool to room temperature before measuring.

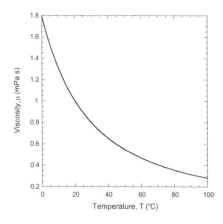

Experiments

Now on to the actual experiments. If you have an espresso maker, wonderful – you can do Part A. If you don't, skip part A but go to your favorite coffee shop and try an espresso! Save some of it or buy two and measure the TDS, pH, and viscosity to compare! Beware, the crema will rapidly dissipate.

Even if you don't have an espresso machine, you definitely can still do Part B where we make use of an AeroPress to make "pseudo-espresso." As mentioned earlier, there is no way to duplicate the pressure of an espresso maker with an AeroPress. However, one can shift from using the AeroPress in typical coffee brewing mode with brew ratios of 15 to 18 to the espresso range of brew ratios around 3 and make pseudo espresso. If you search the web, there are a lot of different recipes out there to try with an AeroPress.

Part A – High Pressure Espresso Maker

Our experiments will focus on trying to match the SCA guidelines. First, determine if your filter cup is for a single or double espresso. If you have both, compare the single and double filter cups. Is there a difference in L and A? Measure them. Recall, the single shot uses 7-9 grams and the double uses well double! Let's use 8 or 16 grams for these experiments.

1) Select an appropriate grind size to obtain particles about the size of table salt. Carefully weigh (9 grams or 18 grams) and fill the (single or double) filter basket. Try to tamp so the coffee is level. Recall we want to obtain a volume between 25 to 35 mL (about 25 to 35 grams) in 20 – 30 seconds. If you are pulling double shots, you want to obtain a volume between 50 to 70 mL (about 50 to 70 grams) in the same amount of time, 20 – 30 seconds.

2) First do a test run. Set up a timer and brew directly into a cup tared on a scale. There are some small scales designed precisely for this purpose and include a timer. No worries if you don't have one, but that means your first test run might be more like 3 or 4 test runs. Stop at 25 seconds. Measure the weight of the espresso.

3) Was the volume/mass between 25 to 35 grams for a single or 50 to 70 grams for a double shot? Pull additional shots varying the grind size until you hit the target. Try for the middle 30 mL or 60 mL for the single or double, respectively.

4) Once you think you have the appropriate conditions, save samples of 3 different shots: the first sample at 20 seconds, the second at 30 seconds, and the third at 40 seconds. Keep all the conditions the same, only vary the time at which you stop pulling the espresso. Measure the mass and height of the crema in each shot immediately after you pull it, by pouring the entire espresso into a clean graduated cylinder.

5) Next, pour out some of the espresso to taste each sample. Record your sensory evaluations. Does one of the shots taste better? What makes it stand out?

6) Repeat the same experiment with the three different times, keeping all brewing conditions constant. These will be the samples for quantitative measurements of pH, TDS, and viscosity.

7) After the shots are cooled to room temperature, measure the viscosity of each sample using the Canon-Fenske viscometer. Use the suction bulb to draw the espresso out of the glass and past the second bulb (to the top line). Release the suction, and record how much time it takes to drain by gravity to the bottom line near the first bulb.

 Note that most digital refractometers are calibrated for regular coffee, not espresso. This means that if you put strong espresso in the refractometer, you will get an erroneous reading. To overcome this problem, simply dilute your espresso with water before measuring it. For example, dilute it by a factor of two (add 10 grams of water to 10 grams of espresso), measure the dilute TDS, and then multiply the TDS by two to obtain the original espresso TDS.

Part B – AeroPress Pseudo Espresso

Here, we will focus on the typical recipes/methods to make espresso like coffee with an AeroPress. If possible, use the same coffee for all six brews.

1) First, we will compare brew ratios of 3, 4, and 5. Use the same coffee and fine grind size for the three brews. The ground coffee should have particles a little larger than table salt. Once you have the grind size dialed in, grind 60 grams of coffee. Each of our brews will use 20 grams of coffee. We will change the brew ratio by increasing the amount of water from 60 grams to 80 and 100 grams.

2) Do the brews one at a time. Use a metal filter and the same brewing conditions for the three brew ratios: add water at 91 – 94°C, stir for 10 seconds, plunge at 60 seconds. Make observations and sensory evaluation after each brew. Make sure you save about 20 mL of each brew for viscosity measurements.

3) Measure the TDS and pH of each and taste the brews. What are your sensory impressions? Can you detect a difference in body / mouthfeel? Was any crema made using the AeroPress? Which pseudo espresso did you like the most? Why?

4) If you don't have access to an espresso machine, make three additional AeroPress pseudo espressos as you see fit to optimize the quality of the brew. Try changing the grind size, or the applied pressure, or the extraction time. Record your brew ratios, stir time, and brew time. As before, taste, measure the TDS, and save samples to measure the viscosity.

5) Once the samples have cooled to room temperature use the Canon-Fenske Viscometer to measure the viscosities.

Part C - Roasting

Finally, do two or more roasts for next time. Keep track of your energy usage! The remaining laboratory experiments will focus on the design competition, so optimizing roasting will be critical. Have you found a roast profile for the available green beans that you like?

Data for Espresso Experiments

Coffee type:_____

Viscometer time constant: $C =$ _____ *cSt / second*
(This value should be provided with the calibration sheet for your viscometer.)

Short Espresso Pull

Total dispensing time with pressure applied: _____ *seconds*

Mass of brew: _____ – _____ = _____ *grams*   (filled cup – empty cup)

Flowrate: _____ *cm³* ÷ _____ *seconds* = _____ *cm³ / second*

TDS: _____ %   PE: _____ × _____ ÷ _____ = _____ %

Sensory Evaluations:_____

_____

Time to drain in the viscometer: _____ *seconds*

Viscosity: 1 *g /cm³* × _____ *cSt/s* × _____ *seconds* = _____ *centipoise*

Medium Espresso Pull

Total dispensing time with pressure applied: _____ *seconds*

Mass of brew: _____ – _____ = _____ *grams*   (filled cup – empty cup)

Flowrate: _____ *cm³* ÷ _____ *seconds* = _____ *cm³ / second*

TDS: _____ %   PE: _____ × _____ ÷ _____ = _____ %

Sensory Evaluations:_____

_____

Time to drain in the viscometer: _____ *seconds*

Viscosity: 1 *g /cm³* × _____ *cSt/s* × _____ *seconds* = _____ *centipoise*

Long Espresso Pull

Total dispensing time with pressure applied: _____ *seconds*

Mass of brew: _____ – _____ = _____ *grams*   (filled cup – empty cup)

Flowrate: _____ *cm³* ÷ _____ *seconds* = _____ *cm³ / second*

TDS: _____ %   PE: _____ × _____ ÷ _____ = _____ %

Sensory Evaluations:_____

_____

Time to drain in the viscometer: _____ *seconds*

Viscosity: 1 *g /cm³* × _____ *cSt/s* × _____ *seconds* = _____ *centipoise*

Data for AeroPress Pseudo-Espresso Experiments

Coffee type:_____

Viscometer time constant: $C =$ _____ cSt / second
(This value should be provided with the calibration sheet for your viscometer.)

Brew Ratio = 3

Total dispensing time with pressure applied: _____ *seconds*

Mass of brew: _____ – _____ = _____ *grams*   (filled cup – empty cup)

TDS: _____ %   PE: _____ × _____ ÷ _____ = _____ %

Sensory Evaluations:_____

_____

_____

Time to drain in the viscometer: _____ *seconds*

Viscosity: $1 \ g \ /cm^3$ × _____ *cSt/s* × _____ *seconds* = _____ *centipoise*

Brew Ratio = 4

Total dispensing time with pressure applied: _____ *seconds*

Mass of brew: _____ – _____ = _____ *grams*   (filled cup – empty cup)

TDS: _____ %   PE: _____ × _____ ÷ _____ = _____ %

Sensory Evaluations:_____

_____

_____

Time to drain in the viscometer: _____ *seconds*

Viscosity: $1 \ g \ /cm^3$ × _____ *cSt/s* × _____ *seconds* = _____ *centipoise*

Brew Ratio = 5

Total dispensing time with pressure applied: _____ *seconds*

Mass of brew: _____ – _____ = _____ *grams*   (filled cup – empty cup)

TDS: _____ %   PE: _____ × _____ ÷ _____ = _____ %

Sensory Evaluations:_____

_____

_____

Time to drain in the viscometer: _____ *seconds*

Viscosity: $1 \ g \ /cm^3$ × _____ *cSt/s* × _____ *seconds* = _____ *centipoise*

Data for AeroPress Pseudo-Espresso Experiments (if no espresso machine)

Coffee type:_____

Viscometer time constant: $C =$ _____ $cSt / second$
(This value should be provided with the calibration sheet for your viscometer.)

Trial 1   Mass of water: _____ g Mass of grounds: _____ g Brew ratio: _____

Total dispensing time with pressure applied: _____ *seconds*

Mass of brew: _____ – _____ = _____ *grams*   (filled cup – empty cup)

TDS: _____ %   PE: _____ × _____ ÷ _____ = _____ %

Notes and Sensory Evaluations:_____

_____

_____

Time to drain in the viscometer: _____ *seconds*

Viscosity: 1 g /cm^3 × _____ cSt/s × _____ *seconds* = _____ *centipoise*

Trial 2   Mass of water: _____ g Mass of grounds: _____ g Brew ratio: _____

Total dispensing time with pressure applied: _____ *seconds*

Mass of brew: _____ – _____ = _____ *grams*   (filled cup – empty cup)

TDS: _____ %   PE: _____ × _____ ÷ _____ = _____ %

Notes and Sensory Evaluations:_____

_____

_____

Time to drain in the viscometer: _____ *seconds*

Viscosity: 1 g /cm^3 × _____ cSt/s × _____ *seconds* = _____ *centipoise*

Trial 3   Mass of water: _____ g Mass of grounds: _____ g Brew ratio: _____

Total dispensing time with pressure applied: _____ *seconds*

Mass of brew: _____ – _____ = _____ *grams*   (filled cup – empty cup)

TDS: _____ %   PE: _____ × _____ ÷ _____ = _____ %

Notes and Sensory Evaluations:_____

_____

_____

Time to drain in the viscometer: _____ *seconds*

Viscosity: 1 g /cm^3 × _____ cSt/s × _____ *seconds* = _____ *centipoise*

Roasting Data

Coffee type: _____ Roaster settings: _____

Mass of green beans: _____ *grams*   Mass of roasted beans: _____ *grams*

Time spent roasting: _____ *minutes* Energy usage: _____ *kW-hr*

Notes: _____

Coffee type: _____ Roaster settings: _____

Mass of green beans: _____ *grams*   Mass of roasted beans: _____ *grams*

Time spent roasting: _____ *minutes* Energy usage: _____ *kW-hr*

Notes: _____

Lab Report

Each group will submit a report with the following material.

(1) From Part A, generate a scatter plot that shows the viscosity (in centipoise) versus the duration of the shot (in seconds). Did the viscosity increase or decrease with time?

(2) From Part B, generate a scatter plot that shows the viscosity (in centipoise) versus the brew ratio for the three different brew ratios (and additional three trials if done). Use different color markers for trials that had different grind sizes compared to your first three trials at constant grind size. Did the viscosity increase or decrease with brew ratio? What other trends did you observe (e.g., with grind size if you did additional trials)?

(3) Make a scatter plot of all your measured viscosities, from both Part A and Part B, versus the measured TDS. Use different color markers for espresso machine and AeroPress. Is there a simple correlation between TDS and viscosity?

(4) A brief paragraph answering the following questions:

(i) How did the mouthfeel change with the duration of your shots? Is the qualitative trend consistent with your quantitative measurements? Likewise, how did the mouthfeel vary with brew ratio in the AeroPress?

(ii) What would you expect to happen to the viscosity of your espresso if you simply let it keep flowing for longer and longer (say, as long as 60 seconds)?

(iii) How did the viscosities and TDS compare between the espresso machine and Aero-Press?

(iv) What type of correlation do you observe between the TDS and viscosity? Given that refractometers only measure dissolved solids, not colloids, what does your data suggest about the relative contributions of the dissolved solids and colloids to the overall viscosity and mouthfeel?

(v) An AeroPress is approximately $30, while a high-end home espresso machine can cost more than $1000. Based on your data and sensory observations here, is a home espresso machine worth the difference in cost?

Lab 10 Bonus Box – Espresso Drinks and Steamed Milk

If you did have the opportunity to "pull" an expresso shot (about 30 mL using about 8 grams of coffee and 9 to 10 atmospheres of pressure), then you made what's known in Italian as "normale" espresso for normal espresso. A "lungo" or long espresso is the same amount of coffee, but double the water. Lungos are less intense (milder) in flavor, but the extra water also lets you extract more of

the larger molecules and increase the roasted and smokey notes. Conversely, a "ristretto" or restricted espresso uses the same amount of coffee, but half the water. It is a tiny drink with extremely intense flavor. Less water means less larger molecules extracted, which enhances the fruity and acidic notes. A double espresso, which has the same ratio as a normale but with twice as much water and coffee grounds, is called a "doppio" – it's a quick way to get double the caffeine!

Espresso by itself only has water and coffee, but there are a wide variety of different espresso beverages with additional ingredients. In Italy, there's the "caffé corretto," or "corrected espresso," which adds a small amount of liquor to a shot of espresso (thus "correcting" it). Typically the liquor used is "grappa," a brandy made from the pressed grapes leftover from wine making. In some cafés in Italy, they will hand you the bottle of grappa to let you correct your espresso as you see fit! Alternatively, there is the "affogato," made by pouring a shot of espresso over a scoop of vanilla ice cream – an absolutely delicious dessert. Note, neither the caffé correcto or affogato are consumed in the morning!

Of course, the most famous extra ingredient added to espresso is steamed milk, which is featured in famous espresso drinks like the café latte, the cappuccino, the flat white, the macchiato, and the cortado. Each of these has a different ratio of espresso to steamed milk and/or milk foam. Nowadays there is a cornucopia of different milks available, including milks made from soy, rice, almonds, cashews, oats, hemp, and coconut, some of which even have special "barista" blends which are formulated to enhance their ability to"froth" and form a nice foam while steaming. You could try to keep things simple and just stick to espresso and steamed cow milk, but even with this limitation, you still need to choose between skim, 1%, 2%, or regular (whole fat near 3.5%) milk. There's even an espresso drink called the caffé breve that uses using steamed half-and-half(that's half milk plus half cream!), yielding an extremely rich and foamy drink.

Regardless of the exact ratio or the type of milk, what all these drinks have in common is that the milk is steamed. So what's the story behind steamed milk? Espresso machines don't just heat and pressurize water for extraction. Many machines also have a "steam wand", which provides saturated steam (heated water vapor) at a pressure of about 2 atmospheres (or 1 bar gauge). The milk is "steamed" or "frothed" in a metal pitcher by adding steam to the milk. This heats the milk from about 4°C (refrigerator temperature) to 65°C and froths the milk by incorporating small air bubbles (a process known as "aeration"). Why a metal pitcher? It's so the barista can sense the temperature just by touching the pitcher. When the wand is more immersed in the pitcher of milk, the steam is delivering a lot of heat energy to the milk. At 2 atmospheres of pressure, the saturated steam is at 120°C. The steam delivers heat energy, not just because the water vapor is hot, but also because the steam condenses in the milk. When steam condenses from vapor to liquid water, the energy transferred from the water vapor to the cooler milk because of the condensation is actually four times larger than the steam temperature energy. So, if you weigh the milk before and after steaming, the mass will actually increase by the amount of steam that you used! The density of the saturated steam is about 0.0013 g/cm^3. That doesn't seem like much and is almost 750 times less dense than liquid water, but the steam mass flow rate out of the wand in a commercial espresso maker is about 1.75 g/s. To heat 200 grams of milk takes less than 15 seconds and increases the mass in the pitcher by almost 15%.

Now that we understand a little about steaming milk, let's turn our attention to frothing and making microbubbles and foam. If the barista is making a latte, they don't need much foam so they primarily heat the milk by immersing the wand into the middle of the milk, and then near the finish they move the wand closer to the surface to help with aeration (adding air and steam to foam the milk vs. adding steam primarily to heat the milk). For a cappuccino, they need more foam, so they would "froth" and aerate the milk by holding the wand just below the milk surface to build up a nice foam layer. The flowing steam pushes a lot of air into the milk when the steam wand is at the surface. Typically, the volume, not mass, of the milk would be doubled by significant frothing for a cappuccino! If the wand is too close to the surface, instead of microbubbles, one gets macrobubbles. If the wand is too far below the surface, there are less bubbles and the milk is mostly heated vs. frothed (good for a latte, but not a cappuccino). Of course, once a nice foam is made, the barista can further heat the milk by immersing the wand until the temperature is the desired 65°C. Why do baristas sometimes bang the pitcher before dispensing the milk or foam? If there are large macrobubbles, banging the pitcher can help break those open without popping the microbubbles.

What type of milk is best? Well, proteins in the milk "denature" (unravel from a compact structure) when they are heated. These proteins help stabilize the microbubbles by going to the gas bubble-liquid milk interface. Cow milk is about 3.3% protein. Believe it or not, but in the summertime milk typically has less protein content than in the winter since the cow's diet is a bit different. What about the role of milk fat? The difference between skim (fat free), 1%, 2%, and whole milk is the amount of milk fat in the milk. The amount of fat does change the texture of the foam and obviously the creaminess of the foam and taste, but it is the protein that really dictates foam formation. With whole milk (~3.5 % milk fat), the foam is really an emulsion of air, protein, and fat. The fat makes the foam denser and silkier, but only slightly decreases the foam stability. Conversely, skim milk foam is stiffer and "drier" due to the absence of milk fat. For both skim and whole milk, fresh milk froths the best. As milk is stored, different enzymes in the milk start to break down proteins and fats, degrading the frothability.

Ultimately, the choice of milk is a question of personal preference. Cow milk and all of the different vegetable-based milks can all be used to make delicious espresso beverages, since they all contain proteins and can be steamed and frothed! The amount and quality of the froth, however, depends on the composition the nut or grain used to make the vegetable "milk" and any additives in the blend. If you have access to an espresso machine with a steam wand, get several milks and experiment away!

Part III

Design of Coffee

Design Competition Format, Guidelines, & Video Project

The first ten labs of this book have focused on "analysis" to help you understand the various scientific principles that relate to the quality of coffee. We now shift our attention to "engineering design," where our goal is to design a coffee that satisfies specified criteria. In this section, we describe the format for a coffee design competition and video project that has been extremely popular at U. C. Davis. If you are working through the exercises on your own, you don't need to worry about documenting your process by video (unless you want to!). You are still strongly encouraged, however, to think carefully about the design goals, since they will help you think quantitatively about how to design a process – a skill that you can apply to other design goals (for example, making the best tasting coffee for the lowest price).

Here, the main goal of the coffee design project is to make the **best** cup of coffee, using the **least** amount of electrical energy. Each group will receive a score defined by the ratio

$$\text{Final Score} = \frac{\text{Blind Taste Test Score}}{\text{Total Electrical Energy}}$$

Note carefully what this metric implies: it is very possible for you to make the best tasting coffee, but to still lose the design competition because your process used too much energy!

If there are sufficient people competing, then there are two rounds of competition. In the first round (the "playoffs"), groups will compete within their section. The group in each section that receives the highest final score will then advance to the second round (the "championship") to compete for the title of grand champion. The two inputs into the final score are defined as follows.

- The coffee will be judged in a blind taste test on a scale of negative 5 to positive 55 (where –5 is amazingly bad coffee, and +55 is stunningly good.) The point distribution is loosely based on the official tasting guidelines established by the Specialty Coffee Association (cf. Lab 1). All of the blind taste scores for each coffee will be averaged together.

- Your group must keep track of how many kilowatt-hours of electrical energy you used during the entire process of roasting and brewing your coffee. Your roasting energy will be "normalized" by how much mass of any particular roast you end up brewing. That means it is OK to roast too much… you only "pay" for the energy of the coffee beans you end up using.

- Your brewing energy, however, will not be normalized. If you heat up too much water… then you have to account for all of it! Any piece of equipment you plug into an outlet must be monitored using the Kill-a-Watt meter and included in your final tally. This is typically only the brewer or kettle and the roaster; as we saw in Lab 5 the energy of the grinder is negligible so we won't specifically keep track of it here.

Groups who place in the top three in either taste score or taste per energy score will receive some bonus points, but only the winning group in terms of taste per energy will advance to the championship round. The group with the highest taste per energy score in the championship round will receive additional bonus points, as well as a grand prize. If there is a championship round, the bonus points can be doubled for placing in the top three for the overall championship.

The following design constraints must be followed.

1) **Ingredients:** The only ingredients you are allowed to use are green coffee beans and water. No syrups, sweeteners, spices, or other artificial flavors may be added.

2) **Minimum Volume:** For the play-off round, you must prepare enough for three dozen people to each get 1 fluid ounce taste of coffee. This means you must make at least 1oz x 36 people = 36 oz = 4.5 cups ≈ 1 liter of coffee. The precise mass requirement depends on the size of thermal carafe available. Here we will choose 925 grams, to leave a little room in the top of a standard 1-liter thermal carafe. If your group is invited to a championship round, you must modify your design to make just 0.5 liters of coffee (because the championship blind tasting panel is assumed to be smaller).

3) **Energy Penalty:** If you don't deliver the minimum amount of required brew, you will be assessed an energy penalty of 0.005 kW-hr per gram of missing brew. (If you make more than the required amount, the energy penalty is zero.)

4) **Time Allowed:** On the day of the blind tasting, you will have 45 minutes to brew your approximately 1 liter of coffee. Brew too early and your coffee may lose some of its freshness, brew too late and risk being disqualified!

5) **Equipment:** You are free to use any combination of the equipment available in the lab for roasting and brewing your coffee.

6) **Cold Water:** You are only allowed to use regular cold **tap** water, not hot tap water, as your starting point for your brew. The kettles should be empty and cool to the touch before you start.

7) **No Flames:** Absolutely no open flames are allowed in the lab, so no portable stoves or burners.

8) **Negative Infinity:** Clever students will note that if their process uses *zero* electrical energy, then their final score will be infinity (because any tasting score divided by zero is infinity). One example of a zero electrical energy process would be to pour cold water over whole green beans. Although this is a clever idea in terms of energy minimization, note that *negative* tasting scores are possible (because of the 'balance' category). So it is likely that such a low energy process would actually get you a score of *negative infinity* and therefore *last place* in regard to final score.

9) **Creativity:** Most importantly, remember that good engineers think of new ways of doing things... we encourage creative designs!

Final Design Project Video

Throughout the next three labs, you and your group will have time to work on making a video that presents your final design. The video must be less than 5 minutes, and must include the following material.

1) A process flow diagram that shows your unique process. There must be enough detail that somebody else can watch the video and replicate your process. Remember, even if you didn't directly measure a material stream, you can calculate it using an appropriate mass balance.

2) Your overall mass balances for water and solid (coffee). These can be shown on the process flow diagram. Make sure you include all waste streams!

3) Your type of roast(s). What beans did you use, and how did you roast them?

4) Your energy usages. Clearly describe the logic you followed to attempt to minimize energy costs.

5) Your TDS and PE for your one of your final design brews, or your competition brew from the contest. How close were you to the ostensible ideal range?

6) An overview of the sensory evaluations of your final brew as judged your group and by others in the blind tasting.

7) An economic cost-benefit analysis for replicating your coffee design at home, roasting your own green beans and providing a daily half liter of your brew. This analysis will include an associated breakeven point comparison with buying a comparable drink daily at a local café of your choice.

8) A summary of anything you would do differently in a (hypothetical) future design contest to improve your coffee taste or minimize your energy usage.

Throughout the video there should be audio narration or text subtitles that help the viewer understand the information you're trying to convey. Pictures and video taken while you were roasting and brewing in lab are highly recommended but not strictly necessary. Some excellent videos have not used any video recordings from the Coffee Lab itself! You are strongly encouraged to be creative.

You are free to use any software you like, as long as you include the required material. It is easy to download free movie editing software. You can use PowerPoint, PhotoShop, or any other program to make schematics, which can then be embedded in your video. All group members must help make the video, although nobody must appear personally in it. Make sure your names, section number, and date show up on a title screen near the beginning of your video. You can submit your video as a YouTube link (either public or private).

Don't worry about having the perfect design yet – the next few labs are intended for you to hone your roast and brew.

Lab 11 – First Design Trials: Optimizing Strength & Extraction

Objectives: The main goal of this lab is for you and your group to begin designing your process, with an emphasis on optimizing the strength and extraction of your brew.

Equipment:

☐ Brewer(s) ☐ Roaster(s) ☐ Digital refractometer ☐ Kill-a-Watt meter

Activities:

☐ At least three brews, completely quantified (TDS, PE, energy)

☐ At least two roasts, with energy measurements

Report:

☐ Data for three brews

☐ A completed energy scoresheet

☐ Comparison of predicted vs. calculated PE for one brew

☐ Paragraphs discussing tasting notes and proposed gameplan for next design trials

Background

If you think back on the previous eight labs, in each experiment we tried varying some experimental condition and then seeing what happened, with some insight provided by fundamental principles (e.g., conservation of mass, flux, or pressure). In other words, we were performing *analysis* of how the brewing method impacted coffee quality. Now we need to change our focus to *design*, where we use the knowledge gained via analysis to create a process that satisfies design goals.

In our case, we want to make the best-tasting coffee using the least amount of energy. As discussed back in Lab 6, a great deal of sensory analysis experimentation has shown that people prefer the taste of coffee in a pretty narrow range of strength (TDS from about 1 to 1.5 %) and extraction (PE from about 14 to 26%, although different people prefer different ranges of PE and TDS). Refer again to the coffee brewing control chart (next page) that shows the different sensory evaluations one gets from brews prepared to different strengths and extractions. If your coffee tastes too bitter, it is probably over-extracted (PE > 22%), but if it tastes sour or vegetal it is probably under-extracted (PE < 18%). The TDS of the brew tends to amplify the intensity of the extracted flavors for most sensory attributes, but counterintuitively some prized attributes increase in intensity at *lower* values of TDS: sweetness and tea-like/floral notes are maximized at low TDS and low or high PE, respectively. Refer to the articles described in the Further Reading section (Frost et al. 2020 and Batali et al. 2020) for more details on the underlying science.

Heretofore we made some coffee and then measured the TDS and PE after the fact. But what do we do if we want to predict these values *before* we do the experiment, i.e., if we want to design the process to yield coffee in the ideal range of TDS and PE? To tackle this problem, we will combine several of our analytical results into a form that will be convenient for predicting the outcome of a brew.

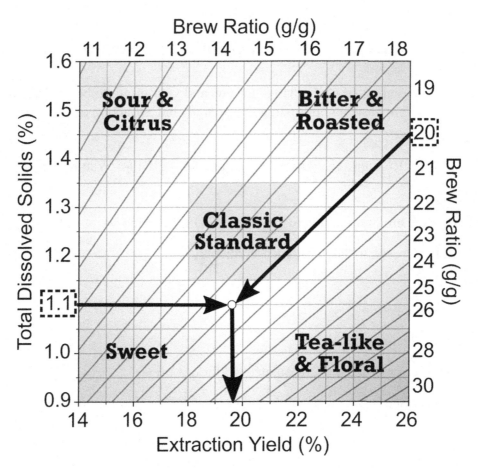

Recall that our mass balance on the coffee solids yielded an expression for the PE (equation 7 from Lab 6),

$$PE = TDS \times \frac{m_{brew}}{m_{dry\,grounds}}. \tag{1}$$

Also recall that our mass balance on the water yielded a prediction for the actual mass of the brew (equation 5 from Lab 3),

$$m_{brew} = m_{feed} - \left(R_{abs} \times m_{dry\,grounds}\right). \tag{2}$$

Substitution of our expression for m_{brew} into our expression for PE yields

$$PE = TDS \times (R_{brew} - R_{abs}), \tag{3}$$

where recall R_{brew} is the brew ratio defined as the mass of hot water fed in over the mass of dry grounds, i.e., $R_{brew} = m_{feed}/m_{dry\,grounds}$. There is a hugely important design implication of equation (3): if you want to obtain a certain value of PE, you *cannot* independently choose a brew ratio and a TDS value. Look at the highlighted point in the control chart above. Here a brew ratio of 20 was used, and the brew had a measured TDS of 1.10%. At the intersection of the corresponding horizontal line (for TDS) and diagonal line (for brew ratio), there is only one possible corresponding PE of 19.6%, as indicated by the vertical downward line.

In other words, once you choose a brew ratio, there is only one possible TDS value that is consistent with the desired PE. This idea is captured in the diagonal lines superimposed on the coffee brewing control chart, which show the possible values of TDS and PE for the specified brew ratio. As you can see, there are only a narrow range of brew ratios that can yield brews within the classic standard zone.

Once you choose a brew ratio, though, how do you specify the TDS? Again, the insights you gained via engineering analysis in the previous labs will now help you design the process. If your TDS (and hence PE) are too small and your brew is under-developed, then you likely had insufficient mass transfer during your extraction. This could be due to a grind that was too coarse, or an extraction time that was too short, or a water temperature that was too low. Likewise, if your TDS and PE are too large and your brew is bitter, you had too much transfer during your extraction: too fine a grind, too long an extraction time, or too high a water temperature. During your design trials today, don't try things randomly: use the insight you gained on mass transfer, as well as equation (3) above, to improve your brewed coffee.

An important question is: should you strive to get your brew within the "classic standard" zone of the coffee brewing control chart? The short answer is: probably not. Although for years coffee industry professionals were taught that it is crucial to get their brew inside that zone, recent consumer preference testing has shown significant variations in what people actually like to drink. In particular, Cotter et al. (2021) showed that black coffee drinkers could be segmented into two cohorts: one cohort strongly preferred coffees brewed to the bottom left corner of the chart (labeled as "sweet"), while the other cohort equally preferred either the top left corner (labeled "sour & citrus") or the far-right side of the graph (between "bitter & roasted" and "tea-like & floral"). See the Further Reading section for more details.

Of course, don't forget that the quality of the brew depends on the quality of the chemical reactions that occurred during roasting. If you under- or over-roasted your beans, it won't matter how well you do the extraction, because you'll just be extracting out unpleasant tasting coffee. **You could extract very, very burnt roasted beans (or even black charcoal) to the 'classic standard' range of 1.3% TDS and 20% PE... but it won't taste very good!** Remember as well, coffee beans are biological products that can vary from lot to lot. What worked for one type of beans won't necessarily work with a different type of beans. For example, the green beans might have different concentrations of sucrose depending on how they were grown, or perhaps they've been stored for different lengths of time and have degraded differently. Coffee is a moving target! You need to adjust your aim, i.e., refine your design, based on your experimental observations for any particular batch of beans. Your ultimate evaluation of brew quality should be based on your sensory evaluation of the taste.

Summary of 1st Design Trial Activities

Unlike the previous labs, we intentionally leave the design trial activities open ended. Use the time to work with your group on making and testing your own process for roasting and brewing the best tasting coffee. You are welcome to use any combination of equipment available in the lab, and you can use the time as you think best. We urge you to think carefully, however, about the following questions.

1) What are the TDS and PE of your brews? Are they close to the classic standard range? Do your own sensory evaluations agree with the taste descriptions on the coffee brewing control chart?

2) What is the best roasting procedure? Make sure you perform at least a couple roasts toward your ideal roast.

3) How much energy is each step using? Is your design energy efficient, or an energy hog? Make sure you get the required data to fill out the sample "energy scoring sheet," which is similar to what will be used in the design competition.

Data for 1st Design Trials

Coffee type_____

Roasting method: _____   Roasting date:_____

Mass of green beans: _____ *grams*   Mass of roasted beans: _____ *grams*

Time spent roasting: _____ *minutes*   Energy usage: _____ *kW-hr*

Brewing method: _____   Filtration method: _____

Mass of hot water:_____ *grams*   Mass of grounds:_____ *grams*   Ratio:_____

Water Temp: _____ °C   Energy usage: _____ *kW-hr*

Extraction time: _____ *minutes*   Grind size: _____

Mass of brew: _____ – _____ = _____ *grams*   (filled cup – empty cup)

TDS: _____%   PE: _____ × _____ ÷ _____ = _____%

Other data:

_____

_____

_____

_____

Sensory Evaluations:

_____

_____

_____

_____

Data for 1st Design Trials

Coffee type_____

Roasting method: _____ Roasting date:_____

Mass of green beans: _____ *grams*   Mass of roasted beans: _____ *grams*

Time spent roasting: _____ *minutes*   Energy usage: _____ *kW-hr*

Brewing method: _____ Filtration method: _____

Mass of hot water:_____ *grams*   Mass of grounds:_____ *grams*   Ratio:_____

Water Temp: _____ °C   Energy usage: _____ *kW-hr*

Extraction time: _____ *minutes*   Grind size: _____

Mass of brew: _____ – _____ = _____ *grams*   (filled cup – empty cup)

TDS: _____ %   PE: _____ × _____ ÷ _____ = _____ %

Other data:

_____

_____

_____

_____

Sensory Evaluations:

_____

_____

_____

_____

Data for 1st Design Trials

Coffee type_____

Roasting method: _____ Roasting date:_____

Mass of green beans: _____ *grams* Mass of roasted beans: _____ *grams*

Time spent roasting: _____ *minutes* Energy usage: _____ *kW-hr*

Brewing method: _____ Filtration method: _____

Mass of hot water:_____ *grams* Mass of grounds:_____ *grams* Ratio:_____

Water Temp: _____ °C Energy usage: _____ *kW-hr*

Extraction time: _____ *minutes* Grind size: _____

Mass of brew: _____ – _____ = _____ *grams* (filled cup – empty cup)

TDS: _____ % PE: _____ × _____ ÷ _____ = _____ %

Other data:

_____

_____

_____

_____

Sensory Evaluations:

_____

_____

_____

_____

Sample Energy Scoring Sheet

If your brew uses beans from just one roast, then fill out only "Roast A" and put zero for "Roast B." If you use three or more roasts, append the data and calculate the total energy of roasting appropriately.

Roast A (bean type): _____

Roast B (bean type): _____

Mass of green beans: _____ *grams*

Mass of green beans: _____ *grams*

Mass of roasted beans: _____ *grams*

Mass of roasted beans: _____ *grams*

Total energy of roast: _____ *kW-hr*

Total energy of roast: _____ *kW-hr*

Energy to roast per gram roasted bean:

Energy to roast per gram roasted bean:

_____ ÷ _____ = _____ *kW-hr/gram*

_____ ÷ _____ = _____ *kW-hr/gram*

Total mass of beans used: _____ *grams*

Total mass of beans used: _____ *grams*

Energy per gram × total grams used:

Energy per gram × total grams used:

_____ × _____ = _____ *kW-hr*

_____ × _____ = _____ *kW-hr*

Total energy for roasted coffee actually used in your brew (Roast A + Roast B):

_____ + _____ = _____ *kW-hr*

Total mass of water heated: _____ *grams*   *(make sure the kettle is cool and empty at start)*

Initial Water Temp: _____ °C   Final Water Temp: _____ °C

Energy used to heat water: _____ *kW-hr*

(Note: don't worry about the energy penalty in this lab since you're not making a whole liter.)

Brewing method(s): _____

Mass of brew: _____ – _____ = _____ *grams*   *(filled carafe– empty carafe)*

If the brew mass is more than 925 grams (0.925 liter), **the energy penalty is zero.** Otherwise, calculate the energy penalty as follows:

Deficient mass: ___925___ – _____ = _____ *grams*

Energy penalty:___N/A___ *grams* × ___0.005___ *kW-hr/gram* = ___N/A___ *kW-hr*

Total energy used to produce your coffee (roast energy + water energy + penalty):

_____ + _____ + ___0___ = _____ *kW-hr*

Roasting Data

Coffee type: _____ Roaster settings: _____

Mass of green beans: _____ *grams*   Mass of roasted beans: _____ *grams*

Time spent roasting: _____ *minutes*   Energy usage: _____ *kW-hr*

Notes: _____

Coffee type: _____ Roaster settings: _____

Mass of green beans: _____ *grams*   Mass of roasted beans: _____ *grams*

Time spent roasting: _____ *minutes*   Energy usage: _____ *kW-hr*

Notes: _____

Coffee type: _____ Roaster settings: _____

Mass of green beans: _____ *grams*   Mass of roasted beans: _____ *grams*

Time spent roasting: _____ *minutes*   Energy usage: _____ *kW-hr*

Notes: _____

Coffee type: _____ Roaster settings: _____

Mass of green beans: _____ *grams*   Mass of roasted beans: _____ *grams*

Time spent roasting: _____ *minutes*   Energy usage: _____ *kW-hr*

Notes: _____

Lab Report

By your specified due date, each group will submit a lab report that includes the following:

(1) For at least three brews, state (i) the brewing method, (ii) grind level, (iii) TDS and PE (show the calculations), (iv) location on the control chart, and (v) tasting notes.

(2) A completed "energy scoring sheet" for whichever process you think is most promising for the competition. (A photo or scan of an energy score sheet is fine.)

(3) For at least one brew, a comparison of your calculated PE using Equation 1 versus the PE predicted by equation (3). How similar or dissimilar are the values?

(4) Finally, a paragraph that describes your main findings today, and a brief game plan for what you will test in your design next week. What logic or experimental data informed your design choices?

Lab 11 Bonus Box – How is Coffee Decaffeinated?

The Lab 2 Bonus Box was titled "Caffeine the Wonder Drug," but what if you don't want caffeine in your coffee? Some folks are extra sensitive to caffeine. Others might like to have an after-dinner cup of coffee deliciousness, but they find it difficult to sleep afterwards. Everyone has heard of decaffeinated coffee, but how do they actually remove the caffeine?

As we mentioned earlier, caffeine is a natural molecule made by *Coffea* plants as a defense mechanism against insects. A lot of folks think that dark roasts have more caffeine than light roasts, but the amount of caffeine is really dictated by the bean – not the roast level. Caffeine is an alkaloid (a nitrogen containing compound) and it is pretty impervious to the roasting process, so a dark or light roast of the same beans has about the same caffeine content. The differences in the amount of caffeine in a typical brew are mainly due to the amount of caffeine that happened to be in the bean to begin with, and how efficiently you extracted it during the brewing process.

Green beans are always decaffeinated **before** roasting. The first step invariably involves steam. The solubility of caffeine in water is highly sensitive to temperature: at room temperature the solubility is about 2 grams per 100 grams water, but it increases dramatically to 66 grams per 100 grams boiling water. As a result, the first step in any decaffeination process is to "swell" the green coffee beans with steam. The beans actually increase in size about 50% during steaming. This opens up the pores in the beans, making the caffeine more accessible. The steaming also helps to solvate and mobilize the caffeine molecules.

After the steaming step, there are four main methods for decaffeinating coffee, which are separated into "solvent-based" processes using chemicals and "non-solvent based" processes using water. (Actually, strictly speaking all of them use solvents since technically water is a solvent as well... but even though water is a chemical, using the phrase "chemical free" is a matter of semantics that is important to many consumers.) In the direct solvent process, a liquid that has a high caffeine solubility but a lower "coffee stuff" solubility (everything else that isn't caffeine) is contacted with the steamed green coffee beans so that the caffeine is selectively dissolved (or "solubilized") into the solvent. The solvents used in modern processes are typically ethyl acetate or methylene chloride. If ethyl acetate is used, the process is often termed "natural decaffeination" because ethyl acetate is found in fruit and can also be obtained from fermentation of sugar cane; it is considered more "natural" than chemically synthesized methylene chloride (called dichloromethane in Europe). Despite the natural name, the ethyl acetate actually used in decaffeination is produced chemically because it is much cheaper to synthesize than trying to extract the chemical from fruit or produce it by fermenting sugar. Regardless, both ethyl acetate and methylene chloride are actually mildly toxic so you don't want them in your cup of coffee. Fortunately, only a few ppm of either solvent remains at the end of the decaffeination process, and essentially none remains after the beans are roasted.

To extract the caffeine, the steamed coffee beans are simply soaked in the solvent for about 10 hours, the solvent is removed, and the green decaffeinated beans are re-steamed to remove any residual solvent. This process is called a "direct solvent" method because the green beans directly contact the solvent. In the "indirect solvent" method, the green beans are steamed and soaked in water, and the water is then separated from the beans. The caffeine-rich water is then mixed with the solvent to extract the caffeine from the water. This procedure keeps the beans from touching the solvent directly, but also tends to cause more loss of flavor compounds.

To help address this problem, and to avoid use of chemical solvents, alternative approaches that "recycle" the water have been developed. One such non-solvent based approach is the "Swiss water process." Named because it was developed in Switzerland (not because it uses Swiss water!), in this process the green beans are soaked in near-boiling water to remove the caffeine, which also inadvertently removes other soluble flavor molecules. The water is collected and the caffeine is removed by filtering through "activated charcoal." The charcoal has a porosity (average hole size) that allows the flavor molecules to get through but traps the larger caffeine molecules. After removing the caffeine, the green coffee "flavored" water is reused to remove the caffeine from the next batch of green beans. The first batch of beans are "sacrificial beans" that help saturate the water with the important flavor molecules that come out in the hot water along with the caffeine. After the caffeine is removed by the charcoal, the second batch of beans "sees" a liquid that already has lots of flavor molecules, so there is little concentration difference to serve as a driving force for the molecules to leave the beans – except for the caffeine, which will rapidly solubilize into the caffeine-free water. Reusing the water in this fashion helps prevent the extraction from the next batch of beans to be processed and so on.

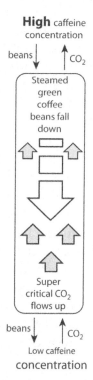

The fourth and final decaffeination technique involves something called "super critical carbon dioxide," which is some pretty interesting stuff. Carbon dioxide (CO_2) is a product of respiration – we exhale this gas as a by-product of using energy – and it is a product from reactions that burn or release energy (including coffee roasting and combustion engines like in cars). Caffeine and most other liquid and solid chemicals are not very soluble in CO_2 gas. However, if you compress CO_2 gas to a high enough pressure (around 250 atmospheres), it can remain in a sort of gas phase, but almost have the density of a liquid, which is why it has the moniker of "super critical." Even though caffeine isn't all that soluble in super critical CO_2, it is much more soluble that the other flavor molecules. After steaming the green beans, the wet, swelled-up beans are contacted with the super critical CO_2 in a "counter current" fashion: beans enter the top of the column and super critical CO_2 flows up from the bottom. As you learned in Lab 6, mass transfer depends on a concentration gradient. By having "fresh" CO_2 contact the already mostly caffeine extracted green beans that have been in contact with CO_2 since the top of the column, the concentration gradient can be enhanced over the length of the column to improve the caffeine transfer. The CO_2 is collected from the top of the tower and contacted with a water spray to leach the caffeine from the CO_2. The CO_2 is then recycled, while the nearly pure caffeine can be sold.

Having said all this, we should note that many folks (incorrectly) believe that there simply is no such thing as a good cup of decaffeinated coffee. The thinking is that no matter what decaffeinating process is used, there is invariably some removal of molecules, which will affect flavor. Whether the loss is good or bad, however, depends on the molecules – sometimes decaffeination can remove molecules that cause flavor defects! Overall, the situation for decaf coffee is improving. In the past much decaffeinated coffee was not that good to begin with – in other words, garbage in, garbage out. With modern techniques, and if you start with a high-quality coffee and use careful processing, a cup of delicious high-quality decaf can be obtained. Decaffeinated green beans are readily purchased online – get some and try your own experiments!

Lab 12 – Second Design Trials: Scaling Up to One Liter of Coffee

Objectives: The main goal of this lab is to plan how to "scale up" your process efficiently to a larger volume, and to continue optimizing your roast and brew for the competition!

Equipment:

☐ Brewer(s) ☐ Roaster(s) ☐ Digital refractometer ☐ Kill-a-Watt meter

Activities:

☐ At least three brews, completely quantified (TDS, PE, energy)

☐ Prepare more roast(s) for the final design competition, with energy measurements

☐ Consideration of time and energy usage

☐ Pictures and/or video as you desire for the final design video

Report:

☐ A completed energy scoresheet

☐ Estimates of how much water, coffee, energy, and time are needed for 1 liter

☐ Paragraphs discussing your proposed design and logic for design choices

Background

There are many processes that work beautifully at "small" scales, but are challenging (or impossible) to implement at "large" scales. For example, a chemist might devise an elegant chemical reaction process for synthesizing some desired compound. Even though the chemist can get the reaction to work in the lab, there might be many engineering challenges to overcome before the reaction process can be used industrially. If the reaction involves too many steps, or requires too many expensive catalysts, or only works at impractically high temperatures, or yields too many waste products, then we might conclude that the reaction can't be "scaled up" efficiently.

The same logic applies to coffee. Perhaps you have perfected a process for making a small cup of coffee that tastes great… but that doesn't necessarily mean you can use the same process to make a larger volume of coffee. Perhaps the process requires an unacceptably large amount of energy; perhaps the taste of the coffee changes when you try to brew over a larger volume; perhaps the process is so slow that it simply requires too much time.

The main goals of this design trial are (1) to hone in on the roast profile for the beans you will be using in the final competition and (2) to plan how to "scale up" your brewing process efficiently to a larger volume. It is crucial that you plan how much water, how much ground coffee, how much energy, and how much time are required. Don't waste time actually making a whole liter today – instead, optimize your design and plan how it will work!

It is crucial – absolutely crucial – that when you and your group walk into the design contest, you know how many coffee grounds you will need, how much hot water you will need, and how much energy it should all require. The materials already discussed in previous labs will help us be quantitative. First, let's think about how much water we'll need. We can calculate exactly how much water we'll need, by rearranging equation (5) in Lab 3, yielding

$$m_{water} = m_{brew} + \left(R_{abs} \times m_{grounds}\right), \tag{1}$$

where m_{water} is the total amount of water you need to feed into our brewer. (Make sure you calculate the quantitative value of R_{abs} for your preferred brewing technique!) How much energy will it cost to heat up this much water? Well, think back to Lab 5, where we showed how the energy is proportional to the total mass, the heat capacity, and the desired temperature increase. Substitution of equation (1) above into equation (6) from Lab 5 yields

$$E_{brew} = \left[m_{brew} + \left(R_{abs} \times m_{grounds}\right)\right] \times C_p \times \Delta T. \tag{2}$$

Think carefully about these equations, and how your choices for $m_{grounds}$ and m_{water} affect your possible ranges for TDS and PE (and the corresponding sensory qualities).

Timing is also important. Obviously, you don't want to run out of time while brewing... you'll suffer a huge energy penalty if you don't brew enough coffee in time, or even be disqualified. Also recall your experience in Lab 4, where the pH of the coffee changed with time, and the discussion in Lab 9 of how brewing techniques without filtration (e.g., the French press) allow the coffee grounds to continue to extract, so the flavor changes with time. Your brew will probably degrade in quality if you finish the brews too quickly and let them sit around for half an hour before anybody tastes them. You'll be combining your brews in a 1 L insulated thermal carafe during the competition, so pH likely won't be too affected, but extraction of any coffee grounds that you let enter the carafe will continue. So, a key goal for this lab is to time how long each step in your process takes, and to estimate the total time required to make a liter of brew. As before, you also need to complete your energy scoresheet.

Summary of 2nd Design Trial Activities

As with the first design trials, we intentionally leave the lab activities open-ended, so that you can work with your group on your own process design. Try at least a couple different overall designs, preferably more. This lab is also a great time to obtain some video for the video project if you so desire. Think carefully about the following questions.

1) If you want to end up with precisely 925 grams of brewed coffee, how much water will you need to heat? You don't want to waste energy heating up water that you don't use. You also don't want to end up short of this amount. Think back to Lab 3... what information do you need to plan a process yielding precisely a desired amount of coffee? Will the data you obtained in Lab 3 apply to your process? (Hint: what is R_{abs} for your brewing method?) If not, what experiment and measurements could you do?

2) Recall that you'll have 45 minutes to brew about 1 liter of coffee. If your process involves any repeated slow steps, will you have sufficient time to make a whole liter? Contrariwise, if your process is really fast, will your brew be sitting around for a long time before anybody tastes it? Record the total amount of time it takes you to complete a brew. Note that extra brewing equipment will be available for the competition.

3) Keep refining your roasts... you are getting very close to the competition!

4) Make sure you record the energies used in every step. You will need to fill out an energy scoresheet similar to the one that you will use in the actual competition.

5) Also get the TDS and PE, but remember those are only guides... your perceived taste evaluation is the most important!

Data for 2nd Design Trials

Coffee type_____

Roasting method: _____ Roasting date:_____

Mass of green beans: _____ grams   Mass of roasted beans: _____ grams

Time spent roasting: _____ minutes   Energy usage: _____ kW-hr

Clock time when started prepping to brew: _____

Brewing method: _____   Filtration method: _____

Mass of hot water:_____ grams   Mass of grounds:_____ grams   Ratio:_____

Water Temp: _____ °C   Energy usage: _____ kW-hr

Extraction time: _____ minutes   Grind size: _____

Mass of brew: _____ – _____ = _____ grams   (filled cup – empty cup)

Clock time when brew finished: _____   Time required: _____ minutes

TDS: _____ %   PE: _____ × _____ ÷ _____ = _____ %

Other data:

_____

_____

_____

_____

Sensory Evaluations:

_____

_____

_____

_____

Data for 2nd Design Trials

Coffee type_____

Roasting method: _____   Roasting date:_____

Mass of green beans: _____ *grams*   Mass of roasted beans: _____ *grams*

Time spent roasting: _____ *minutes*   Energy usage: _____ *kW-hr*

Clock time when started prepping to brew: _____

Brewing method: _____   Filtration method: _____

Mass of hot water:_____ *grams*   Mass of grounds:_____ *grams*   Ratio:_____

Water Temp: _____ °C   Energy usage: _____ *kW-hr*

Extraction time: _____ *minutes*   Grind size: _____

Mass of brew: _____ – _____ = _____ *grams*   (filled cup – empty cup)

Clock time when brew finished: _____   Time required: _____ *minutes*

TDS: _____ %   PE: _____ × _____ ÷ _____ = _____ %

Other data:

_____

_____

_____

_____

Sensory Evaluations:

_____

_____

_____

_____

Data for 2nd Design Trials

Coffee type_____

Roasting method: _____   Roasting date:_____

Mass of green beans: _____ *grams*   Mass of roasted beans: _____ *grams*

Time spent roasting: _____ *minutes*   Energy usage: _____ *kW-hr*

Clock time when started prepping to brew: _____

Brewing method: _____   Filtration method: _____

Mass of hot water:_____ *grams*   Mass of grounds:_____ *grams*   Ratio:_____

Water Temp: _____ °C   Energy usage: _____ *kW-hr*

Extraction time: _____ *minutes*   Grind size: _____

Mass of brew: _____ – _____ = _____ *grams*   (filled cup – empty cup)

Clock time when brew finished: _____   Time required: _____ *minutes*

TDS: _____%   PE: _____ × _____ ÷ _____ = _____%

Other data:

_____

_____

_____

_____

Sensory Evaluations:

_____

_____

_____

_____

Sample Energy Scoring Sheet

If your brew uses beans from just one roast, then fill out only "Roast A" and put zero for "Roast B." If you use three or more roasts, append the data and calculate the total energy of roasting appropriately.

Roast A (bean type): _____

Mass of green beans: _____ *grams*

Mass of roasted beans: _____ *grams*

Total energy of roast: _____ *kW-hr*

Energy to roast per gram roasted bean:

_____ ÷ _____ = _____ *kW-hr/gram*

Total mass of beans used: _____ *grams*

Energy per gram × total grams used:

_____ × _____ = _____ *kW-hr*

Roast B (bean type): _____

Mass of green beans: _____ *grams*

Mass of roasted beans: _____ *grams*

Total energy of roast: _____ *kW-hr*

Energy to roast per gram roasted bean:

_____ ÷ _____ = _____ *kW-hr/gram*

Total mass of beans used: _____ *grams*

Energy per gram × total grams used:

_____ × _____ = _____ *kW-hr*

Total energy for roasted coffee actually used in your brew (Roast A + Roast B):

_____ + _____ = _____ *kW-hr*

Total mass of water heated: _____ *grams*   *(make sure the kettle is cool and empty at start)*

Initial Water Temp: _____ °C   Final Water Temp: _____ °C

Energy used to heat water: _____ *kW-hr*

(Note: don't worry about the energy penalty in this lab since you're not making a whole liter.)

Brewing method(s): _____

Mass of brew: _____ – _____ = _____ *grams*   *(filled carafe– empty carafe)*

If the brew mass is more than 925 grams (0.925 liter), **the energy penalty is zero**. *Otherwise, calculate the energy penalty as follows:*

Deficient mass: 925   – _____ = _____ *grams*

Energy penalty: N/A   *grams* ×   0.005   *kW-hr/gram* =   N/A   *kW-hr*

Total energy used to produce your coffee (roast energy + water energy + penalty):

_____ + _____ +   0   = _____ *kW-hr*

Roasting Data

Coffee type: _____ Roaster settings: _____

Mass of green beans: _____ *grams*   Mass of roasted beans: _____ *grams*

Time spent roasting: _____ *minutes*   Energy usage: _____ *kW-hr*

Notes: _____

Coffee type: _____ Roaster settings: _____

Mass of green beans: _____ *grams*   Mass of roasted beans: _____ *gram*

Time spent roasting: _____ *minutes*   Energy usage: _____ *kW-hr*

Notes: _____

Coffee type: _____ Roaster settings: _____

Mass of green beans: _____ *grams*   Mass of roasted beans: _____ *gram*

Time spent roasting: _____ *minutes*   Energy usage: _____ *kW-hr*

Notes: _____

Coffee type: _____ Roaster settings: _____

Mass of green beans: _____ *grams*   Mass of roasted beans: _____ *grams*

Time spent roasting: _____ *minutes*   Energy usage: _____ *kW-hr*

Notes: _____

Lab Report

By your specified due date, each group will submit a lab report that includes the following:

(1) A completed "energy scoring sheet" for whichever process you think is most promising for the competition. (A photo or scan of an energy score sheet is fine.)

(2) An estimate of the total amount of water and ground coffee that you will need to make 1 liter of brewed coffee at the competition, along with a corresponding estimate of how much energy will be used. Show all of your calculations (with units).

(3) An estimate of how much time will be required to brew a complete liter, based on your measurements of time required here for individual brews.

(4) A paragraph that describes the brewing method, roast information, approximate grind level, your TDS and PE, where you are on the ideal brewing chart, your tasting notes, and any other information you feel is relevant.

(5) Another paragraph that describes *why* you have selected your potential process for the competition. What logic or data informed your design choices?

Lab 12 Bonus Box – How is instant coffee made?

In the United States we don't really think that much about instant coffee. Only a piddling 3% of the coffee consumed in the US is instant, a shockingly small amount given that Americans are well known to be willing to pay a premium for convenience and speed. In contrast, more than 1/3 of the coffee consumed worldwide is instant coffee. Moreover, the consumption of instant coffee is increasing rapidly – it has tripled over the past 15 years. The percentage of instant coffee sold in the US is close to the smallest in the world.

It's not that Americans don't drink coffee. The average American drinks 2.6 cups of coffee a day. Some of the discrepancy is due to the surge in coffee pods in the US. Those single servings of coffee that can be brewed with the push of a button now make up 25% of the American market. They are fast and convenient, but not "instant" coffee.

Anywhere else in the world, instant coffee has a huge footprint. Nestlé (also known as Nescafé) actually buys 15% of all the coffee produced each year. Although "instant" coffee was first reportedly developed around 1771 in Britain, it wasn't till 1938 that Nestlé developed a reasonably palatable version. During that time, Brazil was producing a large excess of coffee and the Brazilian government started an initiative to figure out what to do with the excess coffee. Nestlé came up with a method of drying coffee with carbohydrates that reportedly was drinkable. The timing was perfect. Shortly thereafter, the advent of World War II solidified the place of instant coffee as a quick and convenient method to fuel soldiers.

Today, instant coffee is made by two processes: spray drying or freeze drying. In spray drying, concentrated brewed coffee is sprayed to make a fine mist and dried with hot air. To concentrate the coffee, it is brewed at a high coffee to water ratio. Some of the water is then evaporated off to yield a 50% or greater strength (i.e., TDS). That's pretty concentrated as a typical cup of coffee has a concentration of about 1.3%. The concentrated mist is then sprayed at the top of a tower, and hot air is blown upwards from the bottom of the column (similar to the counter current flow for caffeine extraction in the Lab 11 Bonus Box). At the bottom of the column the dried coffee particles are collected. Those particles are agglomerated (stuck together with a little water) to make larger particles. Sometimes carbohydrates are added to increase the volume and make it look more like ground coffee, and sometimes fresh, finely ground coffee is added for more flavor. Agglomeration is how they make instant coffee powder look more like ground coffee when you open the package. Once the particles have the size and look that the manufacturer wants, it's packaged and ready to go.

In freeze drying, the concentrated coffee is first frozen before drying. It sounds a little like iced coffee, but the starting point is coffee ice cubes. These cubes are broken into small pieces and then put into a vacuum chamber and dried. In the Lab 5 Bonus Box, the phase diagram of water is shown. As you may recall, at pressures below 0.006 atmospheres when you heat ice it doesn't actually melt but instead vaporizes – the water molecules go directly from the solid phase to the gas phase. This process is called sublimation or "freeze drying." Freeze drying costs quite a bit more than spray drying, but most high-quality instant coffee manufacturers use freeze drying because this process retains more of the aroma and flavor molecules than spray drying, resulting in a better tasting instant brew. In fact, those volatile aroma and flavor molecules are so critical to the quality that there are even processes that collect the gases during the extraction (brewing) phase and evaporation phase to try to add them back into the instant coffee. A lot of work to make an instant drink!

Lab 13 – Third Design Trials: Engineering Economics & Coffee

Objectives: The main goal of this lab is to consider the question, "How much will my design cost?" using the concept of a cost-benefit analysis. It is also your last chance to roast your beans for the competition!

Equipment:

☐ Brewer(s) ☐ Roaster(s) ☐ Digital refractometer ☐ Kill-a-Watt meter

Activities:

☐ At least three brews, completely quantified (TDS, PE, energy)

☐ Prepare your roast(s) for your final design competition, with energy measurements

☐ Analyze the economics of your proposed design

☐ Pictures and/or video as you desire for the final design video

Report:

☐ A completed energy scoresheet

☐ Cost-benefit analysis of your proposed coffee design

☐ Paragraphs discussing your proposed design and logic for design choices

Background – Cost Benefit Analyses

The previous labs have focused on fundamental scientific and engineering principles, and how they govern the design of coffee. As we have learned, we can understand a great deal about coffee by considering conservation of mass and conservation of energy, or how chemical kinetics determine the rate at which coffee becomes sour with time, or how pressure and permeability controls the flowrate of water through coffee grounds and affect the flavor.

Understanding principles like these is crucial for really understanding coffee, and for many aficionados that level of understanding is adequate. But, if you're at all interested in using your coffee expertise to *earn money*, then a whole other type of expertise is also required. Specifically, both chemical engineers and coffee professionals must also be able to determine whether or not a certain engineering process or application will be *economically feasible*. Put more simply, you must be able to answer the question "How much is it going to cost?" Most frequently, the goal for some new design is to make a profit, so a closely related question is "How much money are we going to make?"

In this lab, we are going to focus on a type of economic analysis that is particularly useful for economic decision making. Specifically, we will learn how to perform a "cost-benefit analysis." By cost-benefit, we mean "How much will something cost, and how much benefit will it provide in the

long term?" The goal of the analysis is typically to determine which option or course of action is best to implement. Engineers must become adept at quantitative cost-benefit analyses, especially in the context of designing chemical processes. For example, a 20-foot tall distillation column will certainly cost more initially compared to a 10-foot column, but if the larger column yields a higher throughput (i.e., it allows the facility to distill more alcohol more quickly) then it might be worth the extra investment.

To illustrate a cost-benefit analysis, we will examine a scenario highly relevant to many college students: personal coffee consumption. Specifically, let's imagine that you would like to have a large cup of coffee every day during your time at college. Is it better to make your own coffee each morning, or to buy a daily $2 coffee at a local café?

Your preliminary gut feeling might be, "Of course it's cheaper to make your own!" But to an engineer, gut feelings are not sufficient: we need quantitative comparisons. Specifically, how much cheaper is it exactly? Perhaps the cost difference is negligible – in which case it might be better to have a trained barista making your coffee for you each morning. Or perhaps the cost difference is huge, and you would be silly (from an economic perspective) to not make your own.

To address this question quantitatively, let's first consider the costs of buying a coffee each day. As of 2021, a "grande" 16-ounce coffee at Starbucks costs $2.65. Although generally most prepared foods are subject to sales tax (8.25% in Davis, California), there is an exception in California for hot coffee, exempting it from sales tax. (Different states have different sales tax rules). This $2.65 might seem like a small amount, but we want to keep track over the course of a typical undergraduate career, 4 years in duration. It's unlikely that the price will stay constant over 4 years, since *inflation* tends to devalue money over time, but here we will perform the simplest analysis and neglect the possibility of any price increases. If we treat each year as 50 weeks (since hopefully there are about 2 weeks each year when friends or family provide you with coffee!), then over the course of 4 years you will spend a total of

$$\frac{\$2.65}{day} \times \frac{50 \; weeks}{yr} \times \frac{7 \; days}{week} \times 4 \; yrs = \$3,710 \tag{1}$$

That two-dollar coffee turned into a lot of money! Note that we assumed here that you have no additional transportation or other expenses involved in procuring your daily cup of coffee. If you drive your car out of your way each day specifically to get the coffee, then you need to also add the incremental costs of gasoline and wear-and-tear on your car specifically for getting your coffee. These "wear-and-tear" costs are formally known as *depreciation*, meaning the value of the car goes down with time. (Cars depreciate very rapidly, and are thus terrible investments from an economic point of view.) The IRS provides a useful reimbursement rate, including gas, insurance, and depreciation, of $0.56 per mile (as of 2021). That means if you drive just 1 mile out of your way for your cup of coffee each day, the effective price of your daily coffee is $3.21/day, and the total 4-year cost is $4,494. Driving a mile to the coffee shop everyday over college will by itself cost you $784 over four years!

Now that we know the cost of buying coffee at a café each day, we turn our attention to making your own coffee. First, we need to establish the initial costs for buying the equipment necessary to brew your own batch every day. Also known as the "capital investment," a thorough cost-benefit analysis will incorporate all of the pieces of equipment necessary for the entire process. Here we imagine that you initially have no coffee making equipment at all and thus need to buy everything yourself. Specifically, to brew coffee you need a brewer of some sort, a grinder, and an insulated travel mug to put your delicious coffee into. Clearly there are many different types of coffee equipment available, but here let's imagine that you prefer a high-quality brewer that precisely regulates water temperature to deliver an even brew. Your initial capital investments (including sales tax) then might be approximately

- Coffee brewer, $120
- Blade grinder, $20
- Thermos travel mug, $10

This yields a total fixed capital investment of $150. Of course, you then need to account for your "operating expenses," which in this case would be everything you need to purchase on a regular basis to make your coffee. First, let's figure out how much coffee you need. A standard insulated travel mug typically holds about 2 cups (16 fluid ounces), so let's aim to brew up about 2 cups per day. Since there are 237 grams of water in 1 cup of water, that means we need 474 grams of brewed coffee. To determine how much ground coffee we need, we can rearrange equation 2 from Lab 11 as

$$m_{grounds} = \frac{m_{brew}}{R_{brew} - R_{abs}}. \tag{2}$$

As discussed earlier, a good brew will have a brew ratio of about 17, and with the absorption ratio approximately equal to $R_{abs} \approx 2$, that means we need about 32 grams of coffee per day. (Of course, you could make a weaker brew to use less coffee.) Thus, 1 pound of coffee beans (which has 454 grams) will last for two weeks. To recap, our coffee needs are as follows:

$$m_{brew} = \left[\frac{2\ cups}{day}\right]\left[\frac{237\ grams}{1\ cup}\right] = 474\ grams\ , \tag{3}$$

$$m_{grounds} = \frac{474\ grams}{17 - 2} = 32\ grams, \tag{4}$$

$$bags\ needed = \left[\frac{32\ grams}{day}\right]\left[\frac{1\ pound\ per\ bag}{454\ grams}\right]\left[\frac{7\ days}{week}\right] = 0.49\ \frac{bags}{week}. \tag{5}$$

Of course, the next question is: how much does the coffee cost? If you're going to go through the effort of making your own coffee every day, presumably you'd like to use high quality, recently roasted coffee. The price of coffee is highly variable depending on where you are and what quality you purchase, but as a rule of thumb you can purchase excellent roasted coffee (in 2021) for about $15 per pound. At this price, your coffee grounds for each cup per day will be

$$\left[\frac{1\ bag\ of\ coffee}{2\ weeks}\right]\left[\frac{\$15}{1\ lb\ bag\ of\ coffee}\right]\left[\frac{1\ week}{7\ days}\right] = \frac{\$1.04}{day}, \tag{6}$$

This is much cheaper than buying a $2.65 cup of coffee, but we haven't added all the other costs yet. Filter papers are another operating expense. A box of 400 filter papers (designed for a 4-cup basket brewer) costs about $8, so the cost of each filter (assuming 1 used per day) is only 2 cents ($0.02). What about cream and sugar? Let's imagine you like 1 sugar cube per travel mug; typical sugar costs yield a price of about 4 cents per cube. Fresh cream is more expensive, since a pint (16 ounces) of "Half-and-Half" creamer is typically $3. If you use one ounce per cup (two ounces per batch), the cost is $0.38 per day.

What about the water itself? If you pay your water bill, you should also consider its cost. If you're using regular tap, however, the costs are negligible. A gallon of water from your tap typically costs about seven cents per 10 gallons, or $0.0004 per cup. This amount is so small that you can safely neglect the cost of the water; it adds an amount far smaller than the uncertainty in your other cost estimates.

What about the energy cost? As we saw in Lab 5, the energy cost of heating up about 4 cups of water in a drip brewer is approximately 0.08 kW-hr, and since energy costs about $0.20 per kW-hr, the cost of operating your brewer is approximately two cents per day.

Finally, what about maintenance of our equipment? In large production facilities, maintenance will typically be a major expense, but in the context of home coffee brewing maintenance is more straightforward. Your coffee brewer and travel mug should be cleaned periodically, but it is easy to show that, much like water, the cost of soap is negligible. More importantly, we should consider "equipment contingency costs." What happens if the grinder breaks down after a couple years, or if you lose your travel mug? An accurate cost projection will have some budget allocated to the cost of your maintaining or replacing your initial capital investment. There are many complicated procedures for estimating the average lifetime of process equipment; here let's imagine that your expensive brewer is covered by a 4-year warranty, while the grinder has a 2-year warranty and the travel mug has no warranty at all. In this case, we might estimate having to replace the grinder once over 4 years, and to be conservative we can estimate that we might misplace our travel mug on average once every academic year. Together, this adds about $20 + 4×$10 = $60 of expenses over 4 years. On a daily basis, this works out to $60 / (7×50× 4)=$0.05 per day.

Coffee beans	$1.04 / day
Half-and-half creamer	$0.38 / day
Sugar	$0.03 / day
Filter paper	$0.03 / day
Electricity	$0.02 / day
Water (assuming tap)	*Negligible*
Equipment contingency	$0.05 / day
Total:	$1.54 / day

The ongoing operating expenses of making your own batch of coffee every day are tabulated above. Clearly the coffee beans themselves are the major cost, and if you wanted to drive the cost down you should focus on finding less expensive beans. It is straightforward to find lower quality coffee beans around $6 per pound, which would drive the total cost (including sugar, cream etc.) down to $0.92 per day. If you further skipped the cream and sugar and just drank black coffee, then the total cost would be only $0.51 per day… much, much cheaper! Note that we're assuming that you purchase the groceries as part of regular shopping trips, so you don't incur additional transportation expenses just to buy your coffee supplies.

When added up over four years, the total operating cost for brewing your own high-quality coffee is

$$\frac{\$1.54}{day} \times \frac{50 \; weeks}{yr} \times \frac{7 \; days}{week} \times 4 \; yrs = \$2161. \tag{1}$$

Even after adding in our initial capital investment of $150, it is already clear that making your own coffee indeed saves a significant amount of money. Compared to the $3710 total cost of buying a coffee every day, it is clear that in the long run it is much more financially effective to make your own coffee, rather than paying somebody else to do it for you.

This analysis assumed that after the initial investment, you stuck with making your own coffee – but what if after some point you get lazy and start buying it at the café again? How long would you have to make your own coffee for you to break even?

To answer this question, we can prepare a graphical representation of the costs associated with our two different scenarios. We plot versus time the total cumulative expenditure for each scenario, buying or making our coffee, shown here on a weekly basis. Note that the "making coffee at home" starts at week zero at $150 to account for our initial capital investment, whereas the "buying at a café" scenario requires zero initial investment. The cumulative

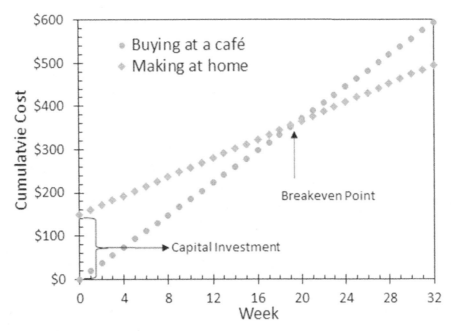

cost of buying coffee increases more steeply than making your coffee, however, reflecting the difference between $1.54 per day for making versus $2.65 per day for buying.

This might appear complicated, but it is straightforward to do in Excel or Google Sheets. Setup your spreadsheet with three columns: weeks, café cost ($), and home cost ($). Note the costs are per week, so multiply the daily costs by seven. (We could also do monthly or daily if desired.) To find the cumulative cost we incrementally add the cost of brewing the coffee from the row above to the row below, as shown in the example spreadsheet at right. This is easy to do use a formula and dragging to fill in the columns (see Appendix A).

We can see that the two curves intersect near week 20. This point, which is the "break-even" point, represents the time at which the two courses of action require the same cumulative amount of money. In other words, as long as you stick to making your own coffee for more than 20 weeks (about five months, just one semester), then you've come out ahead – you'll have more money in your pocket. (Or more specifically, in your savings account!) Clearly, if you keep making your own coffee over a longer time period, say four years, then you come out very much ahead.

Note that our analysis here completely ignored the cost of your time (i.e., your labor), which in a large business is typically one of the main expenses. We implicitly assumed here that the amount of time spent waiting in line would be roughly comparable to the time you spend brewing your own coffee, so that a more detailed analysis would yield no significant difference in time. This is a conservative estimate, since brewing your own coffee at home typically will take much less time than going out of your way to a café and waiting in line.

Week	Café	Home
0	$ 0.00	$ 150.00
1	$ 18.55	$ 160.80
2	$ 37.10	$ 171.61
3	$ 55.65	$ 182.41
4	$ 74.20	$ 193.22
5	$ 92.75	$ 204.02
6	$ 111.30	$ 214.83
7	$ 129.85	$ 225.63
8	$ 148.40	$ 236.43
9	$ 166.95	$ 247.24
10	$ 185.50	$ 258.04
11	$ 204.05	$ 268.85
12	$ 222.60	$ 279.65
13	$ 241.15	$ 290.46
14	$ 259.70	$ 301.26
15	$ 278.25	$ 312.07
16	$ 296.80	$ 322.87
17	$ 315.35	$ 333.67
18	$ 333.90	$ 344.48
19	$ 352.45	$ 355.28
20	$ 371.00	$ 366.09
21	$ 389.55	$ 376.89
22	$ 408.10	$ 387.70
23	$ 426.65	$ 398.50
24	$ 445.20	$ 409.30
25	$ 463.75	$ 420.11
26	$ 482.30	$ 430.91
27	$ 500.85	$ 441.72
28	$ 519.40	$ 452.52
29	$ 537.95	$ 463.33
30	$ 556.50	$ 474.13
31	$ 575.05	$ 484.94
32	$ 593.60	$ 495.74
33	$ 612.15	$ 506.54
34	$ 630.70	$ 517.35
35	$ 649.25	$ 528.15
36	$ 667.80	$ 538.96
37	$ 686.35	$ 549.76
38	$ 704.90	$ 560.57
39	$ 723.45	$ 571.37
40	$ 742.00	$ 582.17

Summary of 3nd Design Trial Activities

As with the first two design trials, we intentionally leave the lab activities open-ended, so that you can work with your group on your own process design. Try at least a couple different overall designs, preferably more. This lab is also a great time to obtain some video for the video project if you so desire.

Very importantly: this is your **last chance** to roast beans for the contest. Definitely bring your A-game… the beans you roast now are what you will be using in the contest! Make sure you carefully record the energies of roasting.

Although the main point of this design trial is to finish honing your design for your contest brew, the theme is economics. The design competition only depends on taste and energy, not costs – but this lab is your chance to think more deeply about the economics of coffee consumption. Accordingly, we urge you to think carefully about the following questions.

1) If you hired somebody at minimum wage to do all the steps for making your 1 liter of coffee, how much would that cost? To answer this, make sure you time the roasting, grinding, brewing, and cleanup associated with the entire process.

2) As described in the text, brewing clearly has capital equipment costs and many operating expenses. What about roasting? What additional expenses are there for roasting your own green beans?

3) Again, this is your last chance for roasting! Do the most excellent roasts possible.

4) Make sure you record the energies used in every step. You will need to fill out an energy scoresheet similar to the one that you will use in the actual competition.

5) Also get the TDS and PE, but remember those are only guides… your perceived taste evaluation is the most important!

Data for 3rd Design Trials

Coffee type_____

Roasting method: _____ Roasting date:_____

Mass of green beans: _____ *grams*   Mass of roasted beans: _____ *grams*

Time spent roasting: _____ *minutes* Energy usage: _____ *kW-hr*

Clock time when started prepping to brew: _____

Brewing method: _____ Filtration method: _____

Mass of hot water:_____ *grams* Mass of grounds:_____ *grams* Ratio:_____

Water Temp: _____ °C   Energy usage: _____ *kW-hr*

Extraction time: _____ *minutes*   Grind size: _____

Mass of brew: _____ – _____ = _____ *grams*   (filled cup – empty cup)

Clock time when brew finished: _____   Time required: _____ *minutes*

TDS: _____ %   PE: _____ × _____ ÷ _____ = _____ %

Other data:

_____

_____

_____

_____

Sensory Evaluations:

_____

_____

_____

_____

Data for 3rd Design Trials

Coffee type_____

Roasting method: _____   Roasting date:_____

Mass of green beans: _____ *grams*   Mass of roasted beans: _____ *grams*

Time spent roasting: _____ *minutes*   Energy usage: _____ *kW-hr*

Clock time when started prepping to brew: _____

Brewing method: _____   Filtration method: _____

Mass of hot water:_____ *grams*   Mass of grounds:_____ *grams*   Ratio:_____

Water Temp: _____ °C   Energy usage: _____ *kW-hr*

Extraction time: _____ *minutes*   Grind size: _____

Mass of brew: _____ – _____ = _____ *grams*   (filled cup – empty cup)

Clock time when brew finished: _____   Time required: _____ *minutes*

TDS: _____ %   PE: _____ × _____ ÷ _____ = _____ %

Other data:

_____

_____

_____

_____

Sensory Evaluations:

_____

_____

_____

_____

Data for 3rd Design Trials

Coffee type_____

Roasting method: _____   Roasting date:_____

Mass of green beans: _____ *grams*   Mass of roasted beans: _____ *grams*

Time spent roasting: _____ *minutes*   Energy usage: _____ *kW-hr*

Clock time when started prepping to brew: _____

Brewing method: _____   Filtration method: _____

Mass of hot water:_____ *grams*   Mass of grounds:_____ *grams*   Ratio:_____

Water Temp: _____ °C   Energy usage: _____ *kW-hr*

Extraction time: _____ *minutes*   Grind size: _____

Mass of brew: _____ – _____ = _____ *grams*   (filled cup – empty cup)

Clock time when brew finished: _____   Time required: _____ *minutes*

TDS: _____ %   PE: _____ × _____ ÷ _____ = _____ %

Other data:

_____

_____

_____

_____

Sensory Evaluations:

_____

_____

_____

_____

Sample Energy Scoring Sheet

If your brew uses beans from just one roast, then fill out only "Roast A" and put zero for "Roast B." If you use three or more roasts, append the data and calculate the total energy of roasting appropriately.

Roast A (bean type): _____   **Roast B** (bean type): _____

Mass of green beans: _____ *grams*   Mass of green beans: _____ *grams*

Mass of roasted beans: _____ *grams*   Mass of roasted beans: _____ *grams*

Total energy of roast: _____ *kW-hr*   Total energy of roast: _____ *kW-hr*

Energy to roast per gram roasted bean: Energy to roast per gram roasted bean:

_____ ÷ _____ = _____ *kW-hr/gram*   _____ ÷ _____ = _____ *kW-hr/gram*

Total mass of beans used: _____ *grams*   Total mass of beans used: _____ *grams*

Energy per gram × total grams used: Energy per gram × total grams used:

_____ × _____ = _____ *kW-hr*   _____ × _____ = _____ *kW-hr*

Total energy for roasted coffee actually used in your brew (Roast A + Roast B):

_____ + _____ = _____ *kW-hr*

Total mass of water heated: _____ *grams*   *(make sure the kettle is cool and empty at start)*

Initial Water Temp: _____ °C   Final Water Temp: _____ °C

Energy used to heat water: _____ *kW-hr*

(Note: don't worry about the energy penalty in this lab since you're not making a whole liter.)

Brewing method(s): _____

Mass of brew: _____ – _____ = _____ *grams*   *(filled carafe– empty carafe)*

If the brew mass is more than 925 grams (0.925 liter), **the energy penalty is zero.** *Otherwise, calculate the energy penalty as follows:*

Deficient mass: ___925___ – _____ = _____ *grams*

Energy penalty: ___N/A___ *grams* × ___0.005___ *kW-hr/gram* = ___N/A___ *kW-hr*

Total energy used to produce your coffee (roast energy + water energy + penalty):

_____ + _____ + ___0___ = _____ *kW-hr*

Roasting Data

Coffee type: _____ Roaster settings: _____

Mass of green beans: _____ *grams*   Mass of roasted beans: _____ *grams*

Time spent roasting: _____ *minutes*   Energy usage: _____ *kW-hr*

Notes: _____

Coffee type: _____ Roaster settings: _____

Mass of green beans: _____ *grams*   Mass of roasted beans: _____ *gram*

Time spent roasting: _____ *minutes*   Energy usage: _____ *kW-hr*

Notes: _____

Coffee type: _____ Roaster settings: _____

Mass of green beans: _____ *grams*   Mass of roasted beans: _____ *gram*

Time spent roasting: _____ *minutes*   Energy usage: _____ *kW-hr*

Notes: _____

Lab Report

By your specified due date, each group will submit a lab report that includes the following:

(1) A completed "energy scoring sheet" for whichever process you think is most promising for the competition. (A photo or scan of an energy score sheet is fine.)

(2) A paragraph of text that describes *why* you have selected your chosen process for the competition. What logic or data informed your design choices?

(3) A set of calculations of the approximate labor costs if you were being paid minimum wage for all the time required to make 1 liter of coffee using your process. How does the labor cost compare to the cost of the supplies (beans, filters) and the energy costs? You can use the approximate costs listed in the background of this lab for comparison.

(4) A cost-benefit analysis for roasting your own coffee for daily consumption. Follow a procedure similar to that presented on in the background for this lab, but add the capital investment of a roaster and the weekly expenses of buying your own green beans. Get approximate prices for green beans from a website like Sweet Maria's. Also include the costs of buying your own brewing equipment. <u>Don't forget to account for the mass lost during roasting!</u> Prepare a graph with three curves showing the cumulative cost per time of: (i) buying coffee daily in a local café, (ii) buying roasted coffee in a store and brewing it daily yourself, and (iii) buying green coffee to roast weekly and brew daily yourself. Label the two break-even points with respect to buying coffee in a café. Also label the break-even point for roasting your own green coffee versus buying roasted beans. Which course of action is best?

Lab 13 Bonus Box – How much does a cup of coffee cost?

More than a century ago, it was easy to walk into a diner or restaurant pretty much anywhere in the United States and order a cup of coffee for 5 cents. That nickel got you more than just a cup… the convention was as many free refills as you wanted, with as much sugar and milk as you like too. What a great deal! By 1921, a cup of coffee in a high-end San Francisco restaurant typically cost about 10 cents.

Of course, 100 years ago that dime was actually worth much more in terms of its buying power, due to inflation. In 2021 dollars, those ten cents are worth about $1.50, so the coffee back then was just a little less expensive than the coffee served in modern coffee houses and cafés, which average between $2 and $3 for a standard cup of drip brew coffee. A natural question from an economic perspective, then, is what sets the price of a cup of coffee? Why isn't a cup of coffee some other price?

The key thing to realize is that the cost of delivering a cup of hot coffee to a customer involves many more costs than just the coffee beans themselves. Recall that the TDS of coffee is about 1%... which means that 99% of it is water. Thus, the actual cost of the coffee, at least to a retail café operator, involves many other costs, including rent, utilities, labor, and other supplies like milk, sugar, and cups. How much do all these costs contribute to the price that a customer pays? This is a complicated question, because market conditions vary so wildly from location to location. The rent and labor costs of running a retail café in an expensive location like San Francisco, for example, will be very different from a coffeehouse in a more rural location. As a representative example, we can examine some recent data compiled by reporters for the Financial Times (Bruce-Lockhart and Terazano, June 3, 2019). The pie charts below show an example of average costs associated with a cup of coffee being sold for $2.99. They found that shop costs (rent and utilities) accounted for almost 40% of the cost of a cup of coffee, with labor comprising another 25%. The beans themselves accounted for only 4% of the cost of the cup of coffee, or 12.5 cents. Of that 12.5 cents, about 10 cents go to the roaster (representing their costs and profit margin), and fractions of a penny go to the exporter, the shipping company, and the processors (who wet and dry mill the beans). Only 1.3 cents of the $2.99 retail price paid by the consumer go to the farmer who grew the coffee.

Recognizing this disparity, many consumers and cafés choose to purchase "Fair Trade" coffee, which aims to provide a better price to the farmer. Many specialty cafés also have "direct trade" relationships with specific farmers that provide pricing structures more favorable to the farmer. Even though the vast majority of the retail cost of the cup of coffee isn't actually for the coffee itself, small differences in the margins make a big difference to farmers in developing countries. Keep that in mind next time you go out for a cup of coffee!

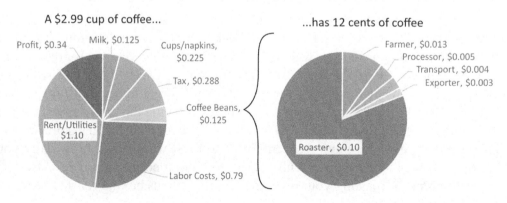

Lab 14 – Design Competition & Blind Taste Panel

Objective: To obtain fame, glory, and bonus points by winning the grand prize!

Equipment:

☐ Brewer(s) ☐ Kill-a-Watt meter ☐ Large insulated carafes ☐ Gong (optional!)

Activities:

☐ Part A – Brew 925 grams of coffee and fill out energy scoresheet in 45 minutes

☐ Part B – Measure TDS of your final brew, and submit your carafe and scoresheet

☐ Part C – Blind taste test of everybody's coffee

Report:

☐ Video report of your final design

Summary of Contest Activities

There are two parts to the design contest. First, you'll have 45 minutes to brew almost one liter of coffee (925 grams to be exact) and fill out your energy scoresheet. You will also measure your final TDS. Then, everybody will participate in the blind tasting. Before you leave, you will know the winning group!

Part A – Brewing 1 Liter of Coffee

As soon as you arrive in lab, wash your hands as usual, and feel free to organize your station and get your roasted beans out. **Empty and rinse your kettle with cool water if it's not already cool to the touch.** DO NOT, however, begin to weigh anything, or grind anything, or heat any water. The contest coordinator will first give an overview of the contest guidelines and rules, and then ask for a volunteer to perform the ceremonial ringing of the gong. As soon as the gong rings, your group has 45 minutes to make your coffee! Each group will be provided with a thermally insulated carafe that holds up to 1 liter of coffee, but to avoid spills or overflows you will only brew 925 grams. (Note that other target masses are possible; a fun variant is to use a random number generator, or some dice, to make a target brew that is announced right before ringing the gong!)

Once the gong rings, zero your Kill-a-Watt meter. Any device you use **must** be plugged into the meter and not re-zeroed until you complete your brew. While you are brewing, continue to measure your energy usage, and completely fill out your energy scoring sheet. If you have extra beans, it's a good idea to do a test grind to make sure the grind size is what you want for the competition, and also to flush out any residual grounds. It's probably also a good idea to rinse out your carafe thoroughly before you put your brew in. If you rinse it with warm water (why might you want to do that?) make sure you include the energy usage!

Design Competition Energy Scoring Sheet

Group name: _____

    Station number: _____   **Section number:** _____

If your brew uses beans from just one roast, then fill out only "Roast A" and put zero for "Roast B." If you use three or more roasts, append the data and calculate the total energy of roasting appropriately.

Roast A (bean type): _____	**Roast B** (bean type): _____
Mass of green beans: _____ *grams*	Mass of green beans: _____ *grams*
Mass of roasted beans: _____ *grams*	Mass of roasted beans: _____ *grams*
Total energy of roast: _____ *kW-hr*	Total energy of roast: _____ *kW-hr*
Energy to roast per gram roasted bean:	Energy to roast per gram roasted bean:
_____ ÷ _____ = _____ *kW-hr/gram*	_____ ÷ _____ = _____ *kW-hr/gram*
Total mass of beans used: _____ *grams*	Total mass of beans used: _____ *grams*
Energy per gram × total grams used:	Energy per gram × total grams used:
_____ × _____ = _____ *kW-hr*	_____ × _____ = _____ *kW-hr*

Total energy for roasted coffee actually used in your brew (Roast A + Roast B):

_____ + _____ = _____ *kW-hr*

Total mass of water heated: _____ *grams*   *(make sure the kettle is cool and empty at start)*

Initial Water Temp: _____ °C   Final Water Temp: _____ °C

Energy used to heat water: _____ *kW-hr*

Brewing method(s): _____

Mass of brew: _____ – _____ = _____ *grams*   *(filled carafe– empty carafe)*

If the brew mass is more than 925 grams (0.925 liter), **the energy penalty is zero.** *Otherwise, calculate the energy penalty as follows:*

Deficient mass: __925__ – _____ = _____ *grams*

Energy penalty: _____ grams × __0.005__ *kW-hr/gram* = _____ *kW-hr*

Total energy used to produce your coffee (roast energy + water energy + penalty):

_____ + _____ + _____ = _____ *kW-hr*

Blind Taste Score: _____   **Final Score:** _____ $(kW\text{-}hr)^{-1}$

(The contest coordinator will fill out the blind taste score and final score.)

TDS Data for your Contest Brew

Total mass of all coffee grounds used for your contest brew: _____ *grams*

Mass of all brew in carafe: _____ *grams*

TDS: _____ %   PE: _____ × _____ ÷ _____ = _____ %

Part B – Measure TDS and submit your carafe and energy sheet

After you're done with the 1 L, take a quick sample to get the overall TDS and overall PE. (Let your small sample cool to room temperature before you measure the TDS!) If you combined different brew types each might have a different PE, but this measurement will let you know what you ended up with.

As soon as you're done, bring both your filled carafe and completed energy sheet to the contest coordinator. Once all of the carafes are submitted, the carafes will be randomized by assigning a random letter known only to the contest coordinator.

Part C – The Blind Taste Test

After the randomized carafes are brought back out, it's time to taste. You'll have about 45 minutes to taste the coffee in each carafe. Everybody will taste every carafe, and each group will *collectively* decide on a score for each of the sensory attributes. (For example, your group will submit 12 scores for 12 carafes.) Refer to Lab 1 for a reminder on how each of the attributes is defined. If it's available, we recommend using the Cropster Cup app to record the taste scores… this allows rapid tabulation of the winners and the contest statistics.

For each tasting, dispense only about 1 ounce (half an espresso glass)… that's all you need. In fact, a small sip or two of each is all that's necessary. Discard any remaining coffee. It's recommended that you drink some water in between coffees to help prevent 'taste fatigue.' Some people find it useful to bring some plain crackers to help cleanse the palate.

For our purposes, high numbers are always better. In the case of acidity, for example, don't give a high score if the coffee is unpleasant because it's extremely sour – that would be a low score. Likewise, a dull flat coffee without any acidity is also a low score. Give a high acidity score if the acidity is pleasantly 'bright' without being overwhelming. As soon as your group is done tasting, submit your score sheet to the TA, who will then go back and compile all the scores. You can clean up your station and take additional pictures or video while you're waiting. Before you leave, our volunteer will ring the gong again, and the winning groups will be announced. With good luck – and good engineering design – your group might take first place!

Design Competition Tasting Score Sheet

Group name: _____

Station number: _____   **Section number**: _____

All categories are ranked 1 to 10 (1=terrible, 10=excellent), except balance, which is ranked –10 (gut wrenching terrible) to +5 (excellent).

Carafe	A
Fragrance	
Acidity	
Flavor	
Body	
Aftertaste	
Balance	
Total	

Carafe	B
Fragrance	
Acidity	
Flavor	
Body	
Aftertaste	
Balance	
Total	

Carafe	C
Fragrance	
Acidity	
Flavor	
Body	
Aftertaste	
Balance	
Total	

Carafe	D
Fragrance	
Acidity	
Flavor	
Body	
Aftertaste	
Balance	
Total	

Carafe	E
Fragrance	
Acidity	
Flavor	
Body	
Aftertaste	
Balance	
Total	

Carafe	F
Fragrance	
Acidity	
Flavor	
Body	
Aftertaste	
Balance	
Total	

Carafe	G
Fragrance	
Acidity	
Flavor	
Body	
Aftertaste	
Balance	
Total	

Carafe	H
Fragrance	
Acidity	
Flavor	
Body	
Aftertaste	
Balance	
Total	

Carafe	I
Fragrance	
Acidity	
Flavor	
Body	
Aftertaste	
Balance	
Total	

Carafe	J
Fragrance	
Acidity	
Flavor	
Body	
Aftertaste	
Balance	
Total	

Carafe	K
Fragrance	
Acidity	
Flavor	
Body	
Aftertaste	
Balance	
Total	

Carafe	L
Fragrance	
Acidity	
Flavor	
Body	
Aftertaste	
Balance	
Total	

Lab Report: Final Design Video

No regular lab report is necessary for Lab 14. Instead, as described in detail on page 124, you and your group will submit a video that presents your final design. The following checklist is provided for your convenience.

Design Video Checklist

Video contents:

☐ Your group name, individual names, ID numbers, and section number (if applicable)

☐ Process flow diagram, with enough detail for others to replicate your process

☐ Mass balances, for water and coffee solids, including waste streams

☐ Type of beans and roast level(s)

☐ Energy usages for each step, and your logic for energy minimization

☐ TDS and PE for one of your final design brews (or competition brew)

☐ Your sensory evaluations of your brew and overview of scores from the blind tasting

☐ Cost-benefit analysis for replicating your brew daily at home (if you did Lab 13)

☐ Summary of what you would do in a future hypothetical contest to improve

Video format:

☐ Includes sufficient audio narration and / or subtitles to explain visuals

☐ All images and calculations are shown long enough to be understood (no quick flashes)

☐ Is less than five minutes total duration

☐ Is submitted as a YouTube link (public or private)

Finally, when you are done with your video, we recommend you sit back with a nice cup of freshly brewed coffee and reflect on all of the engineering and science concepts you have learned about during this course. Hopefully you have a better sense now of how to think like an engineer – and how to make excellent coffee!

Appendices

Appendix A – Spreadsheet Analysis & Plotting Scientific Data

A crucial skill, regardless of your career path, involves the analysis and communication of data. Even if you become an award-winning author or artist, you need to be able to understand your royalties – a kind of financial data. The lab reports in "The Design of Coffee" are aimed at developing your expertise in analyzing and plotting scientific data, with a focus on using standard spreadsheet software (e.g., Microsoft Excel or Google Sheets). The skills are translatable to other types of data as well (if you can plot temperature versus time, you can plot royalty income versus time). In this section we summarize some helpful tips to perform the necessary data analysis, and to make your plots easily understandable by others.

We focus here on three topics: recording data, plotting data, and performing linear regressions (or "best fits") of data.

Good Practices for Recording Data

You will often record data in your lab manual – but to analyze the data you will need to put them into a spreadsheet. Examine below the two example spreadsheets. Both of them contain exactly the same data, but there is a tremendous difference in clarity and legibility. Specifically, the one on the left is an example of "bad practices (what not to do!), while the right is an example of good practices. You can see most of the differences visually, but for the sake of clarity some of the basic good practices for recording and analyzing data are as follows

1) **Units.** The most important rule: when you put down numbers in a spreadsheet, it should be obvious to any other reader what the units are. (There is a huge difference between grams or kilograms!) Always clearly label the units at the top of a column (or somewhere else very clear).

2) **Labels.** Along with the units, some descriptive label (e.g., "Time") for each column of data is necessary.

3) **Metadata.** It is good practice to place some information about the data at the top of the spreadsheet, including for example the type of data, who took it, when, where, etc. Also give descriptive names to your workbook and all worksheets. The name "mydata" could mean anything, whereas "coffee_pH_trial_3" is extremely specific.

4) **Significant digits.** It is easy in Excel to include way too many digits. Don't include seven or eight digits in a number if only the first 3 are significant. A rule of thumb is that your calculated numbers should contain the same amount of digits as your measured numbers (not more).

5) **Formulas.** Any constants that are used in calculations should be clearly entered and labeled nearby with appropriate units. Then, your calculations should refer to the cell containing that constant. (In Excel, you use the $ prefactor to hold the cell fixed in a formula.)

(Bad Practice)

18.0 fine		
	1	2
0.5	4.8000	4.5000
2.0	4.1080	3.7113
4.0	3.8298	3.1460
6.0	3.5421	2.6575
8.0	2.8952	1.8771
10.0	2.9921	1.8926

(Good Practice)

Caffeine Experiment, Trials 1 & 2		
12-Jul-15 2:30pm		
Experiments by J. Lee & A. Gomez		
Brewing Ratio:		18
Grind size:		Fine
	Trial 1	Trial 2
	(25°C)	(90°C)
Time	Caffeine Concentration	
[minutes]	[g / L]	[g / L]
0.5	4.8	4.5
2	4.1	3.7
4	3.8	3.1
6	3.5	2.7
8	2.9	1.9
10	3.0	1.9

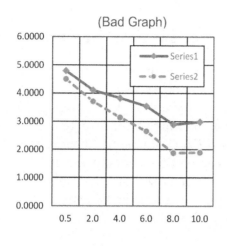

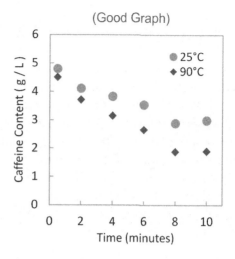

Good Practices for Plotting Data

Examine the two graphs above: they have the same info, but one is clearly better. When graphing data, it's traditional to always state the plot as "y" versus "x", so that a plot of "mass" vs. "time" will have mass on the vertical axis and time on the horizontal axis. Good practices for plotting data include the following.

1) **Axis labels.** The worst possible mistake is to forget to label what the horizontal and vertical axes represent. How else will the viewer know what they're looking at?

2) **Units.** Again, include the units on the axis labels (and legend if appropriate).

3) **Legend.** If your plot includes multiple trials or conditions, use a legend to differentiate them. Make sure each curve has a descriptive label. "Series 1" means nothing!

4) **Markers vs. lines**. The standard convention is to use individual markers to represent individual experimental measurements. Don't connect them with a line (even though that's the default in Excel). Only use solid lines for best fits or for modeling.

5) **Visibility.** Use bold and bright colors for your data. It is difficult to see yellow on white.

6) **Aesthetics.** Most people find a gray background and/or horizontal gridlines quite "ugly" and distracting. You are urged to get rid of the gridlines and use a simple white background. The focus should be on the data – not the background.

Procedure to Perform a "Best Fit" to your Data

Oftentimes we are interested in calculating the slope of your data, which is just another way of asking "how quickly does my data change with respect to some variable?" For example, in Lab 4 you have to determine the slope of the pH versus time. There are several ways to calculate the line that best fits the data (also known as linear regression), but the easiest way in Excel is to follow this procedure. First, plot your data in a standard scatter plot. Click on your plot, then select "Add Chart Element." One of the options should be "Trend line", and select the series of data you want to fit. A best fit line will appear on the graph. Click on the line, and select "Format Trend line," then click "Display Equation on Chart." An equation of the form $y = mx + b$ will appear on the chart. The slope you want is the m value. If you are comfortable using functions in Excel, you can instead use the "slope" function directly in the spreadsheet itself (so that you don't clutter up your graph).

Appendix B – General Guidelines for Brewing

For those of you who are less experienced coffee brewers, the information below provides a quick and handy summary of "Coffee Basics" and "General Rules of Brewing". Coffee basics covers general information about getting the best results by starting with good quality roasted beans and water. The general rules of brewing are based on common taste perception and preferences. As you work through the labs and explore your own personal taste preferences, keep these general rules of brewing in mind in order to more rapidly optimize towards your own individual "nirvana in a cup." Happy brewing.

Coffee Basics

- Use freshly roasted whole beans: To make good coffee you need to use fresh beans. After roasting, the coffee is at its best a couple of days after roasting and up to two weeks if stored properly. Roasted coffee should be stored in an airtight one way valve bag. Note: do not brew beans for at least 1-2 days after roasting. Chemical reactions continue after roasting that are crucial for the flavor and aroma profile.

- Grind immediately before brewing: Grinding releases trapped volatile components. That great smell of freshly roasted coffee means you are losing those great flavor molecules rapidly, so use ground coffee immediately. Ground coffee becomes stale within a few hours of grinding. The smaller the grind, the more rapid the loss. For example, a fine espresso grind will be stale within a few minutes.

- Use good water: water is almost 99% of brewed coffee. The coffee stuff in your cup is only a little more than 1% of the total, so starting with good water is essential.

- Use the right "brew ratio" and the proper grind size: The right ratio of water to ground coffee and the grind size are based on the brewing method. The goal is to optimize the extraction of the good flavors without over-extracting the bad flavors.

General Rules of Brewing

- Ratio of ground coffee to water: For an automatic drip or pour over method of brewing a water to coffee ratio of 15 to 20 grams of water to every gram of ground coffee is typically recommended.

- Water temperature: The suggested water temperature range is 90-95°C (194-203°F).

- Grind size: A narrow particle size helps with an even brewing extraction and more consistent brewing results. The grind should also be optimized to the type of brewing method. For example, espresso uses a very fine grind while a French press uses a coarser grind.

- Extraction time: Typically, most brewing methods use 2-6 minutes (espresso is about 30 seconds). The goal is to extract 18-22% of the ground coffee mass into the brew to obtain approximately 1.15-1.35% total dissolved coffee solids in the brewed coffee. (You study this in more detail in Labs 6 and 11!)

Appendix C – Useful Units and Conversions for Coffee

Mass & volume conversions for <u>water</u> at room temperature

1 milliliter water = 1 gram   (1 mL = 1 g)

1 liter = 1000 milliliters = 1000 grams = 1 kilogram   (1 L = 1000 mL = 1000 g = 1 kg)

1 cup = 237 grams

1 cup = 8 fluid ounces

1 fluid ounce of water = 29.6 grams

4.25 cups of water = 1000 grams = 1 liter

Temperature

To convert from Celsius to Fahrenheit, multiply by 9/5 and add 32.
To convert from Fahrenheit to Celsius, subtract 32 and multiply the difference by 5/9.

°C	0	10	20	30	40	50	60	70	80	90	100	110	120
°F	32	50	68	86	104	122	140	158	176	194	212	230	248

°C	130	140	150	160	170	180	190	200	210	220	230	240	250
°F	266	284	302	320	338	356	374	392	410	428	446	464	482

Brew Ratio Table

	Desired Brew Ratio						
	14	**15**	**16**	**17**	**18**	**19**	**20**
5	70	75	80	85	90	95	100
10	140	150	160	170	180	190	200
15	210	225	240	255	270	285	300
20	280	300	320	340	360	380	400
25	350	375	400	425	450	475	500
30	420	450	480	510	540	570	600
35	490	525	560	595	630	665	700
40	560	600	640	680	720	760	800
45	630	675	720	765	810	855	900
50	700	750	800	850	900	950	1000

Mass of Dry Grounds (grams) — left axis

Mass of Water to Use (grams)

Glossary

absorption – the process by which a liquid soaks into a porous medium; for example, the process of water moving into a sponge or paper towel.

absorption ratio – the ratio of the mass of water absorbed into coffee grounds during brewing, per mass of initial dry coffee grounds; see equation (4) on page 37.

acidity – a sensory attribute of coffee associated with sourness; often described as "bright" when favorable, "sour" when unpleasant, or "dull" or "flat" when missing.

adsorption – a process in which molecules in a gas or liquid physically bind to a solid surface (not to be confused with absorption).

AeroPress coffee maker – a specific brand of cylindrical full-immersion brewer with a plunger that is hand-pressed to apply a desired pressure; similar to a large syringe but with a filter.

aftertaste – a sensory attribute associated with the duration of flavor (both taste and aroma) emanating from the back of the mouth and remaining after the coffee is swallowed.

alkalinity – a measure of a water solution's ability to neutralize acids, described in terms of the total concentration of carbonate, bicarbonate, and hydroxides in the water; typically represented in milligrams of calcium carbonate equivalent per liter.

aroma – a sensory attribute associated with the smell of a coffee sample.

atm – a unit of pressure, equivalent to atmospheric pressure at sea level; 1 atm = 14.7 psi.

baking soda – the common name for sodium bicarbonate ($NaHCO_3$); often used in baking of food.

balance – a sensory attribute that reflects an overall impression of the coffee, considering all the attributes together without any one particular attribute dominating over any other; not to be confused with mass balance.

batch reactor – a closed system reactor with no continuous flow of reactants entering the system or products leaving the system while the reaction takes place.

blade grinder –an inexpensive coffee bean grinder that breaks apart roasted coffee by spinning a thin metal blade; grind size uniformity is improved by pulsing and shaking it during use.

body – a sensory attribute associated with the tactile feeling or mouthfeel of the coffee liquid; closely coupled to the viscosity of the liquid.

breakeven point – in a cost-benefit analysis, the point in time at which the cumulative costs of one course of action equal the cumulative costs of another course of action.

brew ratio – the ratio of water mass put into a brewer per mass of initially dry coffee grounds put in the brewer; see equation (1) on page 30.

brewer – an apparatus that performs brewing, by combining water with ground, roasted coffee beans to create a coffee beverage.

brewing – the act of adding water to coffee grounds to extract soluble material and make a coffee beverage.

Brownian motion – the random jiggling movement exhibited by colloidal particles; readily observed in a microscope.

burr grinder – type of coffee bean grinder that produces more uniform particle sizes by controlling the spacing between two flat rings with serrations.

caffeine – the common name for the chemical compound with formula $C_8H_{10}N_4O_2$ present in high concentrations in coffee beans; responsible for positive psychoactive effects in humans; see pages 35 and 133.

calcium citrate – the common name for the chemical compound with formula $Ca_3(C_6H_5O_7)_2$; it is commonly used as a food preservative and is a good source of calcium in the diet.

capital investment – the amount of money necessary to purchase equipment and/or initial supplies necessary to begin a process or operation.

carafe – a container to hold liquid coffee for serving, typically made either of glass or vacuum-insulated stainless steel.

centipoise – a unit of dynamic viscosity, equivalent to 0.01 kg m^{-1} s^{-1}; abbreviated as cP; water at 20°C has a viscosity of about 1 cP

centistoke – a unit of kinematic viscosity, defined as the ratio of the dynamic viscosity and density of a fluid; equivalent to 1 square millimeter per second (mm^2/s); often abbreviated as cSt; water 20°C has a kinematic viscosity of about 1 cSt.

chaff – the fragile, paper-like skins of the green coffee beans that flake off during roasting; typically considered a waste material, but contains antioxidants and is edible.

check valve – a mechanical apparatus that allows fluid to flow only in one direction.

chemical engineering – the branch of engineering that focuses on analyzing and designing processes for converting matter into more useful forms.

citric acid – the common name for the chemical compound with formula $C_6H_8O_7$; it is a weak and odorless acid typically found in citrus fruits.

Clever Coffee Dripper – a specific brand of full immersion coffee brewer, shaped like a cone with a spring valve at bottom to allow precise control of extraction time.

coffee – depending on context, "coffee" can refer to the plant, the fruit, the green beans, the roasted beans, or the beverage.

coffee bean – the seed of a coffee fruit, that is postharvest processed, roasted, ground, and brewed to make a coffee beverage.

carbon dioxide – the common name for the gas CO_2 that is exhaled by animals and generated inside coffee beans during roasting.

Cannon-Fenske viscometer – a specific type of glass capillary that is calibrated such that the time required for liquid to drain through it is directly proportional to the kinematic viscosity.

Coffee Brewing Control Chart – a graphical representation of the relationship between total dissolved solids (TDS), percent extraction (PE), and brew ratio overlaid with sensory descriptive attributes of the brewed coffee. By specifying any two parameters (e.g. TDS and brew ratio) the remaining parameter (PE) is fixed; see pages 64 and 126, and back cover.

Coffee Taster's Flavor Wheel – a graphical representation of dozens of coffee flavors, arranged in the shape of wheel, to facilitate identification of flavor notes in coffee; as the chart is viewed radially outward, the descriptive words transition from general to more precise.

colloidal particles – small solid particles suspended in a fluid phase, typically 1 to 10,000 nanometers in size (0.001 to 10 microns).

concentration – a measure of the number of molecules per unit volume; typically measured in moles per liter or grams per liter.

concentration gradient – a spatial difference in concentration, from high concentration to low concentration over some specific distance.

conservation of energy – the principle stating that energy cannot be created or destroyed in a closed system, only transferred from one form to another.

conservation of mass – the principle that mass cannot be created nor destroyed in a closed system.

control chart – a graphical representation of how different control parameters affect a desired outcome; see Coffee Brewing Control Chart.

control parameters – aspects of a process that can be altered or "controlled" to manipulate the desired outcomes.

control volume – an imaginary box around a unit operation or collection of unit operations, used to perform a mass or energy balance on all material streams entering and exiting the volume.

cooling cycle – a time period after coffee roasting that helps cool down the beans and allows the roaster machine to cool down.

cost-benefit analysis – a systematic approach to estimating the strengths and weaknesses of alternatives used to determine options that provide the best approach to achieving benefits while preserving savings.

crema – a thin and typically short-lived layer of foam on top of a shot of espresso.

cupping – the coffee industry term for the traditional method of tasting coffee using only hot water and coffee grounds in a cup; typically, the brew is slurped loudly with a spoon.

Darcy's law – an equation that describes the flow rate through a porous medium in terms of the applied pressure difference; see equation 1 on page 88.

dark roast – a roast level of coffee characterized by beans with a very dark brown color, approaching black, and an oily surface; typically achieved during second crack while roasting.

decaffeinated coffee – coffee made with green coffee beans that were additionally processed (before roasting) to preferentially remove caffeine.

defects – sensory attributes associated with negative or "off" flavors that detract from the taste and perceived quality.

density – a measure of how much mass a substance has per volume; often measured in grams per milliliter (g/mL) or equivalently grams per cubic centimeter (g/cm^3).

depreciation – an economic term for the decrease in value of something with time (e.g., a new car quickly depreciates in value).

dispensing time – for full immersion brewers, the time period after the initial extraction period during which the brewed coffee is dispensed through the filter.

distilled water – water from one container that has been boiled into steam and then condensed back into a liquid in a second container; this process leaves behind salts and impurities, so that the water in the second container is very pure.

drip brewer – a type of brewer that slowly drips hot water through a bed of coffee grounds and allows it to filter into a carafe.

dry processed – a style of postharvest processing of coffee cherries where the coffee cherries are allowed to dry completely before the seeds are removed from the fruit; sometimes referred to as "natural" processed.

economically feasible – the desirable situation in which the economic benefits of a proposed activity are greater than the economic costs.

emulsified oils – small droplets, typically on the scale of microns, suspended in water.

emulsion – a mixture of two or more immiscible liquids, such as mayonnaise or well-shaken oil and vinegar (salad dressing).

endothermic reaction – a chemical reaction that requires/consumes heat energy.

energy – the quantitative property that describes the amount of work (force applied over a distance) or heat in a system; typically measured in joules or kilowatt-hours.

engineering – the discipline that involves taking our scientific understanding of the natural world and using it to invent, design, build, and operate machines or processes that solve problems and achieve practical goals.

Epsom salt – the common name for magnesium sulfate ($MgSO_4$); often used as a bath salt and readily purchased in drug stores; safe to consume diluted in water.

equipment contingency – funds set in reserve in case equipment needs to be replaced.

espresso – highly concentrated coffee beverage made by forcing a small amount of nearly boiling water under pressure through finely-ground coffee beans.

espresso machine – a specialized brewing apparatus that includes a boiler to generate high pressure steam for making espresso.

exothermic reaction – a chemical reaction that generates/releases heat energy.

extraction – a specific type of mass transfer where molecules move from a solid or liquid phase to a different phase; coffee brewing is technically "leaching," a specific type of extraction, where molecules dissolve from a solid phase (coffee grounds) to a liquid phase (water).

extraction time – the total amount of time during which coffee solids were extracted into the liquid.

fermentation – the biological processes by which yeast or bacteria convert sugars into different chemicals; responsible for removing mucilage from the exterior of coffee seeds prior to drying.

filter – an object that separates solids from a liquid; typically made of paper or a metallic mesh.

filtration – the process by which solid particulates are physically blocked from moving through smaller holes while allowing liquid to pass.

first crack – the first instance of audible "popping" or cracking sound during roasting of coffee beans, due primarily to increased gas pressure associated with water vapor expansion during heating; typically occurs near the start of a light roast.

flavor – a sensory attribute of a food or liquid derived from its taste and smell; in coffee flavors are often described in comparison to other sensory references (see Coffee Taster's Flavor Wheel).

fluid mechanics – the branch of physics dealing with the properties and motion of fluids.

flux – the rate at which molecules undergo mass transfer, in terms of the amount of molecules moving through a particular area per unit of time.

foam – a collection of small gas bubbles formed in a liquid.

force – any interaction that changes the motion of an object; related by Newton's laws to mass and acceleration, $F = ma$.

fragrance – a sensory attribute associated with the smell and aromatic aspects of the coffee, as detected by an initial smell before tasting in the mouth.

French press – a specific type of full immersion coffee brewer, typically cylindrical with a metal filter attached to a plunger; the grounds are pushed to the bottom prior to dispensing.

full immersion brewer – a type of brewer where all of the water is added to the coffee grounds at once, then filtered after extraction.

fuse – an electrical circuit component designed to fail if the current is too high, to protect the entire circuit from electrical power surges; a thermal fuse melts at a specific temperature, making an 'open circuit' and stopping the flow of electricity.

germination – the biological process by which a seed develops into a plant.

gong – a circular metal plate that is fun to hit with a padded mallet to make a deep, ringing sound.

green coffee bean – the seed of a coffee fruit, after postharvest processing has removed the fruit and outer hull, but before roasting; typically dried to about 12% moisture content, down from about 50% originally in the seed.

grind size – the average particle size of coffee grounds; often describe as "fine" for very small grounds, "medium" for intermediate size grounds, or "coarse" for very large grounds.

grinder – a machine used to break the coffee beans into smaller particulates before brewing.

grounds – the small brown particulates that result from grinding roasted coffee beans.

hardness – a measure of the total calcium and magnesium ion concentrations in water; often measured in milligrams per milliliter (mg/mL).

heat – a type of energy, associated with the molecular ("thermal") motion of individual molecules; typically measured in joules or kilowatt-hours.

heat capacity – a physical property of a substance, defined as the total amount of energy necessary to raise the temperature of the substance by one degree; see also specific heat capacity.

hydronium ion – a water molecule that is positively charged because it has an extra hydrogen atom attached to it, denoted as H_3O^+; water that has a high concentration of hydronium ions is acidic and has a low pH; see equation (1) on page 45.

inflation – an increase in prices corresponding to a decrease in the value of money.

insulated – covered or coated with something to prevent heat loss or electrical current flow.

joule – a unit of energy, equivalent to 1 $kg \cdot m^2/s^2$; often abbreviated as J.

Kill-a-Watt meter – a specific brand of electricity monitor that measures cumulative energy usage in kW-hr, but also measures real-time voltage in volts, frequency in hertz, and power in watts.

kilowatt – a unit representing one thousand watts of power (1 kW=1000 W), equivalent to 1000 joules per second (1 kW = 1000 J/s).

kilowatt-hour – a unit of energy, equivalent to the amount of energy consumed by a process using 1 kilowatt of power for exactly one hour; equivalent to 3.6×10^6 joules; abbreviated as kW-hr.

light roast – a roast level of coffee characterized by a light brown color and no oil on the surface; typically associated with roasts near just entering first crack.

mass balance – the application of conservation of mass to analyze a physical system, with consideration of mass inputs and outputs through a control volume around a unit operation or process.

mass flow rate – a measure of how quickly mass passes through a particular unit operation; for example, measured in grams per second.

mass transfer – the process by which molecules move from one phase to another (e.g., from solid to liquid).

mass transfer coefficient – a parameter that relates the rate of mass transfer (i.e., the flux) to the overall concentration difference in a system.

material stream – a flow of any material (either liquid, solid, or gas) into or out of a unit operation.

medium roast – a roast level of coffee characterized by a dark brown color and little oil on the surface; typically achieved between first and second cracks during roasting.

micron – a unit of length equivalent to one millionth of a meter (one thousandth of a millimeter); also known as a micrometer; often abbreviated as µm (1 µm = 0.001 mm = 10^{-6} m).

milliliter – a unit of volume, equal to one thousandth of a liter; equivalent to one cubic centimeter (1 mL = 1 cm^3).

moisture content – the amount of water in a substance, typically expressed as the ratio of water per total mass of the substance; green coffee beans typically have 10 to 12% moisture content.

Mr. Coffee – a specific brand of drip coffee brewer, with a built-in water heater.

newton – a unit of force, equivalent to 1 N = 1 kg·m/s^2; see equation (1) on page 52.

off-gas – the process by which gas molecules escape out of a solid or liquid phase into the surrounding air.

operating expenses – the ongoing costs necessary to perform a process, such as labor, supplies, and maintenance.

organic compounds – molecules containing carbon; not to be confused with "organic" meaning grown without pesticides.

over-extracted – a characteristic of brewed coffee associated with very high percent extractions, often characterized by an overly bitter taste.

PE – see "percent extraction."

percent extraction – the percentage of solids originally in the coffee grounds that were transferred to the liquid phase; also known as the "yield" or "extraction yield."

permeability – a measure of the ability of fluids to pass through a porous material; larger holes or gaps in the porous material yield high permeability; small holes or gaps yield low permeability.

pH – a measure of acidity; specifically, the negative logarithm of hydronium ion concentration in water in moles per liter $pH = -\log_{10}[H_3O^+]$; lower pH is more acidic; see eq. 1 on page 45.

pH meter – an apparatus that measures the electrical voltage across an electrode to determine the amount of hydronium ions present in the solution.

portafilter – a metal filter basket with a handle that is inserted into the "group head" of an espresso machine; it is filled with coffee grounds and then tamped prior to insertion into the machine.

porous media – a material containing interconnected small or tiny holes, which allow fluid or gas to pass through.

postharvest processing – the steps involved transforming fresh coffee cherries to green coffee.

power – the rate of energy usage, typically measured in joules per second (also known as "watts").

ppm – a measure of concentration, "parts per million"; see page 72.

pressure – the force per unit area applied to some object; at sea level, the pressure due to the weight of air in the atmosphere is 14.7 psi = 1 atm.

pressure gradient – a spatial difference in pressure, from a high pressure to a lower pressure, over some specific distance.

process flow diagram – a diagram commonly used in chemical and process engineering to illustrate the general flow of processes and equipment, typically without showing minor details.

psi – a unit of pressure, "pounds per square inch," where 14.7 psi = 1 atm.

refractometer – an instrument that measures how quickly light moves through a liquid ("the refractive index"), which is proportional to the total dissolved solids (TDS) in coffee.

reverse engineering – the process of disassembling an apparatus to determine how it functions.

roast level – a measure of how darkly coffee beans were roasted (e.g., light, medium, or dark).

roast profile – the procedure used to roast coffee beans, often described in terms of the temperature versus time inside the roaster.

roasted coffee bean – coffee beans after they have been heated to high temperatures to cause physical and chemical changes.

roaster – (1) a machine that applies heat to transform green coffee beans into roasted coffee beans; or (2) the person who operates a coffee roasting machine.

roasting – the process of applying heat to green coffee beans such that they undergo significant chemical and physical changes to yield roasted coffee beans.

scale – an instrument that measures the mass of an object, typically in grams or ounces.

scaling up – the process of increase the size, amount, or rate of some process, ideally without changing other properties of the product.

second crack – the second instance of audible "popping" or cracking sound during roasting of coffee beans; typically occurs near a dark roast; very dark roasts go well into or completely past the second crack.

sensory analysis – the scientific procedure applying principles of experimental design and statistical analysis for the purpose of evaluating characteristics of products perceived by human senses.

shear stress – a force per unit area applied tangentially to a surface (typically of liquids); compare to a pressure, which is a force per unit are applied perpendicular to a surface.

sodium – in the context of water quality, the concentration of sodium ions (Na^+) in the water.

specific heat capacity – a physical property of a substance, defined as the total amount of energy necessary to raise the temperature of one gram of that substance by one degree.

spent grounds – the used and moist coffee grounds that remain after coffee brewing; typically considered a waste stream and disposed of as compost.

spring valve – a mechanical apparatus that allows fluid to flow only when it is pushed in; typically present in brewers to ensure a carafe is present before allowing coffee beverage to drip out.

sucrose – the scientific name for ordinary table sugar, with molecular formula $C_{12}H_{22}O_{11}$; sucrose is a naturally occurring sugar in plants, including coffee seeds.

sweetness – a sensory attribute associated with the perception of sugars; typically considered highly desirable in black coffee.

table salt – the common name for sodium chloride (NaCl), which is ordinary salt typically found in kitchens and restaurants.

tamping – the use of a cylindrical metal object to compress coffee grounds in a portafilter in preparation for making espresso.

TDS – see "total dissolved solids."

thermocouple – an electric device for measuring temperature, consisting of a probe containing two connected wires of different metals whose voltage drop is proportional to the temperature.

total dissolved solids – a measure of the combined content of all dissolved substances present in a liquid, typically expressed as a mass percentage (mass of dissolved species per total mass of liquid); brewed coffee typically has 1 to 2% TDS; for example, $2\% \text{ TDS} = \frac{2\,g}{100\,g} \times 100\%$.

under-extracted – a characteristic of brewed coffee associated with very low percent extractions, often characterized by overly sour or vegetal flavors.

unit operation – a step in a process where a chemical or physical change takes place.

viscometer – an apparatus designed to measure the viscosity of a fluid.

viscosity – a measure of a fluid's resistance to flow; often measured in centipoise (cP) for dynamic viscosity or centistokes (cSt) for kinematic viscosity; for example, water is less viscous than honey.

VOC – see volatile organic compounds.

volatile gases – substances that can escape from a liquid or solid phase to the gas phase, such as steam or carbon dioxide.

volatile organic compounds – carbon-based chemical compounds that have a high vapor pressure at room temperature, which allows them to evaporate or sublimate from the liquid or solid phase to gas phase; any compound that can be smelled is volatile, but not all volatile compounds have an odor.

volumetric flow rate – a measure of how quickly a volume of fluid passes through a particular unit operation; for example, measured in milliliters per second.

waste stream – a material stream out of a unit operation consisting of undesired substances (e.g., spent coffee grounds or chaff).

watt – a unit of power, equivalent to 1 joule per second (1 W = 1 J/s).

wet processed – a style of post-harvest processing of coffee where the coffee fruit is stripped off of the seeds shortly after harvest, and the seeds are fermented and subsequently washed with large amounts of water to remove the remaining fruit mucilage; often referred to as "washed" process.

Further Reading

The Design of Coffee: An Engineering Approach is intended as an introduction to coffee, with a focus on thinking about coffee from an engineering perspective. For readers interested in diving deeper into the rich science of coffee, we recommend the following material. This list is far from exhaustive; think of it as a starting point to continue your explorations.

General Books & Anthologies

Coffee Technology, by Michael Sivetz & Norman Desrosier (1979)

Considered by many in the coffee industry as the "Bible of Coffee," this classic is difficult to find (used copies are available on Amazon for $900!). But if you do get a copy, it is a wealth of information written by a chemical engineer (Sivetz) with tremendous experience in the design and operation of coffee roasteries.

Coffee, volumes 1 through 6, edited by R. J. Clarke and R. Macrae (1987)

This highly technical collection covers the full range of coffee science in great detail. Volumes 1 and 2 focus on coffee chemistry and coffee technology respectively; 3 and 4 focus on coffee biology, and 5 and 6 focus on related beverages and commercial/legal aspects of coffee.

Coffee: Recent Developments, edited by R. J. Clarke and O. G. Vitzthum (2001)

An updated and condensed (but still technical) version of *Coffee* by Clarke and Macrae.

Espresso Coffee: The Science of Quality, edited by Andrea Illy & Rinantonio Viani (2005)

IllyCaffé is one of the leading producers of high-quality espresso in the world. This book, co-edited by Andrea Illy (grandson of founder Francesco Illy) covers all aspects of coffee science, from coffee agronomy to human nutrition, with a focus on espresso coffee. Mandatory reading.

Uncommon Grounds, by Mark Pendergrast (2010)

For those interested in the social and economic aspects of coffee, this book dives deep into the history of coffee, from its discovery in Africa, to the colonial period, to mass consumer culture of the twentieth century, to modern "third wave" café culture.

The Craft and Science of Coffee, edited by Britta Folmer (2017)

This book features twenty detailed chapters on coffee, diving deep into topics ranging from the coffee farm, to storage, roasting, grinding, and cupping, and all the ways to the psychology of coffee consumers. It includes perspectives both from academics and thought leaders in the coffee.

The Curious Barista's Guide to Coffee, by Tristan Stephenson (2019)

An easy-to-read overview of coffee covering the history, growing, harvesting, and roasting of coffee to grinding, brewing and recipes for different coffee beverages.

Peer Reviewed Scientific Articles

About the Coffee Brewing Control Chart:

"Effects of brew strength and brew yield on the sensory quality of drip brewed coffee," S. C. Frost, W.D. Ristenpart, & J-X. Guinard, *Journal of Food Science* 85, 2530 (2020).

"Brew temperature, at fixed brew strength, has little impact on the sensory profile of drip brew coffee," M. E. Batali, W.D. Ristenpart, & J.-X. Guinard, *Scientific Reports* 10, 16450 (2020).

"Consumer preferences for black coffee are spread over a wide range of brew strengths and extraction yields," A. R. Cotter, M. E. Batali, W. D. Ristenpart, & J.-X. Guinard, *Journal of Food Science* 86, 194 (2021).

About postharvest processing of coffee:

"Following coffee production from cherries to cup: microbiological and metabolomic analysis of wet processing of Coffea arabica," S. J. Zhang, F. De Bruyn, V. Pothakos, J. Torres, C. Falconi, C. Moccand, L. De Vuyst, *Applied & Environmental Microbiology* 85, e02635 (2019).

"Exploring the impacts of postharvest processing on the aroma formation of coffee beans – a review," G. V. de Melo Pereira et al., *Food Chemistry* 272, 441 (2019).

"A comprehensive analysis of operations and mass flows in postharvest processing of washed coffee," N. M. Rotta, S. Curry, J. Han, R. Reconco, E. Spang, W. D. Ristenpart, & I. R. Donis-Gonzalez, *Resources, Conservations, & Recycling* 170, 105554 (2021).

About coffee chemistry:

"Correlation between cup quality and chemical attributes of Brazilian coffee," A. Farah, M.C. Monteiro, V. Calado, A.S. Franca, & L.C. Trugo, *Food Chemistry* 98, 373 (2006)

"Sensory and monosaccharide analysis of drip brew coffee fractions versus brewing time," M. E. Batali, S. C. Frost, C. B. Lebrilla, W.D. Ristenpart, & J.X. Guinard, *Journal of the Science of Food & Agriculture* 100, 2953 (2020).

"Acids in coffee: A review of sensory measurements and meta-analysis of chemical composition," S. E. Yeager, M. E. Batali, J.-X. Guinard, & W. D. Ristenpart, *Critical Reviews in Food Science & Nutrition*, in press (2021).

About coffee brewing and espresso:

"Using single free sorting and multivariate exploratory methods to design a new Coffee Taster's Flavor Wheel," M. Spencer, E. Sage, M. Velez, & J.-X. Guinard, *Journal of Food Science* 81, S2997, (2016).

"Effect of basket geometry on the sensory quality and consumer acceptance of drip brewed coffee," S. C. Frost, W.D. Ristenpart, & J.-X. Guinard, *Journal of Food Science* 84, 2297 (2019).

"Coffee extraction: A review of parameters and their influence on the physicochemical characteristics and flavour of coffee brews," N. Cordoba, M. Fernandez-Alduenda, F. L. Moreno, & Y. Ruiz, *Trends in Food Science & Technology* 96, 45 (2020).

"Systematically improving espresso: Insights from mathematical modeling and experiment," M. I. Cameron et al., *Matter* 2, 631 (2020).

"An equilibrium desorption model for the strength and extraction yield of full immersion brewed coffee," J. Liang, K. C. Chan, & W. D. Ristenpart, *Scientific Reports* 11, 6904 (2021).

About coffee roasting:

"Coffee roasting and aroma formation: Application of different time-temperature conditions," J. Baggenstoss, L. Poisson, R. kaegi, R. Perren, & F. Escher, *Journal of Agricultural and Food Chemistry* 56, 5836 (2008)

"Evidence of different flavour formation dynamics by roasting coffee from different origins: Online analysis with PTR-ToF-MS," A. N. Gloess et al., *International Journal of Mass Spectrometry* 365, 324 (2014).

"A heat and mass transfer study of coffee bean roasting," N. T. Fadai, J. Melrose, C. P. Please, A. Schulman, & R. A. Van Gorder, *International Journal of Heat & Mass Transfer* 104, 787 (2017).

Notes

Notes

Made in the USA
Las Vegas, NV
15 October 2023

79117097R00098